LEAVING GOD FOR GOD

ONE PASTOR'S SPIRITUAL PATH BEYOND THE CHURCH

PHIL DAVIS

APOCRYPHILE
PRESS

Apocryphile Press
PO Box 255
Hannacroix, NY 12087
www.apocryphilepress.com

Copyright © 2024 by Phil Davis
Printed in the United States of America
ISBN 978-1-958061-64-0 | paper
ISBN 978-1-958061-65-7 | ePub

Rilke quotations are from *Rilke's Book of Hours: Love Poems to God (100th Anniversary Edition)*, translated from German by Anita Barrows and Joanna Macy (NY, NY: Riverhead Books, 2005). Used by permission of Penguin Random House, New York, N.Y.

Please join our mailing list at www.apocryphilepress.com/free
We'll keep you up-to-date on all our new releases,
and we'll also send you a FREE BOOK.
Visit us today!

CONTENTS

I am larger, better than I thought.
I did not know I held so much goodness.
—Walt Whitman[1]

You are the deep innerness of all things,
The last word that can never be spoken.
To each of us you reveal yourself differently:
To the ship as coastline, to the shore as ship.
—Rainer Maria Rilke[2]

To Stephanie
I couldn't become who I needed to be
without you
and
To my Children
and their Children

PROLOGUE

Speak what we feel,
not what we ought to say.
—William Shakespeare[1]

I was sitting in Father Walsh's office for my counseling session. I'd been seeing him for two years and it had been three years since I resigned my pastorate and left ministry at the age of 43. I had been a part of the Evangelical Christian movement for 24 years. Though I wasn't a Roman Catholic, Father Walsh was recommended to me by a close friend. Fr. Walsh was a local parish priest who also had a counseling practice.

Earlier that week I had visited a different church hoping to find a new place I might occasionally attend. I left that church service feeling like a recovering alcoholic who had fallen off the wagon and had a relapse. I was a wreck; too many bad feelings dredged back up.

After explaining this recent church experience to Fr. Walsh, he stopped me and said, "Phil, you need to _not_ go to church for a long time, because it made you sick."

"What? Did I hear him correctly?" I thought.

Imagine that—my Christian counselor, a Catholic Priest, a fellow professional Christian worker, and by then a good friend, telling me church had "made me sick" and I should not go to church for a long time.

I knew what he meant, even if I couldn't fully articulate it at the time. And I knew he was right. It wasn't a sickness unto death, and it wasn't a sickness for which I needed to be institutionalized or medicated. And though I had been on anti-depressants for about a nine-month stretch two years earlier, under Fr. Walsh's referral, I didn't need them anymore.

Fr. Walsh knew me well. In fact, he probably saved my life in those first three years of turmoil and transition after I left ministry. This was a more subtle and more hidden sickness that he was referring to.

This book is about why I was "sick" and how I got healthy.

INTRODUCTION
"IS IT OKAY?"

Dare to love God
without mediator or veil.
—Ralph Waldo Emerson[1]

Sometimes I think I am the only one who nearly went crazy, the only one with this condition that I have come to call my "Jesus Doppelganger" and "Yahweh-Jesus" conundrum. Maybe I am the only one who invited Jesus into his heart and Yahweh and Jesus wound up crowding me out of my own house. Was I the only one who felt so overpowered psychologically by this Holy-Perfectionist-Savior Son of God within me that it messed with my head? This two-headed schizophrenic "Yahweh-Jesus" deity could mess with my mind: Yahweh, the Old Testament God of wrath, judgment, curses and blessings always seemed to overrule gentle Jesus (who wasn't so gentle anymore). They were like an existential good cop-bad cop team that always won.

It's supposed to be the glorious "mystery" of Christianity and the Gospel: Christ in you. It's right there in Paul's letter to the Colos-

3

sians: "the glory of this mystery...which is Christ in you" (Colossian 1:7).

The Apostle Paul wrote, "I am crucified with Christ...nevertheless I live, yet not I...Christ liveth in me" and that we are "new creations" in Christ (Galatians 2:20-21; II Cor. 5:17). I had studied the Bible and theology at the highest and deepest levels as a layman, a seminarian, and then a pastor for years. How does one mentally, psychologically, and spiritually live with this "Divine Presence" within that I was taught wants to take over and control every aspect of my life? We are supposed to give Christ the Throne of our lives. It sounds ominous and it became threatening.

For anyone truly serious about following Christ and Christianity (or any religious faith for that matter), you will face a gauntlet of challenges and choices that will test the limits of your innermost thoughts and the delicate balance of your psychology. For Christians, it's a double-edged sword, because the very meaning of the word "Gospel" is "Good News." The paradox of that became more and more disturbing to me. After years of Christian ministry, more and more of the details, doctrine and dogma of my Evangelical Christianity seemed to be bad news to me.

Father Walsh would remind me more than once during our counseling sessions, "You're not a Fundamentalist. And it's okay." Remembering that would always help me as I worked through leaving the fold and reconstructing my faith.

WAS IT OKAY?

But was it okay? I could repeat his words to myself when I needed to, but it wasn't quite so easy to give myself permission to change my beliefs. Why was that? How is it that it took me quite a few years to allow myself to feel that "It's okay"? I wasn't leaving God. But was it okay to leave the church? To leave my first faith?

For one thing, after 24 years of being a dedicated Evangelical layman and then professional, full-time minister, it's not as easy as just changing churches. It's not as simple as just switching member-ship from an Evangelical church to an Episcopal or Catholic Church, or whatever I might decide.

✝ My Christianity had become my profession, as well as my char-acter and my belief system. If I had been a college professor teaching history or economics, my religious beliefs wouldn't be an integral part of my job and I could change Universities as easily as one changes jobs. But being a Christian worker meant that it was all about my religious beliefs, my sincerity of conviction about them, and my character and performance.

I knew I could go to any number of different denominational Christian churches if it was just a matter of the preference for a few different doctrines. I knew enough about all the differences of our theologies to know that I didn't just want to swap a Ford for Chevy.

What I was going through was a deconstructing of my beliefs and convictions and reconstructing different ones. I knew I couldn't work that out while preaching or teaching in another church posi-tion or denomination.

Deconstruction of my beliefs, conscience, and the inner workings of the spirit and soul made it all extremely personal and existential. I was a product of the Evangelical Movement that I committed myself to when I was 19 years old.

After over twenty years in the movement, I realized that I didn't like who I was becoming. I realized that some of the beliefs I used to think were so important were no longer important to me. After years as a Conservative Evangelical, I didn't like where we were all headed and didn't want to hang around and see where it led.

More importantly, I felt in some ways betrayed by God and my beliefs. But was my beef with God? Or was it *my* beliefs, *my* image of God that I was wrestling with?

My story (or journey) is about how I gave myself permission to be honest—I was no longer comfortable in the Christian circle and the Evangelical movement that I had lived in for most of my adult life.

My journey had a whole second half as I came to terms with the changes in my beliefs and the nature of my faith that led me to leave Evangelicalism for a wider spiritual path. I never "left" or abandoned my pursuit of spiritual truth, authentic faith, and a desire for a connection with "The Presence"—a term I prefer over the generic name "God."

This book is organized into these general stages of my decades-long journey:

- Faith at a Crossroads
- Constructing my Faith—In these chapters I briefly review how I got involved in the movement and became a local church pastor.
- Deconstructing my Faith—In this section I go through my years of reconsidering and being honest about my beliefs.
- Reconstructing my Faith – In this section I review some of the steps and events that helped me put it back together for myself.
- Enlarging my Faith—In these closing chapters I review where I am now.

FAITH, DOGMA AND TRADITION

In one of my favorite movies, "Fiddler on the Roof," we watch Tevye as his three oldest daughters successively challenge his religious beliefs and traditions. Tevye is a local milkman whose family are Russian Jews living in a small rural village at the time of the Russian Revolution of 1905.

Each daughter comes to him in succession to ask Tevye's blessing on their romantic choices for partners. Each daughter's choice causes Tevye to question whether he can give his blessing based upon Jewish beliefs and traditions. The first two daughters challenge his thinking and religious traditions, but he manages to distinguish between tradition and his core beliefs, so he gives them his blessing, however reluctantly.

But by the time the third daughter comes to him, it is a leap too far for Tevye. She is breaking not just tradition, but what he believes is a core belief. So he refuses to give his blessing and effectively disowns his daughter for crossing a line he felt was etched in stone. But as the story ends, we know Tevye will find a way to show love to his third daughter, tradition or no. We know Tevye now, so we know for him, love will ultimately win.

It's a wonderful character study of a devout, sincere, and good man, who has a conversational relationship with his God and who honestly applies his mind to these challenges to his faith.

He compares his religious faith to a fiddler playing a tune while trying to keep his balance on a pitched rooftop without falling and breaking his neck. It's an apt analogy for me as well.

Tevye's challenges are ones every spiritual person must face if we are to honestly and maturely distinguish a religious tradition or belief from an honest relationship with a Higher Being.

It is so easy for religious people to fall back on their religious traditions, dogma etched in stone, and cultural applications of beliefs, thereby losing sight of the spirit of their religion. We tend to be compelled to defend the Letter of the Law at the expense of the Spirit of the Law.

I'd like to think that Tevye, after initially rejecting his third daughter, remembered an Old Testament verse that sums up all of what God really wants:

"What does the Lord require of thee, but to do justly, and to love mercy and to walk humbly with thy God?" (Micah 6:8).

Was it okay if I left the Evangelical camp and those "orthodox" beliefs that I had codified, "concretized" and "deified" for another set of spiritual beliefs? I know for many it is never okay to "leave the fold" of their Faith, Church, Religion. For many Evangelicals and Fundamentalists there is no other way but their way.

Was it okay for me to challenge these long held beliefs, deconstruct my belief system, and rebuild it in a way that I believed was truer to a bigger God than just the God of the Evangelicals, or the Protestants, or the Judeo-Christian Faith?

It was not going to be easy for me to say: "It is okay that I am not an Evangelical or a Fundamentalist any longer."

What would God think?

What would the Church think?

I decided I didn't care what the Church thought.

I did care what God thought.

I knew it would mean a wrestling match.

PART ONE
FAITH AT A CROSSROADS

CHAPTER 1
HERE BE DRAGONS

The ultimate leave-taking
is the leaving of god for God.
—Meister Eckhart[1]

I have two close friends that went through a journey similar to mine. We have known each other for over 40 years now; we still live nearby and see each other often. All three of us made painful decisions to leave the fold and make major changes to the religious beliefs we had followed since we were young men.

We all had a "born again" experience and became devout Christians before we were twenty. We were active in serving in ministries, in evangelism, in discipleship ministries, in weekly Bible studies and church leadership. Two of us were in full-time Christian ministries as paid staff. All of us served as deacons, one was a church elder, and one was a Pastor.

Each of us came to a moment in life where we made major decisions to drastically change our spiritual paths, our beliefs, and our church affiliations. None of us were rejecting God. Each of us came to a point where we felt we had outgrown our churches and beliefs; we needed a spiritual life and faith that was not so confining. It would have been easier to stay and stuff it. It takes courage to think for yourself and question.

Today, years later, all three of us feel much healthier spiritually and do not regret the changes we made. It wasn't easy for any of us. Two of us went through divorces. All of us felt like outcasts and heretics during the initial period of leaving and searching. We were "shunned" by most of those who stayed. The church is not always kind toward people who dare to leave. A noted pastor once said: "The church is the only hospital that shoots its wounded."

A CULT OR A CULTIC EFFECT?

Over the years since changing our courses and religious beliefs, my friends and I have shared and compared notes. There is one partic-ular question that we answer differently. I asked them: "Do you think you were in a cult?" Both of them answered: Yes. My answer was: No.

The reason I disagreed with them is that for me the churches and ministries we were part of are not considered cults. These churches and ministries were fairly standard conservative Evangelical churches. My friends' answers reveal more about the effect their involvement had upon them. This is why I prefer to distinguish between being *in* a cult versus a church having *a cultic effect* upon a person. I would argue that none of the churches or ministries we were a part of would be considered cults by mainstream Christianity. However, it's very easy for the ministry, church, or religion to have a cultic effect on you. In other words, the ministry or church has exces-sive control over you.

I do not believe I was ever in a cult. But my two friends and I all had a great sense of needing to be reprogrammed.

In recent years there have been more and more books published about the trauma of leaving the fold and changing one's religious beliefs. Back when I was leaving in the early 1990's I couldn't find any books to help. I recently came across Marlene Winell's book *Leaving the Fold*. I wish I had had her book when I left! She calls the experience for some a "shattered faith syndrome." Some have talked about the abuse of some church groups, while others have talked about the experience of coming out as a kind of PTSD (post-traumatic stress syndrome) and have called it post-religious stress syndrome (PRSS).

Winell writes:

"...leaving a cherished faith is much like the end of a marriage. The symptoms of separation are quite similar—grief, anger, guilt, depression, lowered self-esteem, and social isolation."[2]

I was surprised at how much of Marlene Winell's church experience when she left her fold was like mine. She writes:

"Leaving the fold was then a long and wrenching process which tore at the fabric of my existence. 'Losing' God was like losing my parents."[3]

Winell researched her topic extensively, and she was able to recount numerous cases of people going through the trauma of leaving their fold. Reading her book helped me realize that my two close friends and I were not alone in the deconstruction and reconstruction of our faith.

"People from a wide variety of religious groups were struggling with self-esteem and needed to reclaim the ability to think for themselves, to understand and accept their own feelings, and to take more responsibility for their own lives."[4]

I went through a few dark years initially after leaving. I went back to college in order to prepare for another profession. I went through a painful divorce; I was on medication for depression and suicidal ideation. I lost many "friends" who couldn't accept what I was doing. I went to three different Christian counselors and did not feel like they helped. I finally found Father John Walsh, a local Catholic parish priest, and he helped save my life and my mental and spiritual state. But I was criticized by others from the old fold for seeing a Catholic priest! I met another woman, got married and wound up divorced again. It took a few years before I was able to feel stabilized again. I met another woman who was a Godsend. We have been together now for over 20 years.

Out of respect for my first wife, the mother of my children, and personal privacy issues, I will not go into all the details of my divorce. It is enough for me to say that the personal struggles I was going through related to my faith and whether to continue a career as a pastor; the personal issues we were facing together culminated in a painful separation and divorce.

TOXIC RELIGION

My story is a cautionary tale. I take full responsibility for all the decisions, twists, turns and detours. If my religious experience had a cultic effect on me, that is because I allowed it to. No one twisted my arm or forced me to get involved in Christian ministries or become as committed as I did. I was honestly seeking and genuinely committed to Christ and Christianity.

Perhaps that is part of the mystery. Sometimes religion can be hazardous to your health. What I hope to show is that each of us needs to think critically about the effects that our zeal, our faith, our dogma, and our religion and church involvement have upon us in a holistic way. Sadly, today in America, Jesus himself would not be welcomed in many of his churches.

The psychology of our inner spiritual life is something that is not addressed often enough in churches and ministries. Most of my spiritual journey these last thirty years has been a path of discovery to understand and reconstruct a healthier relationship with God, the Presence.

I found that the biggest obstacle was dogma and doctrine. When dogma becomes concretized or deeply entrenched, it can be exceedingly difficult to root out.

Winell writes:

"A dogmatic religion is one that does not truly honor the thoughts and feelings of the individual."[5]

I remember reaching the point in my life when the very first verse that brought me to Jesus and his Gospel message no longer rang true for me.

What went wrong? Was it me or was it God? The church will always say it's your fault.

Before Europeans crossed the Atlantic, on some old maps, when many still thought the world was flat, at the edge of the known sea the mapmakers put a warning: here be dragons. It was their way of warning seafarers that no one yet knew what was in that unknown, uncharted part of the sea. They figured it was dangerous. That can also be said of the realms of the spirit, the mind, the soul.

Those adventurous ancient explorers who went beyond the limits of the known maps of their day are not unlike spiritual seekers. Some men and women grow restless with the staid, predictable limits of safe domesticity. Some by nature want to take on the dragons or discover there are no dragons at all, only new and fascinating lands and seas yet to be discovered. For those brave enough to launch out into that uncharted sea, brave enough to face their own dragons and those tough questions of faith, there is a new land to be found. I think of the novelist Thomas Wolfe's words:

"To lose the earth you know, for greater knowing; to lose the life you have for greater life; to leave the friends you loved, for greater loving; to find a land more kind than home, more large than earth."[6]

I knew after twenty years in the Evangelical Movement that some things didn't feel comfortable anymore. Some of the doubts I had that I never voiced were murmuring louder inside.

CHAPTER 2
THREE SCENES

Only by embracing the truth
of our past histories can any of us hope
to be free of pain in the present.
—Alice Miller[1]

I'll pick up in the middle of my story with three brief scenes.

SCENE 1: AT THE BACK OF THE CHURCH (1992)

I stood at the back of the storefront church we had converted into a sanctuary. I was the founding pastor who had planted the church six years earlier. It was Sunday and everyone had left but me. I was straightening up, cleaning up a bit, and then I walked back to the sound board to make sure it was turned off.

I stood for a moment and scanned the room—the riser we'd built, the walls we'd painted, the curtains we'd hung, and I thought we'd made it a very welcoming place. I loved the particular blue that

17

Linda had chosen for the curtains, and then I was amazed at how Marvin had matched the color with an identical blue in the paint he mixed by hand out of the back of his van. I had planted the church with only two other families, and we had grown to 125 people. It was slow going after six years.

I stood there as a flood of snapshot memories and a kaleidoscopic of emotions rushed before my eyes—the way one sees their life pass by in that instant before a car crash.

I was 43, husband and father of three children under 14 (twin boys and a ten-year-old daughter). I had been an ordained pastor for almost 12 years. Two years earlier I had published my first Christian book and my second was in rewrites with the publisher; I had been interviewed on radio and TV about the book, and I was the guest speaker at a conference where I would be teaching from my book. Additionally, I had written and directed a successful missions video —I had spent two weeks in the Venezuelan Amazon jungle where, as the director and second cameraman, I had had an adventurous time with the missionaries among three primitive tribal groups.

Since the time I was a nineteen-year-old Airman, I had dedicated my life to Christ; I had served in ministries to get to this point. I was on a successful trajectory in a profession I felt called to as a conservative Evangelical minister.

But standing at the back of the sanctuary that day, I knew something was shifting. I didn't really see it coming the way it did, but then again it had been brewing for a while. It didn't just happen. But like the big wooden bookcase wall in those movies where someone pulls the right book out and the bookcase revolves, revealing a secret doorway that opens to another room, the shift came. The bookcase was revolving.

I formed the words that had been seeking expression: "I don't like who I am becoming." This had more to do with the internal shifts that were going on than with my external accomplishments. I didn't like who "Evangelicals" were becoming as a movement. I didn't like who I was becoming as an Evangelical.

I didn't like the narrow confines of the theology, the Jesus-only myopia, the self-satisfaction and spiritual arrogance that our Evangelical elitism breeds, the judgmental eyes through which we profile people and shun them when we choose, the general close-mindedness of the average Christian toward those (writers, artists, philosophers, musicians, etc.) who are not of "our tribe," and the cold, casual ease with which we dismiss and disparage those who "don't see the light"—those we categorically write off as "pagans" who are "going to hell." We were always "profiling" people, sizing them up based upon our litmus tests: are they saved, did they pray the prayer, are they carnal or spirit-filled, backslidden or, God-forbid, "lukewarm?"

Evangelical/Fundamentalist Christianity has a dark shadow that few Evangelicals ever glimpse—nor do they recognize themselves as its breeding ground. I saw where all this is going now, and I didn't really want to become that any more than I already had.

I felt a great heaviness and sadness. It was as if a close friend was telling me: "I don't like who you are anymore." I didn't form any other words in that trance—those were the only words.

I knew what I had to do. A few months later, I resigned and left the ministry.

SCENE 2: AN OLD STUDY BIBLE (1993)

A few months after leaving ministry, I sat on the edge of the bed holding my big leather study Bible I'd used for the last few years. I knew what I was going to do with the Bible. I was in the bedroom I was renting from a good friend, John, who was also going through some major life changes. I was separated from my wife and dealing with all the fall-out from leaving my position as a pastor of that church I planted.

It was a time of great turmoil—personally, spiritually, socially, and career-wise. I knew it would be difficult, but that didn't mean I was ready for all of the difficulties. People change careers all the time, but leaving "ministry" carries its own special baggage and recriminations, the biggest being the "tag" that one had failed God and ditched his "calling."

I sat on the bed, tears welling up in my eyes. I was angry, sad and felt betrayed by this "God" I'd constructed, this "Bible" I had embraced in my training and studies. I felt tired and unhappy with this "Yahweh-Jesus" that had dominated my adult life.

Why had my 24 adult years of staid Christian living and ministry brought me to a place of unhappiness? How had it fractured my self? Why after years of what I thought was selfless ministry and following Jesus' Great Commission did I find myself an outsider—alone and rejected?

Leaving ministry, separating from my wife of 19 years, restarting my life and career were unbearably difficult. I was not regretting the decision to leave. I was feeling uncertain about how it would all turn out. It really didn't seem like there was anyone but myself to blame.

Major tectonic spiritual shifts were taking place inside me. What began at the back of the church in "Scene 1" was continuing. Putting it all into words that others could understand at the time was nearly impossible. I barely understood it myself.

Sitting there on the edge of the bed, I began to calmly tear in half my thick, gold-edged study Bible, section by section. This was a ritual moment for me, a symbolic act to mark a moment.

I tore chunks of the thin pages, slowly and deliberately. My tears flowed. I knew that some people view this act as blasphemous or sacrilegious. But deep down I knew the real God understood. This was between me and Him. In spite of my turmoil, my issues with God, and my anger, I knew or hoped the real God understood.

I knew one thing for certain, one thing had to change: I needed to change the voice of "God" in my head. Somehow over the course of years of zealous, dedicated Christian service, that voice – a voice that had largely come from all my studies of Scripture, the Bible, and readings and interpretations – got distorted and it was not who God was. This was not a simple fix. How do I change my belief structure that had been ingrained in me for decades? Is God just my beliefs? Is God this Bible?

I thought of those men who lived before there was a written Scripture that they could hold in their hands, a book, a Bible. I thought of Jacob who lived before Scripture and a Book. I thought of him wrestling the Angel of the Lord all night long, taking God to the mat, rolling around in the dust and dirt to get a blessing.

"The Voice" that had filtered through to me from this book—this Bible—that I had studied for so many years, the "Voice" that I heard in my head as He had taken shape in my theological thought—that "God" no longer seemed like an accurate reflection of who I knew God must be. I knew that much. If that voice in my head was who God actually was, then I wanted it out of my head. I needed to change the voice of God in my head.

I needed the voice of God to ring true in my head, but somehow, I had lost it. The Voice of God in my head had become more and more the annoying, grating voice of an old, angry, furrowed-brow, hard-nosed, impatient, judgmental, intolerant, never satisfied disciplinarian—a God of dogma and beliefs too narrow for such a transcendent being. *I can see this.*

All the initial reasons I was drawn to Christianity and Jesus—the grace, peace, love message—seemed hollow. I felt crushed and disillusioned. Though I had preached about God's goodness and grace to others, I wasn't experiencing that in my own head and heart. I believed that "Yahweh-Jesus" held me to a higher standard, and there was little grace or margin for error for me.

I didn't like who I had become and who I was becoming after years in this movement and I didn't like who "my" God had become in my head. *It's all in your head!*

I sat and slowly tore my whole Bible in half, section by section, the thick Old and New Testaments, concordances and all.

I would not read my Bible again for many years. *Sad*

SCENE 3: "WHY HAVEN'T I HEARD THIS BEFORE" (1994)

I had gone to three different Christian counselors in the year since leaving ministry, hoping to find someone to help me make sense of what I was going through.

After each successive counseling session with these three "Christian" counselors over a period of six months, I left feeling "tell me something I can't tell myself." It wasn't out of arrogance. But I realized something about the three counselors and myself. We had all read the same books, taken similar approaches to counseling, and had similar views on human psychology from our similar Christian training. We were all part of the Evangelical Movement. They really couldn't tell me much I couldn't tell myself.

Then my close friend John said, "You need to see Father Walsh." He had been seeing Father Walsh for several months. John and I had known each other for about 12 years through the same local churches. We were both going through similar upheavals in our faith, divorces, leaving the church and looking for a more adequate, richer, real-life spirituality. He had been on Campus Crusade staff and I came up through The Navigators ministry. We were both parachurch converts and disciples who went on to have careers and ministries in the community church.

So I found myself sitting in Father Walsh's counseling office for my first session. Father Walsh was in his mid-sixties, a handsome Anthony Hopkins look-alike. He had a mellifluous baritone voice, nearly white gray hair, twinkling blue smiling eyes, and a calm presence that immediately set me at ease.

I would come to know Father John Walsh as the most gracious, wise, and deeply spiritual person I've ever had the privilege to know and eventually call my good friend. He would become a major figure and mentor for me in the second half of my journey.

After explaining my general situation and why I was sitting in his office, Fr. Walsh drew a simple diagram of my "inner self" on a flip chart. He clearly described how I got where I was. (I will return to this diagram and what he had to say about it later in this book.)

I sat in disbelief at the clarity and wisdom of his words and the simple diagram (which I copied into my notebook there in his office). It seemed so simple, yet I had not heard it in such clear terms. Then as he finished his diagram and explanation, I stood up, almost unconsciously, pointed at the diagram and in disbelief (mixed with some long, pent-up anger), I said, "Why haven't I heard this before?"

THREE BRIEF SCENES...AND three key reasons why I decided to change my life course:

Scene 1—I didn't like who I was becoming.
Scene 2—I didn't like the voice of God in my head.
Scene 3—What else did I miss?

That session with Father Walsh began a long road to recovery.

PART TWO
CONSTRUCTING MY FAITH

CHAPTER 3
DOG TAGS

If God lived on earth,
people would break his windows.
—Yente, the Matchmaker
"Fiddler on the Roof"[1]

Y ou've probably seen them in movies. Those silvery pieces of tin dangling from beaded chains around U.S. soldiers' necks. We called them dog tags. Impressed into the thin steel metal of dog tags are the soldier's name, serial number, blood type and religion. The G.I.'s in "Saving Private Ryan" casually sitting with a few stacks of dog tags looking for a "Ryan" needed to be reminded that each dog tag represented a dead or missing soldier. Sometimes when an American soldier dies, his dog tags are the only way he can be identified.

Before receiving my dog tags as an Airman in the U. S. Air Force, I had to indicate officially that I was a "Protestant." Back in 1968 the only choices I think I had for my dog tags were Protestant, Catholic,

Jewish, or NO. So by default and my parents, I was Protestant. The choice had been made for me. I was 18 and grew up in Lutheran and Methodist churches on Long Island, New York. I was christened as an infant in a Presbyterian Church and attended confirmation classes in a Methodist Church.

Recently, I was sitting with a friend having a casual lunch. We were talking about our spiritual paths and interests; we talked about prayer and trusting God. He grew up in India as Hindu and I grew up in America as a Christian. But neither of us used the particular language or "trappings" of our respective religions. We shared common ground and language in our spiritual seeking and in our similar spiritual disciplines, so we could talk freely about prayer or meditation or trusting God. It didn't matter the particular names of our deity—we shared the common words, like Lord and God, and we both had spiritual foundations of faith.

At our heart and soul levels our image of the Divine Being was that this divine being was good and benevolent. Our devotion and our desire for wisdom and truth were the same, and the way we prayed and meditated were similar. Our particular religions were just the external dressings. We both respected each other's religion without any sense of one being superior to the other. The nature of spiritual life for both of us was similar, and the longing or desire to connect with a divine Presence were the same.

My friend was born in India to Hindu Indian parents. I was born in America to Scottish-English-German Protestant parents. Did I choose my religion? Or did it choose me?

Much of our initial and introductory religion comes to us based upon where and to whom we are born. Geography is a major part of the "starter religion" we are introduced to from our ethnic and religious family traditions. *True*

I was born and grew up on Long Island, New York, not a city kid, but a suburban baby-boomer kid back when just about everyone I knew went to church or synagogue. My ancestry is a heavy combination of English Puritan, German Lutheran, and Scottish Presbyterian.

These are all Protestant Denominations, each originating from a specific ethnic and geographic place.

I have to admit that, growing up on Long Island as a Protestant, I had the easiest gig as far as religion went. My Roman Catholic and Jewish friends had way more to do for their religion than I did. The Methodist and Lutheran Churches didn't ask as much of me as the religions of some of my Catholic and Jewish friends asked of them. But there were times I envied my Catholic buddies because they had "confession." They all seemed way more relaxed or unburdened after Friday confession. It seemed like it wiped the slate clean, and they were free to have fun again for a week.

MY STARTER RELIGION

Initially, my faith was constructed for me. Most of us wind up being handed a religion from our parents: a starter religion. My parents took me to church when I was young. When I was 13, I took Confirmation classes at the Methodist Church. The Pastor led a group of about 15 of us in studies of church history, the Old and New Testaments, and some church theology. It was all a blur to me partly because the girls at that time easily stole the show.

I thought about becoming a minister because I liked Pastor Johnson; he was kind, warm and caring. The idea of the Confirmation process is that it gives youth who are "coming of age" a chance to make a commitment or confirm their beliefs in their church's doctrine. For me as a Methodist, Confirmation was basically saying, "Yes, I'm a Methodist, like my parents." But what did it mean beyond that? I wasn't sure.

After my Confirmation, my parents let me decide if I wanted to go to church any more. It was kind of cool they did that. For me, at the time, church wasn't relevant. First off, my parents had stopped going, dad dropped us off at church and came back and picked us up when it was over. Second, there weren't any cool youth groups at any of the churches in town, so why would I be interested? So at 13, having just memorized the order of all 66 books of the Bible and recited them in front of the whole church to receive my "Confirmation," I decided not to go to church.

My family officially became members of the C&E Club. We were nominal Protestant Christians, who mainly went to church on Christmas and Easter.

My early religious construction of faith came fully constructed. I didn't have to think about it. It was all figured out by others and all I had to do was sign up.

SPIRITUAL DNA

My religious DNA goes back to the first Davis Protestants who fled England and religious persecution, crossed an ocean, and settled in Massachusetts in the 1630's. I know from tracing my genealogy that my ancestors that came to America in the 1630's were Puritans from Marlborough, England. They were among the earliest ships of Puritans that came to Massachusetts and settled along the coast. They were seekers of religious freedom.

I literally have Puritan DNA in my blood. I have felt this deep Puritan strain in me my whole life. It's like it came with the package —body, soul and mind. It is not something I consciously cultivated, but it seems it's hard to drain out that strain.

The genealogical search for my family roots had a big kick-start from a huge Family Bible handed down to me with birth and death records of the Davis side dating back to 1804. But its roots are not purely Puritan, as it turns out.

The Davis family came from Marlborough, England, which is close to the ancient stone structures of Stonehenge and Amesbury. This area in distant times was inhabited by people who oriented their worship toward the stars and sun.

At some point, the star worshippers gave way or gave into the Christian Roman Catholics and Protestants who took over the region. By the 1630's, those Christian Puritans now found that *their* religion was under attack, so they crossed the Atlantic Ocean to Massachusetts for religious freedom.

My early religious education and the imprint on my soul was Protestant Christianity; my scriptures were the Revised Standard Bible and the King James Bible, which included 66 books in the Old and New Testament. I was very much a product of my time, family, ethnicity, and geography. *As are we!*

CHAPTER 4
IN MY ROOM

Please Let Me Wonder
—The Beach Boys[1]

'm looking at two old photographs, still trying to figure them out, without any real success for a few decades now. It's like those perennial great mysteries of our planet—Easter Island, the Great Pyramids, the Lost City of Atlantis. Except my great mystery is a personal one. The only person in both photos is my father, Charles Davis. In one photo he is about 18 years old and in the other photo he is 48.

In his younger photograph, he is surrounded by four of his buddies seated on a picnic table. My dad is the only one sitting on the bench, while the others are sitting on the picnic table around him. My dad looks happy, lean, athletic, and confident; and he is leaning back into the other guys with his arms draped over their knees and legs looking as comfortable as brothers. Dad was an only son, but I have a few photos of him and these same friends.

In the second photograph, my dad is surrounded by his four sons. I am twenty years old dressed in my Air Force Uniform; my three younger brothers are 16, 8 and 4. My dad, in a white t-shirt, looks twenty years older than his 48 years, already a little stooped, muscles gone in his arms. He still has his hair in a pompadour, and it's only thinning slightly. The illness that would take him down is already settling in. What strikes me about the photo is that none of us are touching.

This contrast between two snapshots of my father remains a mystery to me to this day. What happened to that affectionate youthful Charles? How was it he could be so casual and affectionate with his buddies, but could barely put his hand on the shoulder of his young sons?

I have many photographs of my father over the years. His parents took good photographs when he was young, and my dad became an excellent photographer who built his own darkroom in the basement of our home and developed his own photographs, teaching me photography along the way as a kid. I am fortunate to have a wealth of family photographs documenting my youth.

My father passed away many years ago, before I was old enough to ask him all the questions I now wish I had known to ask earlier. But I didn't know I had those questions then. So I am pondering in the dark, and staring at old photographs like some homicide detective looking for a hidden clue that I missed last time I looked at this photo.

It's clear from all the old photos of my dad before, during and right after his Army years, that my Dad was affectionate with his buddies. In one he seems proud and exuberant, with his arms around a friend on either side of him, like some proud dad with two grown sons as they pose on a bridge somewhere during WWII. In another shot with a few neighbors at his downstairs homemade bar, dad is the jovial bartender carousing with his own Rat Pack of suburban buddies in white shirts and ties with their whiskey, beers and Tom Collins. This was the dad that I never knew.

The title of the first book I authored (*The Father I Never Knew*, NavPress, 1991) was based on my relationship with my father, which I felt was cut off abruptly when he died at 54.

I know it is said of my dad's generation, those men who grew up during the Depression of the early 1930's, fought in World War II and gave birth to the Baby Boomers and the affluent 1950's, that many of these fathers were not known for being affectionate or talkative, not given to expressing their inner thoughts. My dad didn't talk much. But as the years have gone by, I realize my dad did a lot for me as I was growing up in his home.

DEVELOPING AN INNER LIFE

When I was twelve, my dad finished off one side of the attic and made it into a bedroom with its own bathroom (there was only one other bathroom in the house). I helped him with a lot of the remodeling. It was to be my room. With a fourth son on the way, the eldest son got the best room in the house—all to myself.

I look back now and see how significant it was that in my adolescence my dad gave me my own bedroom and my own car.

In 1963, the pop song *"In My Room"* by The Beach Boys became my bedroom hymn. Written by Brian Wilson, the sensitive genius of The Beach Boys, and Gary Usher, the song captures the emblematic youthful hymn-like sound that drew me to their music. Brian sings about his room as a haven, where he can get away and pray. I may have stopped going to church at 13, but I started praying in my room. The beautiful harmony and arrangements on those Beach Boy songs in the 1960's conveyed a whole feeling to me. They felt to me like secular hymns about youth. They gave voice to something in my soul. There was a celebration of youth in the sounds.

My Dad's gift, my own bedroom, as I was coming of age gave me a chance to develop an inner life. In a rather small home with three younger brothers, there was rarely a place to get away to be alone.

My father lost his father when he was twelve; he and his mother had it tough for a few years.

This is what my dad put in my new bedroom: my own TV, my own record player, a large desk, a reel-to-reel tape recorder, an artist's easel, a full-size bed. My room became a sanctuary and a studio. I could close out my younger brothers and all that was going on downstairs—which I did often.

This was when I began to write stories, poems, and song lyrics, to take painting lessons, to read lots of books of my own choosing, and to listen to all kinds of music. There in my own bedroom I began to develop an interior life.

Eventually I would learn how to play guitar in my room, start my first rock band, and start my first recordings with the reel-to-reel tape recorder my dad bought for me.

When I was sixteen and could drive, my dad bought me a car. And it was not an old car, it was a beautiful 1963 Chevy Impala, the two-door cool coupe style. My car was the other world my dad gave me and entrusted to me.

Looking back now, I see so much more of how my dad let me be me and gave me the two best things an adolescent coming-of-age kid could want: his own bedroom and a cool car.

Like Brian sings in the song, my bedroom was where I could let loose, let down, sing out, think, and pray. At the time, I mainly prayed the only prayer I memorized from church, The Lord's Prayer. I did start free-style prayer; simple requests about school tests, dates, girlfriends.

In my room was where I consciously remembered praying at night before bed, right when I was turning thirteen. I didn't really appreciate how significant it was for me at the time, but my own room gave me a chance to develop a private, inner world where I could think, where I could develop a private space to wonder and be myself.

I remember that in that private space, alone, I watched movies on my own TV that made a deep impression. I remember being moved by some of the early "sword and sandal" movies; movies about Biblical times. I remember some famous actor in tears clutching the robe of Jesus at the Cross. Watching those movies alone in my room, I had a different reaction than if I had been downstairs with my little brothers running around or making noise. I shed some tears.

This was the early and mid 1960's, so rock and roll music made a big impression. I was building my own record album collection, learning guitar, and playing music with my friends. I was a huge fan of The Beach Boys, The Beatles, The Rolling Stones, Bob Dylan, Simon and Garfunkel, Neil Diamond, and on and on.

However, it was a lesser-known song by Johnny Rivers that really hit me one day. We were all in the middle of a turbulent time in America with the assassinations of leaders, the Vietnam War, the civil rights movement, and the counterculture challenges. I was on course to graduate in June of 1968. I wasn't at all sure what I would do. Would I go to college right away? Would I get drafted or should I enlist? It was a disconcerting time.

Johnny Rivers sang a line that caught my attention. The title of the song said it all: "Look to your Soul."[2] It was as simple as just looking to your soul for the answers. It doesn't sound so earth-shattering now, but at the time, looking to my soul was something I hadn't heard put that way before, and I took it seriously. At the time, I wasn't going to church and didn't know any of my friends who were (unless they had to). The church in my hometown didn't seem relevant. So how would I look to my soul? I wasn't going to look for a conventional church-type solution. Rock music opened some doors.

So, I made a mental note to continue to look inward, to be as spiritual a kind of person as I could. My bedroom, my private space and sanctuary, gave me a place apart, a place closed off from the rest of the house downstairs and the world outside to be alone, to wonder, to dream, cry over that broken date, ponder over lyrics from songs I listened to in the dark on my bed, and to pray.

CHAPTER 5

CIGARETTES OR A BIBLE?

Gotta serve Somebody.
—Bob Dylan"[1]

BASIC TRAINING, AMARILLO AIR FORCE BASE, TEXAS

I didn't know what day it was. It was one of those days in the first week of basic training in the U.S. Air Force when it doesn't matter what day it is. I felt like I was suddenly in someone else's bad nightmare; drill instructors were shouting obscenities in between relentless orders and I'm being rudely awakened at all hours of the night for no good reason. I was in basic training at Amarillo Air Force Base, Texas.

I was sitting in a chapel—or auditorium made to look like a chapel—and it was something called Chaplain's Orientation. All I remember as I sat trying to get used to my new shaved head was that the Chaplain said, "You are allowed to carry this New Testament in the shirt pocket of your fatigues. So if you don't smoke you can carry your Bible with you."

Cigarettes or the Bible? It was an easy choice for me since I didn't smoke; I chose to put the little New Testament in my fatigue pocket. Johnny Rivers' words rang in my head: "look to your soul." I needed all the help I could get.

I started reading "The Gospel of Matthew" that day. I remembered the order of books of the Bible from my confirmation class, and I knew Matthew was the first book and he was one of Jesus' twelve disciples.

I decided to enlist while in my senior year of high school during the Vietnam War. Most of my friends went off to college, but I decided to enlist in the Air Force for four years so I wouldn't get drafted out of college, plus I could get the G.I. Bill and use it to pay for college after my four years' service for Uncle Sam.

Basic Training is designed to break you down and build you up, designed to get you to follow orders and jump when the drill sergeant says jump. I was 18 years old, far away from home for the first time and in a hostile military environment. It was disorienting. So I found myself praying more.

THE LONGING

A couple of friends who signed my high school yearbook wrote similar lines: "I hope you find what you're looking for." They saw it in me even more than I was aware of it in myself. I was looking for something. I was 18 and starting my adventure into the world, I was an idealist and a romantic in Air Force fatigues.

I graduated high school the month Bobby Kennedy was assassinated, not long after Martin Luther King was assassinated in April, which was not long after the Tet Offensive upped the war effort in Vietnam. The social unrest, civil rights movements, the war in Vietnam, and the assassinations of our best and brightest left me feeling unmoored spiritually when I was launched out into the world the summer of 1968.

The old barracks at Amarillo Air Force Base had big wooden lockers built into the walls of each of our rooms. In the lockers, above the drawers, in the large space for hanging our clothes and placing our shoes and boots, there was a sturdy place large enough for me to sit curled up and close the locker door, leaving it open just enough for the light to filter in so I could read.

That pocket New Testament Bible from the Chaplain's Office helped me. I read through the Gospel of Matthew in Basic Training. The verse that I underlined and stood out to me the most was:

"Come unto me all ye who are burdened and heavy ladened and I will give you rest. For my burden is easy and my yoke is light."[2]

It represented to me Jesus' main invitation. He was offering spirituality that is not based upon laws, traditions, and regulations. He was offering a spirituality that was not a burdensome religion but something that gave you rest, grace and comfort.

This was in reality the first time I was making a decision as an adult to seek comfort from the religion of my youth. It was a step at constructing a faith that I could practice in private, with my own prayers and needs.

THE PRESENCE AND "THE CRIPPLER"

When I was five years old, I woke up one morning and I could not move. I was paralyzed and terrified. I had never experienced anything like this before. I was a typically active five-year-old boy. But that morning I couldn't move from my neck down.

Instead of calling out to mom, I prayed. This was at the height of the polio epidemic—"The Crippler" —that was hitting Long Island, and I had not yet been vaccinated. I immediately thought I had polio. I was terrified. So I prayed and asked God to take it away. Within moments I was able to move. I got up freely and was fine.

I'm not claiming it was a miracle, but in my five-year-old brain it was God who responded and heard me pray that morning. God became personal for me that day.

. . .

How do we construct our faith?

For many of us our religion is constructed for us. We just decide to go with what the church decided. But at some point, we decide as adults what we will believe.

It's a decision at some point: (1) to acknowledge a Divine Presence and (2) to believe that the Divine is either personal or not. America's Founding Fathers were said to have been "deists" as opposed to "theists." Deists believe there is a Supreme Being, but don't believe the creator intervenes in his creation. Theists believe that the Supreme Being does intervene in our world and is personally involved.

I believed that had God intervened. He was personal from an early age. It is a religious construct that I chose. We don't have empirical proof of the existence of a Divine Being, so it's a mental decision. We can choose to believe scriptural texts that tell us about God.

I wanted a spirituality that was more than a label on a Dog Tag. I wanted to find something personal in religion, so I started with what was most familiar, relevant, and appealing: Jesus' words and message.

The church may not have been cool when I was young, but Jesus was always kind of cool. He was the long-haired outsider who challenged the religious people of his day.

Jesus made the Divine personal and human.

CHAPTER 6
MY WOODSTOCK

Far over the misty mountains cold
To dungeons deep and caverns old
We must away ere break of day
To seek the pale enchanted gold.
—J.R.R. Tolkien[1]

COCOA BEACH, FLORIDA, MAY 1969

I was sitting on a pristine beach a short walk from my barracks on my first Air Force duty assignment after ten months of training. Patrick Air Force Base, Cocoa Beach, Florida, sat on a narrow strip of a barrier island bounded by the Atlantic Ocean on the east and the inland waterways Banana River and Indian River Lagoon on the west. The land was not much more than a big stable sand bar, barely above sea level.

The Apollo space program, just a few miles up the road, was a few weeks away from landing its first men on the moon. Cocoa Beach and Titusville were party towns for the area back then. I had my own room in the barracks which was probably a par five from the beach at what is now the main gate on A1A.

It was my first week on base and I was sitting on the beach wondering why I had enlisted in the Air Force when all my friends were enjoying college life. I wasn't sure what I'd do to occupy myself for the next three and a half years of being an Airman.

That night one of the guys I worked with invited me to a party at a house on the dunes in Satellite Beach. As we pulled up in his car it was already dark and the small, concrete-block, one-story house sat on top of the modest dunes between the beach and A1A. Back in 1969, the beach coast from Vero Beach to Merritt Island had none of the condos or high-rises that have since sprung up.

There were about twenty cars parked in haphazard fashion around this lone house that was bathed in dull light from a single light pole. Music was blaring from the house as we approached. I was told as I entered, that if there was anything I wanted, just ask...drugs, alcohol, sex...just ask. I walked through the house in what seemed to me something from a movie: every room was dark and filled with people on the floor and on furniture in various states of sexual activity, and alcohol or drug induced highs or lows.

I lost the buddy I was with pretty quickly as he disappeared into a dark room. I meandered through the hallways and made my way out the back of the house to clear my breath. This was not for me. I waited outside and walked the beach alone until my ride was ready to leave.

I quickly found out at Patrick AFB there were two basic paths Airmen were on: the drugs, alcohol and topless bars and houses on the dunes, or the straight and narrow.

A KNOCK ON THE DOOR

The following weekend on a Saturday morning, a knock on my door at 7:00 in the morning woke me. As I got up to open the door, I thought, "This better be important if somebody is waking me early on my day off."

I opened the door to see two blond guys, dressed nicely, with smiles on their faces. One of the guys said cheerfully: "We're inviting guys to an informal Bible Study, volleyball, and free lunch at a home off the base. If you'd like to go, we meet at the Airmen's Club at 8:00 and hop in a few cars."

They didn't pressure me. I stood there and tried to fathom what had been said. First off, I'd never met guys my age who were interested in the Bible, let alone a Bible Study. Second, I thought, "If these guys have enough nerve to wake me this early on a Saturday, maybe I should check this out." Third, the idea of volleyball and lunch at a family home sounded good enough. I said to the two guys, who would become my good friends (Ray and Bill), "Sure. I'll see you over there."

That day changed my life. There were about twenty-five guys at the house, and we broke into five or six groups for a one-hour Bible Study. The guys were all young, friendly, and mostly current and ex-military guys. There were four married couples that directed the ministry. It was a parachurch ministry team who worked for The Navigators, a Christian organization similar to Campus Crusade and Young Life. We played volleyball for about two hours at a nearby park on the Indian River Lagoon in Eau Gallie. Then we had lunch and hung out for a while.

In the afternoon, Ray (one of the guys who invited me) shared the Gospel with me and I prayed a prayer to invite Jesus into my heart. I'd never quite heard the Gospel message like this in my churches back home. I thought I was a Christian because of my family and I believed in Jesus (my dog tags indicated Protestant). But this idea of making a decision for Christ and asking him to come into my life was something I had not heard before.

I came back to my barracks that afternoon feeling light and hopeful for the first time in months. For the next three and a half years that ministry fellowship became like family.

THE APPALACHIAN FOOTHILLS, GEORGIA, AUGUST 1969

Three months later, I was standing in a chapel in the north foothills of Georgia with about 200 others, mostly young men and women like myself. The building was modest, but had sliding glass doors on either side providing a gorgeous view of the pastoral setting: pine trees so tall that the view down to the mountain lake was blocked by their tall thin trunks. It was a sunny morning and the lake beyond the bed of pine needles at the foot of the hill was a peaceful, sparkling greenish-blue. We were singing hymns prior to a speaker's lecture. I had never heard hymns sung so beautifully in person. I remember feeling this was possibly one of the most peaceful places I could be in that week.

I was on leave attending a Christian Conference in the foothills of the Appalachian Mountains in north Georgia, a few clicks from the North Carolina state line. I came to the conference with a group of about twenty others from the ministry at Patrick Air Force Base.

It was August, 1969, the Vietnam War was raging, there were protests against the war all around the country. The U.S. space program had successfully landed Neil Armstrong and Buzz Aldrin on the moon, and somewhere upstate in my home state of New York there was a music festival taking place that I didn't know much about at the time—Woodstock.

We had caravanned in several cars to get to the Toccoa Falls conference grounds, which was actually a Bible College campus that became a retreat and conference center during the summer break. This was one of the regular Southeastern conferences sponsored by The Navigators, a parachurch ministry that worked primarily on ministry bases and college campuses (at that time).

I was surprised at how close I felt in such a short time after meeting this collection of ministry people from the Base fellowship in Florida. I rode in Don's late model green Oldsmobile that was as heavy as a tank. Don was from West Virginia; he had attended a couple of years of college before he enlisted. Ray, who rode with us, was from Connecticut. He too had a couple of college years under his belt. Both of them had become like brothers to me in three months.

Standing there singing with all those voices of devotion and dedication was such a contrast to the singing in the churches I had grown up attending on Long Island. Back home it seemed the churches were poorly attended or were populated by mostly older people and only a handful of young people my age. People mumbled through the hymns, the men rarely sang, it seemed—if they were there at all.

That morning and each of the sessions over the week-long conference reminded me that I was on a good path. These were good people, as friendly as I'd ever met, sincere, genuine, and good-humored. Some of the young guys who came with us from Florida were ex-military. Still in their twenties, they had been in the Air Force, Marines, Navy, or Army. A couple of the guys had been to Vietnam and a couple had been wounded in combat. During that week there were classes and workshops on things like the devotional life, prayer, Bible study, witnessing, discipleship, as well as plenty of free time for sports, volleyball, basketball, football. This was "muscular" Christianity, as some might say; heavy doses of sports and competition. But it was very relationship based as well. You made real friendships, and this was like a college fraternity of brothers and mentors.

What I also liked about this ministry was that it was non-denominational; there were Presbyterians, Catholics, Baptists, Methodists, former agnostics, nonchurchgoers—you name it. It didn't matter what church you were from or went to. This was about the basic Gospel and Christian message. It was Jesus that drew us together. We would have been called "Jesus Freaks," as the term was used then, except we all had short, military-style haircuts. Even the ex-military guys kept their hair short.

As I stood there singing that morning, it all seemed romantic in its own way: the pastoral setting, the nature retreat, the Walden Pond to walk around, the young people, the spiritual devotion, the idealism, the peacefulness of it all. It was a welcome contrast to the unsettling times happening in the world outside and faraway.

Most of the hymns we sang were new to me. The one that really stuck with me was "The Sands of Time." The melody and words seemed more poetic and a bit more modern than most of the typical dusty old and ancient hymns. This was the verse I remember:

> *"O Christ, He is the fountain,*
> *The deep, sweet well of love!*
> *The streams on earth I've tasted,*
> *More deep I'll drink above:*
> *There to an ocean fullness His mercy doth expand,*
> *And glory, glory dwelleth In Emmanuel's land."[2]*

The song reminded me of why I had become a Christian, or as they say, "prayed the prayer" three months earlier. It was because of the Jesus of the Gospels and his grace and love. At this point, my theological acumen was thin.

I had become a frequent visitor to the pristine, open stretches of soft sand and gentle surf there on Cocoa Beach, a short walk from my barracks, where the Atlantic Ocean view stretched for an unobstructed 180-degree span. The line that stuck with me was: "There to an ocean fullness, His mercy doth expand."

The previous year, June 1968, I had graduated from Kings Park High School, New York. When we were getting our Yearbooks signed, I remember one girl saying she didn't want me to sign her yearbook. When I asked her why, she said, "Because you'll write something too serious."

She was probably right. I was the serious kid, the romantic sentimentalist. I was the music lover, the kid playing guitar and secretly writing his first songs. It was not that I didn't have fun. I had a great time. But I was also thinking about more than just careers and college. I was the kid telling my friends about this Johnny Rivers song called "Look to your Soul." The counterculture movement was challenging our thinking and the norms of the 1950's and early 1960's.

I knew in that chapel in the foothills at Toccoa conference grounds overlooking the pines and the lake, singing those hymns that morning with all those other dreamers and seekers, that I thought I found something. I was on to something and not some faddish thing. I was on to a relevant, contemporary Jesus.

The Beatles sang "Give Peace a Chance" and "All you need is Love." Suddenly Jesus and religion could be cool. This wasn't about politics, the war, or all the controversy swirling around in the culture. This was about something more seminal, more eternal.

Almost a year earlier in Basic Training in the Air Force, I was huddled in that locker reading a pocket New Testament before falling out for morning drills in the Texas panhandle. That verse that first caught me with the invitation from Jesus I had by now memorized, along with other verses: "Come unto me, all ye that labour and are heavy laden and I will give you rest."

I had finally found a way to "come unto me" and to connect with Jesus. And it was these people who were helping facilitate that for me. It was a way that didn't involve a particular church or denomination, or a set of doctrines and rules, but was focused on Jesus and his message of forgiveness, grace, peace and love. I had now gone all in and decided to be a disciple, a follower of Jesus.

CHAPTER 7

THE MONKISH BOYS

For unto whomsoever much is given,
of him shall be much required.
—Jesus[1]

"We'd like you to give your testimony in front of the guys at Saturday bible study next week," Ray said.

"What's a testimony?" I asked, thinking, *Okay, what did I get myself into now?*

Ray and I became close friends over the next year. The little group of guys I met that first Saturday in May all became my friends. Nobody cursed, nobody drank or did drugs. We would go out to dinner together most of the time instead of eating at the chow hall on the Base. The ministry and the fellowship essentially became my fraternity.

After my big "born again" moment sitting on the canal with Ray and "praying the prayer," there were no lightning flashes in the sky, no parting of the clouds, no angels descending, no "Eureka" moment of seeing the light. Yet I knew something changed. There was a sense of something aligning inside, a sense that there was a new inner peace and a path, an opening to spiritual things I had not found before. That secret passage behind the revolving bookcase was revealed.

Ray pointed out the verse that says we become "new creations in Christ" once we are born again. I quickly learned the terminology.

> Jesus answered and said unto him, Verily, verily, I say unto thee, Except a man be born again, he cannot see the kingdom of God.[2]
>
> Therefore, if anyone is in Christ, he is a new creation; old things have passed away; behold, all things have become new.[3]

What does that really mean to be "a new creation?" This is the one that puzzled me for years, because Christians often talk about it quite casually as if to imply that you are no longer human, as if you are a new form of life—you are a "Christian being" rather than a "human being." But scientifically, physiologically, anatomically, and psychologically I am still a human being, of the species *Homo sapiens sapiens*. No matter how you parse it, I am still and always will be a human being. Christians may be "new creations" in a figurative sense, I thought, but by all other literal senses we are still human beings, *Homo sapiens*. We do not change our species when we "become" Christians. However, I didn't make a big deal of it at the time.

"TO WHOM MUCH IS GIVEN"

They wanted me to give "my testimony" in front of the group. Once Ray explained what "a testimony" was, and that it only needed to be three to five minutes long, I was relieved. But I was still nervous about talking in front of all these guys.

A testimony was simply explaining a little bit about why I

decided to invite Jesus into my heart. So I was to share a little bit about my family background, church background and what brought me to this point of commitment. Keep it simple.

So I went back to my room in the barracks and thumbed through some verses. Ray had also given me another assignment, which was not mandatory, but it was something the other guys were doing: memorizing Bible verses. The Navigators had something called the Topical Memory System, which was a series of verses printed on small business-size cards.

I was given a stack of small cards with verses printed on them. One of the verses really caught my attention; it was the verse that says "to whom much is given, much is required" from Jesus' words in Luke's Gospel (12:48). I have already discussed how fortunate I felt growing up and having great parents, a great family, and how much I felt my dad and mom had done for me. *To whom much is given.* That was me.

So that was the verse I used in "my testimony" about why I responded to the Gospel, along with the verse that had struck me in my readings in Basic Training in the pocket New Testament the Chaplain gave me (Matt. 11:28). I nervously stood before about twenty people at the ministry house and stumbled through "my testimony."

I will point out an important part of this that I didn't see quite clearly at the time, but which I understood better later: the "much is required" part of the verse. I was genuinely interested in Jesus and his message of peace and grace. Even though it was "free," there was a sense of responsibility, duty, and a good kind of paying back. It was similar to my mindset as an Airman in the U.S. military: a sense of "duty" to Uncle Sam, the Air Force, my country. This sense of giving back to Jesus, of requirements and obligations, weighed heavily on me. He died on the Cross for me; I kind of owed him, a kind of gentleman's agreement and honor.

THE MONKISH BOYS

For all the talk of grace and the free gift of salvation by faith, there was the other side of the coin. Right away this fellowship of believers I had entered had a list of things I could do. Within a week of my being "born again" and becoming a "new creation" I was asked to give my testimony, I was given a stack of verses to memorize, I was enrolled in a series of Bible Studies (with workbooks), and I was expected to come back next week. With my enlistment in the U.S. Air Force, Uncle Sam had plenty of requirements for me also, and a different set of disciplines to adhere to. So now with my enlistment in the "Lord's Army," I had a bundle of new steps for how to grow as a Christian, how to become a "disciple" of Jesus.

It was made clear to me that there are "nominal" Christians, which are those who "call" themselves Christians and go to church occasionally. Then there are "practicing" Christians or "disciples," who take their Christianity seriously and walk the walk as well as talk the talk.

Well, I wanted to be an exemplary Christian. I wanted it to matter and make a difference in my life. I wanted to show Jesus that I appreciated what he did for me and that I took his words to heart. So sign me up for the discipleship program!

This was something I could really sink my teeth into. My job as an Airman at the hospital was fairly routine; I was an X-Ray technician at the base hospital. Sometimes I was on call nights and weekends, sometimes I would have to work in the emergency room, and occasionally I drove the ambulance for emergencies. However, I had plenty of time off to myself.

For the remaining three and a half years of my Air Force duty, I was essentially in a layman's fraternity, a self-enrolled pre-seminarian, a discipleship training program. On the Air Force base we were sometimes called "the Never-daters" (a play on The Navigators name) because most of us were walking a straight and narrow path and didn't smoke, drink, do drugs or date (although some of the guys had girlfriends back home). I should mention this: there were very few female "airmen" on the base, so it's not like there were a lot of available women to date on base.

I have nothing but fond memories of The Navigators fellowship during those early years. It was in some ways like being in Bible College and having a job at the same time.

I kept busy with ministry activities. We had bible study and sports on Saturdays, Sundays was Airmen's Chapel and hanging out at The Navigator reps house playing sports, watching sports, having meals. Within no time I was going through the barracks knocking on doors on Saturday mornings and inviting guys to Bible study. Soon I was going through the barracks on Wednesday nights and inviting guys to the Base Chapel services. Within a year I was leading Bible studies and teaching Sunday school at the Base Chapel. We had developed an important supportive role with the Base Chapel ministry; one of the Chaplains worked real closely with us.

I became close friends with Darrell, the Nav rep for Patrick Air Force Base. When Darrell was reassigned to north Florida, I became close friends with Bob, the Nav rep who took over the ministry. Both Darrell and Bob became important mentors in my life. I am deeply indebted to them for their wisdom, kindness, and generosity. Both men had come to Christ later in life, so they had a balance and wisdom that I did not always see in many of the younger ministry reps. Both men had wives and young children, so they had a great sense of family and middle-age maturity. I admired Darrell's easy warmth and southern grace. I admired Bob's mind, critical thinking, and great sense of humor. Bob was also from New York, so we had that in common. Bob had been in the U.S. Army and was a Ranger, as he would say "jumping out of perfectly good airplanes."

Both men and their wives opened their homes to me as if I were family. To welcome all us service men into their home was a generosity of spirit that was unusual.

Ray, who led me to Christ, was two years older than me and had enlisted after a couple of years in college to avoid the draft. Ray was a great companion. We were both fans of the British rock band the Moody Blues, so during those two years, every time a new Moody Blues album was released, we'd each buy it and sit together and analyze the lyrics to the songs. Our time was cut short when Ray received orders and was transferred overseas.

Patrick AFB was a happening place to be during these years because the Apollo program was in full swing. I was there at ground zero when Apollo 11 launched, and I felt the rumbling of the ground from the power of the lift-off. I was there on base watching the first steps on the moon before heading to Bible Study. I was tapped to be on the medical support crew for two of the Apollo Missions. All that meant was that in the event of a crash, the astronauts would be brought to our hospital for treatment. I participated in exercises where astronauts were helicoptered in outside the hospital and I pretended to X-ray them.

The ministry would grow in numbers and eventually would include McCoy Air Force Base in Orlando, and Florida Institute of Technology in Melbourne. The quality of the men and women I would meet always impressed me.

On Sundays everyone was free to go to whatever church they wanted. Most of the guys on the base went to the Base Chapel, which had two worship services: one Protestant and one Catholic.

This was Christianity stripped down to the essentials of the faith. It wasn't about how we did communion, how we did baptism, or whether you were a Protestant or a Catholic. There was a decidedly conservative, evangelical flavor to The Navigators ministry, rather than a liberal one.

When I "came to" Jesus it was not so much because I was told I was a sinner and going to hell. That was not the emphasis of the message. The Gospel was presented to me as "Good News": Jesus is knocking on the door of my heart (Rev. 3:10), he wants to give me eternal life (John 3:16) and abundant life (John 10:10).

Since I'd always believed in Jesus and was brought up in the Christian Church, it was not a big stretch for me. It seemed the next step; it seemed like what I'd been looking for. I felt a great sense of purpose and mission.

The message of the Gospel also came with an invitation to be a "disciple" of Jesus and join the Great Commission of Jesus.... "Go ye into all the world and make disciples." (Matt. 28). I hit the ground running and wanted to be the best "disciple" I could be.

I had not battled drugs, alcohol, promiscuous sex, or been a troublemaker; I had been the good kid, the good son. So my "conversion" or "coming to Jesus" moment wasn't because I needed to be saved from some vice or bad habits.

"To whom much is given...much is required." Okay, I thought, I owe God. He had given me much, and now he was asking much of me. We had a mission: the Great Commission. So I was ready to do my part. I was one of the monkish boys.

CHAPTER 8
"SINNERS IN THE HANDS OF AN ANGRY GOD"

Christianity and Judaism are religions of exile:
Man was thrown out of the Garden.
—Joseph Campbell[1]

Patrick Air Force Base was not a big base. The center of the base where the barracks and service facilities are located was small. So it was easy to run into one of the guys from the growing ministry when I was out and about.

"What's your latest verse?" was often the greeting we offered fellow ministry guys when we ran into each other.

We carried little "verse packs" with Bible verses printed on small business cards that we were memorizing. There was a whole series of verses we all memorized. I had to be ready to quote the "latest" verse I was memorizing. It was all part of the camaraderie and our own ministry *esprit de corps*.

It was part of our discipleship program, and it was a good way to learn scripture. We would hold each other "accountable" as a way to maintain discipline. After months of memorizing verses, some of us began memorizing long sections of scripture. It was surprising to me how much we could memorize.

The Christianity I was drawn to was a rather generic "conservative Evangelical" theology. Back in the late 1960's and 1970's, "conservative Evangelicalism" didn't have all the extra political and cultural baggage it has today in the twenty-first century. The ministry fellowship at Patrick AFB had an interdenominational feel. The people were from all denominations, and it wasn't an issue.

We were careful in the 1970's to distinguish "Fundamentalist" Christians from conservative "Evangelicals." We were the latter. There wasn't a lot of legalism in the ministry fellowship. We didn't prohibit dancing, playing cards, rock music, smoking, etc., etc. We were "conservative" in a theological sense, not necessarily in a cultural, political sense.

That being said, there were a good number of Southern Baptists in the ministry; this was, after all, the southeast, part of the expanded Bible Belt.

After a few years in the movement, I became uncomfortable with some of the theology. Some of it I eventually just didn't believe, but I managed to avoid confronting people with the issue. When I became a pastor, I avoided teaching or talking much about some of those uncomfortable or debatable doctrines. I'd had quite enough of those circular discussions in seminary.

The most disturbing was the doctrine that unbelievers would be sent to Hell and face eternal damnation. This teaching, along with the contrast of Yahweh in the Old Testament and Jesus in the New Testament, was a great source of existential and emotional angst for me for years. I enjoyed the Old Testament for its stories and characters more than its theology.

DISCIPLESHIP 451

The Good News of the Gospel was "good news" because of the grace offered by Jesus in salvation by faith, not works. But it seemed the good news and free part drifted into the background of my discipleship regimen. The "amazing grace" that accepted me "just as I am" soon morphed into the "much is required" reminder from Paul and a "what have you done for me lately?" expectation from God. Suddenly one of the early verses we memorized loomed over everything, Paul's exhortation to "work out your own salvation in fear and trembling" (Philippians 2:12). The relief of the good news gospel was replaced with fear and trembling.

I didn't think of it in such blatant terms during those early years. Rather, for me, I was on a path of devotion and dedication. I was soaking up a lot of the good teachings and good fellowship of the ministry. I wanted to serve God with an honest heart. But the inner workings of my mind grappled with the fundamentalist world of teachings, preaching, and theology that I was being immersed in.

The discipleship program I was in for about eight years was based upon the concept of "multiplying" disciples to help fulfill Jesus' Great Commission (Matthew 28). The plan was, first you become a "new believer," then you become a disciple, then a disciple-maker, then a maker of disciple makers, and so on. Pyramid scheme disciple-making made logical sense strategically.

Being a disciple entails growing as an "infant" believer (I Corinthians 3:1) into one who then is "thoroughly equipped" (II Timothy 3: 16-17) to follow Christ, defend the faith, lead others to Christ, able to disciple one-to-one new believers. As a disciple of Christ, the keyway to growth is through the Christian "disciplines." The "disciplines" are not new; but the ministry fellowship really helped make them practical and gave me tools to get started. Obviously, the key word is discipline. The military is already big on its own disciplines for its troops. The goal in Christian disciplines is to know Christ and the path.

We memorized:

"Study to show thyself approved unto God; a workman that needeth not be ashamed, rightly dividing the word of truth."[2]

"Approved unto God?" Does this mean I have to prove myself? Is this conditional? I wondered.

I was thoroughly schooled in the "disciplines" of the faith. Study was a big part of this. Disciplines included: morning devotions (Quiet Time); prayer and meditation; weekly Bible Study, Bible Reading Program (reading through the whole Bible), memorizing scripture regularly, learning to witness and sharing the Gospel regularly, going to church regularly and being part of a local fellowship of believers. It kept me busy and kept me out of trouble, particularly during those first four years. We would go out "witnessing" and sharing the gospel on the base one night a week. I was taught how to share "the Bridge" illustration and how to counter objections. We held rap sessions in rooms in the barracks where we'd have open discussions. We all read Josh McDowell's *Evidence that Demands a Verdict* (and the follow-up: *More Evidence that Demands a Verdict*) which was great tool for apologetics, so we could be prepared to answer any objection someone threw at us.

I was told to share the gospel on airplanes when I went anywhere. This was one of those big guilt trips that was laid on me: What if you're the last person who had the chance to share the gospel with this person? I was told that their blood would be on my hands from the verse in Ezekiel 3:21:

"When I say unto the wicked, 'Thou shalt surely die,' and thou givest him not warning, nor speakest to warn the wicked from his wicked way to save his life, the same wicked man shall die in his iniquity; but his blood will I require at thine hand."[3]

I bought into this at first. Imagine being told that because you didn't share the Gospel with a stranger on a plane and he never had another chance to hear it before he dies, his blood is on your hands.

That didn't seem right. Their blood is on my hands? Wait. What does that mean for me? Do I go to Hell too, then? I thought.

What I was being taught in a subtle and unfortunate way was that Bible verses could be lifted completely out of context and applied directly to me. This literalism and application of verses directly to each person can often be a misuse of Scripture. Sadly, this type of cherry-picking Bible verses for one's own use or admonition of others is a form of interpretation used by many Christian groups. Scriptural malpractice runs rampant in many circles. The Church (and Fundamentalists and Evangelicals) often weaponized scripture. We often called the scriptures "the sword."

After my first year as a disciple, I went from one Bible Study group a week to two a week; the second Bible study was one I was teaching. So lots of my spare time went into these discipleship studies and activities.

I was reading things like the sermons of Jonathan Edwards, the Puritan minister from Colonial America; biographies of John Wesley, George Whitfield, David Brainerd; Christian classics written by the classic authors. Jonathan Edwards was highly revered in these circles. But there was little comfort in messages like Jonathan Edwards' "Sinners in the Hands of an Angry God."

"The God that holds you over the pit of hell, much as one holds a spider, or some loathsome insect over the fire, abhors you, and is dreadfully provoked; his Wrath towards you burns like fire, he looks upon you as Worthy of nothing else but to be cast into the Fire; he is of purer Eyes than to bear to have you in his Sight... You are thus in the Hand of an angry god..."[4]

Wait a minute. God "abhors" me? This is terrifying, I thought.
God abhors man is what Edwards tells us in his most famous sermon. My only consolation was that: "Well, at least I am saved."
But deep down I am thinking: *"So God is really an angry God, and*

it's only because of Jesus and his intercession and advocacy on my behalf that God's anger is averted."

It's kind of like living with a Dad who you know at any minute can be volatile and explosive. So I better tiptoe around those eggshells so I don't set him off. At least Jesus seemed like the "good cop," so let me deal with his side of the Yahweh-Jesus deadly duo.

But I was living in America's southeast, Bible belt country, and though I was not a Southern Baptist, there was a lot of that hellfire and brimstone preaching and emphasis going on around me. The Gospel is really only "Good News" *after* you hear the "bad news" of God's anger, judgment, Hell, and damnation.

On top of that I learned that some Christians believe you can lose your salvation.

Wait a minute. So which is it? You mean I can become an "un-son" of God? You mean I can be kicked out of the family? So how can I be sure of my salvation? I pondered with much existential angst.

The Apostle Paul's whole lawyerly discourse on how Christians are adopted into God's family and how Jesus is our advocate before God the Father in *The Book of Romans* was not so much comforting as it was scholarly. I felt like my relationship with God the Father was only possible because Jesus reminded him that I was on the "okay" list.

The case presented by Paul makes it sound like I am in a courtroom or a King's chamber and I am just another case number. Jesus is my attorney and I am contrite because I need Jesus to help me get my sentence lightened or my prayer answered by God. I am an "adopted" son of God, so I don't have full rights like Jesus. God would hardly know who I am if not for Jesus.

How can God the Father and God the Son be One and part of the same Trinity? It sounds like the two opposite faces of God. It made me wonder what happened to Jesus' warm invitation: "Come unto me all ye who labor and are heavy laden and I will give you rest."

If we are scaring people into salvation, if we are simply giving them two choices—Hell and a Lake of Fire, or Eternal Life and Heaven—then of course some people will say "Sure, I'll pray the prayer. I'll believe in Jesus. Why not? Sign me up. Put my Name in the Book of Names. I don't want to go to Hell."

I couldn't help thinking about how the Emperor Constantine had turned the tables: before his rule Christians were being killed for their faith, but once he came along, you could be killed for *not* being a Christian believer. It all makes this "Christian God" look like a sadistic cosmic terrorist.

I never could reconcile myself to all the talk of Hell and the Lake of Fire and sinners being sent to burn in Hell for all eternity. What kind of God would come up with such a cruel, sadistic kind of perpetual torture? Even Adolph Hitler and his Nazis just put undesirables out of their misery in gas chambers—at least it was over quickly. (Of course, he also tortured and prolonged many people's death in the concentration camps.) Is the Christian God nothing more than a Cosmic Hitler, delighting in eternal torture? That's not who I will ever believe God is. But that was the messaging in many of the Fundamentalist and Evangelical circles.

It seems many Christians and churches delight in the image of sinners in the hands of an angry God who will drop them in a lake of eternal fire as judgment. Christianity has a murderous history, which we casually forget. Christians have tortured unbelievers in vicious ways throughout the centuries. Where did these Christians come up with burning people at the stake as they did for centuries? God and their interpretation of scripture gave them the idea. They figured that they were just sending them on their way early to where they said God will send them anyway: to Hell and to the lake of fire. I heard Christians all the time talk about people they thought should be sent to Hell to burn for eternity. How sinister and macabre. They were simply quoting their theology of damnation and Hell.

Make no mistake: I believe the truly evil will be judged. But I have no idea how that will transpire. However, once they are judged, they will not be eternally tortured in fire. No matter how nice and gracious God may be to those he loves, I for one would not be comfortable accepting all God's kindness and grace knowing that this same God has a dark, sadistic bent, that like a Medieval prison guard he has a private torture chamber with the cries of the damned and tortured eternally ringing in his ears. That's not my God.

The evil "will perish" is what scripture says (Psalm 37:20). Their judgment will be no afterlife; they will cease to exist consciously. God will ultimately decide which people are "wicked" and "evil"; that is not our job. God is love, light, goodness, compassion. That is the God I know, not the Angry God dangling humans like spiders over a fire. My God does not abhor human beings.

However, it took many years to exorcize that image of God from the stone tablets of my inner mind and heart.

- How do I really trust an Angry God?
- How do I reconcile the Angry God the Father with the Kind and Gracious Jesus?
- Why is it only because Jesus is my "advocate" that I am able to approach this God who is supposedly "love" and loving?
- I get the impression that I am not really accepted by God; it's only because of Jesus that he can even look at me.
- How did the "Just as I Am" Good News altar call invitation to Jesus and Grace become "What have you done for me lately, Phil?" discipleship program?

BEGINNINGS OF MY OBSESSIVE-COMPULSIVE RELIGIOUS DISORDER

At first, I was just a young believer who was drawn to Jesus' message of peace, forgiveness, and grace. At first, during those initial four years, I was glad to be a follower of a religion that had such deep historic roots. At first, during those initial eight years, I thought: "Who am I to question any of this? I can't question God, Jesus, my leaders and pastors."

The disciplines I learned helped me in many ways over the years, and discipline itself has served me well in life and on my spiritual path. But the downside is the excessive guilt that came with it all. I knew I was developing an overly sensitive Christian conscience influenced too heavily, perhaps, by the rigors of this particular discipleship ministry.

One example is "Quiet Time," what we called morning devotions. The idea was to get up early enough to have devotions as part of your normal daily routine. I started this practice and kept faithful at it for years. It's not a requirement; it's something you choose to do as a believer: some Bible reading and prayer before work. Not long after starting this routine, I remember seeing one of the many Bible tracts I had. The tract basically pictured Jesus waiting patiently in the morning to meet with the believer, and the believer forgets and leaves Jesus waiting. The point is:

You stood up Jesus. You had an "appointment with God" and you forgot or ignored it, or worse yet, you overslept. Jesus was sad. You made Jesus sad.

I never quite agreed with the guilt-trip to this extent; but the arrow of guilt it conveyed still stung. If I missed a Quiet Time, I'd feel like I let Jesus down. Was it a sin? No, it wasn't a sin, but it gnawed at my conscience. Guilt manipulation is one of the biggest sins of the Church and it comes in many, many forms.

I was already reading about church history, apologetics, and eschatology before ever thinking about going to seminary. I built a decent library of books while in the Air Force: Bible commentaries, Greek and Hebrew lexicons, biographies and autobiographies of missionaries and Christian greats, Christian psychology, books of famous sermons, books on end-times, etc. I knew from church history that the Fundamentalist movement was a late-comer and it had fueled the anti-science, anti-higher learning rhetoric that became deeply entrenched in both the Fundamentalist as well as much of the Conservative Evangelical Movement.

I learned from church history that the Fundamentalist movement's teachings about end-times (eschatology) was "pre-millennialism" and it developed only in the 1800's. I learned that many Christian denominations held to completely different Biblical interpretations of end times. There were "post-millennialists" and "millennialists," as well as "pre-millennialists."

I also knew that not all Christians believed in the Literal interpretation of Scripture; particularly as it relates to the Creation story in Genesis. I learned during these years that Fundamentalists and Evangelicals were persistent in their "literalism" and their pre-millennialism. Pre-millennialism is basically the belief that believers will be "raptured" (taken off the earth) before the "Tribulation" period and that Christ will establish a literal thousand-year reign on earth.

Hal Lindsey's best-selling book *The Late Great Planet Earth* was instrumental in popularizing pre-millennialism and its end-time events. We were literally expecting Christ to return in our lifetime. I read the book, but I wasn't completely on the End-Times bandwagon. There's a little too much literalism on that wagon for me.

During my first year of college, I remember walking into a Campus Ministry fellowship group and hearing a speaker talking about end-times. He said what a number of others were purporting: that Henry Kissinger was the Anti-Christ (Kissinger was a noted politician at the time). I heard that and walked out and never went back to that Campus ministry. These were the same crazy Christians who in the 1980's changed their minds: by then they claimed Mikhail Gorbachev, the President of the Soviet Union, was the anti-Christ. He even had a mark (a birth mark) on his head to prove it. Others got on a kick that ATMs and cashcards were the beginning of the "mark of the beast," another sign of the Anti-Christ. I had no use for such nonsense. God help us.

I knew after eight years of initial Christian discipleship and training, I had developed what I will call OCG Disorder: Oppressive-Compulsive Guilt Disorder. I had developed an overly sensitive, oppressive, excessively guilty inner "Big Brother Holy Spirit." I was always ready and capable of upbraiding and badgering myself over some sin or slippery slide into sin, sins of both "omission" and "commission." I always and forever would be a poor "wretch" whose only hope of avoiding the fires and damnation of Hell was because Jesus paid for his desperately wicked soul.

At one ministry conference, I was approached by the Chief Financial Officer of a missions organization who wanted to have lunch with me. I had been giving a lot of money to the ministry and missions as a young Airman. I'm sure this middle-aged CFO was surprised when he saw that it was a twenty-year-old "kid" who was giving so generously, and not some older, more mature Air Force Officer.

The summer after being honorably discharged from the U.S. Air Force, I was one of the team leaders at a summer-long training program. All twenty-four attendees were hired on Disney World's night shift; we were housed in vacation chalets where we shared lodging, shared meals, and enjoyed activities together. This was our summer break. It was a memorable summer making new friends, working at Disney World and leaning into our discipleship programs.

Prior to this, I had only had one date in the previous four years. She was one of only a handful of eligible single girls involved in our ministry. I remember Christian couples trying to be match-makers and saying: "You need to marry a solid, committed Christian girl. You'll learn to love each other."

I thought to myself: *I'll have none of this "learn to love" each other talk.*

That summer I met my first wife among the eight college-age young women at a summer "training program" organized by the ministry. We hit it off right away and I was so ready to date after four years of celibacy and never-dating that we were married the following summer. One of the first serious questions I asked her was: "Would you be willing to go to the mission field if that's the direction God leads?" She was.

I was in my full zealot years.

CHAPTER 9
ROMANCING THE FAITH

Spirit in the Sky.
—Norman Greenbaum[1]

PRIMED

Let me step back and comment on my early initiation into my "first faith."

I was primed for giving myself in service throughout the 1960's. From President John F. Kennedy's "Ask not what your country can do for you but what you can do for your country" and the civil rights movement, to the peace and love messages of rock and roll and then that Johnny River's tune that stopped me in my tracks and told me: "Look to your Soul"—I was primed.

I was the serious kid in high school. I went to the movie theater by myself to see *A Man for All Seasons* and *The Sand Pebbles* because none of my friends particularly cared to see those movies. I drove twenty miles on slushy, snowy winter roads to see Sir Thomas More face down King Henry VIII over an issue of conscience; he was imprisoned and eventually executed for his principled stand. I went to see a common seaman, played by Steve McQueen, face death to help a missionary family on a U.S. gunboat in war-torn China in 1926.

By the time I was 17, my notions of "heroes" was expanding and shifting—from the western/war heroes of movies and television I'd grown up with, to not only the rock and roll artists I admired, but also novelists, writers and men like the heroes of those two movies. One is a clergyman who dies for his beliefs; the other is an "every-man" who heroically does what's right to help those in need.

It was the dawning of the Age of Aquarius, as well as "The Eve of Destruction," "Something's Happening Here" and "What's Going On?" I was between my junior and senior year in high school when the summer of 1967 became the Summer of Love. "Are you going to San Francisco?" was the hippie call, with flowers in their hair. Flower Power, Peace and Love, Make Love Not War.

Suddenly, The Beatles, The Beach Boys, Donovan, and others were flying to India to sit at the feet of an Indian Guru, the Maharishi Mahesh Yogi. My rock and roll idols were taking up spirituality, other religions and transcendental meditation.

When John Lennon's words about how The Beatles were more popular than Jesus caused a social-religious stir, I knew what he meant. I didn't go out and burn my Beatle records. He wasn't putting down Jesus; it was just an observation. Rock music (The Beatles being the biggest thing at the time) had so captured our collective zeitgeist that the Church (i.e., Jesus, the Father and Holy Spirit) couldn't compete. We were looking for spiritual answers but the church didn't quite seem relevant.

When I moved into the barracks at Patrick Air Force Base the first of May 1969, a sergeant helped me lug a footlocker full of rock and roll LPs up three floors. "What do you have in here? Rocks?" he asked huffing. "Close," I said. "Rock and roll." Rock and pop music had become my "prophets" and preachers. If rock music was looking for spirituality with soul, so was I.

On Broadway, there was Jesus in the leading role in *"Jesus Christ*

Superstar." Neil Diamond sang his gospel-like "Brother Love's Traveling Salvation Show." The Doobie Brothers sang "Jesus is just Alright." George Harrison sang about Hare Krishna in "My Sweet Lord." And The Beatles sang the hymn-like "Let it Be." Only years later did Paul tell us that the "Mother Mary" in the song refers to his own mother Mary who died before he ever met John Lennon as a teenager. The Byrds sang "Turn, Turn, Turn" right out of the Book of Ecclesiastes from the Old Testament. Rock music was catching my wavelength or was it the other way around?

Bob Dylan sang "I Dreamed I saw St. Augustine," and before we knew it, he did a whole album of Christian songs, *"Slow Train Coming."* Norman Greenbaum had a hit with "Spirit in the Sky." Bob Dylan's "The times they are a changin'" was prophetic and the answer was "Blowing in the Wind," as obvious and yet as hard to catch as an "Elusive Butterfly."

On top of that there was the growing unpopularity of the senseless Vietnam War and the rise of the Jesus Freaks, like some hybrid conservative Hippies minus the drugs and free love. Spirituality had become a popular pursuit for my generation. Maybe there was a place opening for me when I needed it most. There was a desire to go beyond what we saw as the dead orthodoxy of the mainline churches. We wanted to find a relevant and contemporary spirituality.

However, my "dream plan" to graduate high school, drive to Los Angeles, California, somehow meet Brian Wilson of The Beach Boys, get into the music industry and be a songwriter and music producer was dashed by the Vietnam War, the draft, and now my four-year stint in the U.S. Air Force.

It's hard to convey the turmoil of graduating high school and being thrust into the adult world of 1968. Vietnam was exploding, the draft was on, college students and Vietnam vets were protesting the war, Martin Luther King was assassinated in April, and Robert Kennedy in June, just a couple of weeks before my graduation ceremony.

I was driving to a girlfriend's house when I heard on the car radio about Robert Kennedy's assassination. It seemed like twenty years of sociocultural conflict were packed into the few years between 1963 and 1969. I felt like my send-off was: "Here's your high school diploma, be careful out there, they are killing all the good guys, but have a nice life."

Most of my friends were going to college after high school. I wasn't sure what to major in. An Air Force recruiter sold me on the Air Force. I had "high enough grades" to get to pick my Air Force job, he said. And after four years, I could go to college on the GI Bill. He was right about one of those two things.

The reality was that at the end of Basic Training in Texas, our Drill Sergeant had us fall into formation, then he raised his arm and lowered it, motioning to separate us into two groups. Then, turning to each group, he said: "You guys are going to be cooks and you guys are going to be medics." I was in the group of medics. (So much for photojournalism.) We cursed our recruiters and dealt with our Air Force fate. Ironically, I did wind up taking photographs: I became an X-ray technician in the military.

I was primed for some cause, some revelation, some "seeing the light" moment, something to give my life and energy to, something to change my life.

I was a nineteen-year-old Airman in May 1969 when I stepped off the small airplane in Melbourne, Florida, with my orders to report to Patrick Air Force Base, Cocoa Beach, Florida. I was being sent to sunny, sandy, sensual, sexy Cocoa Beach during the biggest counter-cultural movement of the century and I was wishing I had gone to college instead of enlisting.

Within two weeks at Patrick AFB, I had my "coming to Jesus" moment, met a fellowship of new friends and was recruited into another army, the "Onward Christian Soldiers."

Fall in formation. Dress right dress. Forward march.

MOUNTAIN TOP EXPERIENCES

I was sitting in a large conference auditorium in the Blue Ridge Mountains of North Carolina near Asheville. Every year there were at least three or four Christian Conferences that we looked forward to attending. This particular gathering at the Ridgecrest Conference Center was a men's conference.

In the main auditorium, I was singing with 700 other Christian men from around the southeast. The singing was more memorable to me than any of the speakers or messages. I felt what may have been the closest thing to an "altered state" of consciousness without taking any particular substance to get there. To hear that many men's voices singing these powerful hymns and choruses transported me. I felt as if any moment the roof of the auditorium would lift off and the heavens would open and Jesus himself would descend into our midst. I felt my heart "strangely warmed," as John Wesley famous commented about his conversion. It was inspirational, emotional, and as close to a divine experience as I had ever had up to then in my life; an early, memorable transformational experience.

That was the goal after all: a mountain top experience. We were in fact in the mountains. We drove up from Orlando in a big tour bus. I remember the excitement and anticipation. I remember the "high" I felt when we left after the weekend. This was of course the goal of the retreat: to get us excited about Christianity and fire us up to go back home and be more dedicated to Christ and look forward to the next conference and the next mountain top experience—our Christian version of an altered-state experience.

It was all part of the design: keep us busy, keep us involved, keep us wanting more. But no one was forcing me; it was all voluntary.

THE CONFERENCES and retreats were something we all looked forward to. The messages, the music, the workshops, the campfires, the walks in the woods with some close friends or mentors, the moments of conviction, the fervent prayers and decisions to change our lives and be more committed were all part of "the experience." Just like the first one I went to in 1969 at Toccoa Falls, in the north Georgia foothills, each one pumped me up and left me on a spiritual high. It was a romancing of the faith.

At one of the early conferences, after participating in a "talent" night, I was honored to become part of a small folk-rock style band (*The Eternal Sound*) that would go on to perform at many conferences over a seven-year period. It gave me a chance to play guitar, perform with a band, and write a couple of original songs we performed. We went on to record an album after one performance before 400 people. After the crowd left, we played live on stage to an empty auditorium with the audio engineers and their equipment recording us.

I met my first wife at a summer-long Christian training program, which was another type of "retreat" or conference that was often offered to us. There were 24 young college-age trainees that summer. We all lived in a few dorm-like places and worked at Disney World, Orlando. When not working, we had training sessions or free time.

I know a lot of people came to Christ as teens, college students, and servicemen through many these types of conferences and retreats and through parachurch organizations that focused on young adults—organizations like Young Life, Youth for Christ, Campus Crusade, The Navigators, etc. And this was a good thing; young people at formative ages looking for something meaningful. We were young people looking to make a difference, help change the world, or at least make our corner of the world a better place.

These conferences and retreats, the Windy Gaps, Ridgecrests, and Toccoa Falls, provided a time away, a time to reflect, learn about our faith and for some to taste a spiritual high for the first time. Those years before marriage and careers were a special time, unencumbered by the weight of adult responsibilities, houses, children, mortgages and such. We had a chance to put down a stake, draw some lines, decide who we wanted to be and become.

A ROMANTIC MYSTIC

Years later, Father Walsh would tell me that I was a romantic mystic. I had a sensitive artist's spirit looking for something grounded yet inspirational to give myself to.

One of the earliest books I read after becoming a Christian was the inspirational story of the five missionaries martyred in Ecuador in the late 1950's. The book was the best seller *Through Gates of Splendor*, written by one of the missionary widows, Elizabeth Elliot. Elizabeth would go on to be a noted Christian author and speaker. What drew me to the story was that these were five young men who were killed trying to bring the Gospel to a tribe of hostile indigenous tribal people in the jungles. They were not people martyred in a distant past; this was recent. Life magazine did a whole photo spread on the story and showed photos from the team that went in and found the bodies.

Jim Elliot became the most notable of the five. (His journals were published posthumously, and that book inspired me as well). Missionaries and "heroes" of the faith became a new source of inspiration and I read scores of biographies about men like Hudson Taylor, Adoniram Johnson, Jonathan Goforth, John Wesley, David Brainerd, George Whitfield, Luther, etc., etc.

MY BACK PAGES

I have always lived by large bodies of water. I grew up on Long Island, a fish-shaped island about 150 miles long and 30 miles wide extending east from Manhattan. The Atlantic Ocean was to the south; to the north was the Long Island Sound, a large body of salt water without waves that was connected to the Atlantic Ocean, with Connecticut on the north side.

Patrick Air Force Base, Cocoa Beach, was surrounded by water: the Atlantic Ocean was directly east, and the inland waterway to the west separated the barrier islands from the mainland of Florida.

Later, in seminary in Chicago, Lake Michigan was east just a few miles away. On summer vacations, my parents would take us to pristine lakes in the mountains of upstate New York and New England.

Somehow for me, these large bodies of water oriented my world. Growing up a few miles from the Long Island Sound and the Atlantic Ocean my world was oriented by the Ocean: North and South. In Florida, where I've since lived most of my life, I lived those first five years a short walk from the Atlantic Ocean to the East and the Indian River Lagoon (and the Banana River) to the West; farther west was the Gulf of Mexico.

I would spend time walking the shores, swimming, hanging out at the beaches and dunes meditating, musing, reading and praying by these large bodies of water. For me, the Ocean was like an ever-present manifestation of God, the Presence. I could understand how the ancient peoples personified Gods and Goddesses of the ocean, lakes, and rivers. The beaches and shorelines of Florida and Long Island for the most part were very accessible, soft sand, and for the most part calm, moderate waters.

MANY YEARS LATER, maybe thirty, I was driving alone down Topanga Canyon Road north of Los Angeles, California. I was there while attending a screenwriters' conference a few years after leaving ministry. I was heading toward the Pacific Ocean listening to a recording of The Byrds cover of Bob Dylan's song "My Back Pages." I kept hitting replay. It was one of those moments when I felt the song was written about me. It's still one of my favorite recordings.

Dylan's lyrics poetically captured my life as a young Christian zealot. A younger me, someone who, by the time I was forty-five, seemed a somewhat different me. The most memorable line is the chorus where the singer acknowledges that he feels younger now. He sees his younger self as an older version.

Younger now? Older then? I had an old soul from a young age. It caused me to skip, pass over and not have enough time for some things, things usually considered part of the life of a younger man. I was older then in some ways when I was twenty-something: the monkish boy, like some older Trappist Monk in hospital whites cloistered in cement-block barracks by soft sand beaches. Older then, younger now? It stirs up for me the riddle of Wordsworth's line "the child is father of the man."

Seems that it's not always wise to skip certain passages of our growth and development; there can be multiple coming of age moments, multiple times of seeing the light. Sometimes when we skip or pass them by, we find the younger man makes a return appearance to school the older man. There are some things in life you come to understand only with time. Dylan's genius as a poet comes out in this song, when the word images say more than an explanation can do justice.

Dylan's image of musketeers triggers in me a whole scene of dashing, uniform dressed Alexander Dumas' musketeers, like I've seen in the movies. I see myself in those ranks. I was a uniformed soldier in the U.S. Air Force, I stood in ranks and marched all of us in dress blues. I was also figuratively uniformed in that fraternity of monkish missionaries in the ranks of God's Army.

And somehow in a few short years the foundational doctrines of Christianity had grown surprisingly deep.

I could go through Dylan's song line for line and show how much it fit my early "zealous" journey, but I'll just touch on a few impressions that hit me so squarely. Like the musketeers of Alexander Dumas' novel, their flashing uniforms, their camaraderie, their sense of duty and military *esprit de corps* paint a romantic image of these dedicated soldiers in flanks of formation. My musketeers were the fellowship of Christian brothers.

The singer (in this case Roger McGuinn of The Bryds) is looking back at his zealous self, whether it was politics, social injustice or whatever the youthful cause, and he sees himself differently. What had possessed him at such a young age to be committed with such devotion and zeal? That was me: the young "old" soul of my youth, zealous beyond my own good reasoning.

I saw my younger self in the mirror of Dylan's lyrics. I have experienced the flames and fires of his imagery, being captured by a cause and the theological whirl of Heaven and Hell carries its own curse of spiritual arrogance. A world of ideas, mental constructs, theological truths, the splitting of fine doctrinal hairs. We were every bit as precise as mathematicians, our formulas were theology; we were wordsmithing how God works. And somehow I was more sure about it all than I had earned the right to be.

The singer looks back and remembers that posture of an angry student pointing his finger at the establishment, the institutions, without any clue that one day he'd become his own enemy.

This is the warrior priest in his soldier's stance pointing a finger and preaching. There is a romantic sense about spirituality, about going into the ministry, being "called," being a seminarian, a priest, ordained, a pastor, minister, rabbi, etc. For those going into ministry in churches that require a certain attire, the robes, the sacraments, the accoutrements, sanctuaries, stained-glass windows, rituals, the oaths, creeds, and vows all become part of the mystique and romanticism of being a "man of the cloth."

Driving down Topanga Canyon Road that day, I don't know how many times I hit replay on "My Back Pages" before I reached Pacific Coast Highway and turned left at the Pacific Ocean and headed south toward L.A. I had the lyrics memorized by the time I got to the Santa Monica Pier.

Even though I was not drawn to the conventional church or any particular denomination, the mystique of being part of something that had such a long history as Christianity was part of the romance. To be part of something bigger than myself, part of something substantial and spiritual was important to me.

· · ·

Romancing the faith is also the idea of changing "the world" through belief and commitment to a higher calling, a crusade, a mission from God, a Great Commission. There is romancing the faith in dedicating oneself to something as supernatural and eternal as a God and His church.

I spent three and a half years stationed at Patrick Air Force Base. It was an idyllic place to be at the time, far away from the war in Vietnam, in tropical Cocoa Beach. As I neared the end of my Air Force four-year enlistment, the question of what was next weighed heavy for me. Should I move back home to New York and start my post military life there? Should I stay in Florida and stay involved in the local ministry? Should I go to a major university or a Bible College? What career path did I want to take? Did I want to go into full-time ministry, become a Christian worker or a minister?

CHAPTER 10
TWO DEATHS

Study to show thyself approved unto God,
a workman that needeth not to be ashamed,
rightly dividing the word of truth.
—Paul to Timothy[1]

A few months before my four-year Air Force enlistment was up, I received a call from my ministry leader. I had been discipling a couple of guys and they had become friends. The ministry leader basically told me that these two guys I'd been discipling were not really going to be worth my time and I should find a couple of better discipleship candidates. Stunned, I wasn't sure how to respond.

I remember saying, "But these guys are my friends." His point was that these were not the kind of guys who would be leaders or disciple-makers. So I should spend less time with them and more time looking for more promising ministry prospects.

Whoa. He is really serious about who I am spending time with, I thought.

I didn't exactly follow his advice. I still hung out with those guys and didn't change my circle of friends. But I knew something had changed.

GROOMED FOR MINISTRY

During that last year in the Air Force at Patrick AFB, I knew I was being groomed for a possible ministry staff role. It was an honor to be given more and more responsibility. By now the ministry had grown to include a local university and another Air Force Base. There were finally some college girls around.

I was seriously thinking about full-time Christian ministry as a profession, maybe with the Navs or as a missionary. But I wanted to keep my options open, so I was already making plans to go to college —not Bible College, but a regular university where the degree would give me options. I didn't want to go into ministry full-time unless I really felt called.

A lot of guys I knew were going to Bible Colleges. But after four years of intense discipleship training, two weekly Bible Studies, and essentially getting a bible college education from all my studies and readings, I wanted a broader education at a secular university. I never viewed a non-Christian liberal education as a bad thing, but as a good thing.

I wanted to stay in Florida where I had made all these friends and where college would be more affordable. So when the local ministry representative asked me if I wanted to move into his family ministry home, I felt honored and accepted the offer.

By the time I moved into the local ministry home upon returning from my two-month visit with my family in New York, I had three roommates who were all a few years older than me. Two guys were ex-military and a third guy was an Air Force officer still on active duty. I knew all three guys well from our mutual ministry involvement.

The two-car garage of the rental house in Indialantic Beach had been finished off into a big bedroom. We had plenty of room and two bunk beds for the four of us. We had our own little bathroom off the utility room. I lived there for about 18 months, during the time I started college and was working as an X-Ray technician at the Brevard Hospital. It was another phase of the "monkish" ministry fraternity. We had a good time together.

There was a chain of command "authority" structure aspect to this ministry, as there are in other ministries, churches, business and the military. If you signed up for the "program" you became part of the structure of leaders, disciple-makers, ministry leaders and local reps and their ministry strategy, etc.

A NEW LOCAL CHURCH MODEL

I lived in the ministry home for about 18 months. Once I married, I moved to Orlando to continue college at the University of Central Florida. I decided to major in English Education with the thought that maybe I would become a teacher, but no matter what, the degree would give me options.

I started going to a non-traditional, contemporary, non-denominational church that met at a local elementary school in the Orlando area. That was a turning point for me. I began to see men my age who were committed Christians, yet had secular careers. Maybe I didn't need to go into full-time ministry. I had not seen myself becoming a local pastor at this time. I was now working with the local Navigator community ministry team after having moved on from their military ministry.

Parachurch ministry appealed to me more than the local church or missions. Parachurch ministries were those Christian organizations that operated outside of church denominations. Ministries like The Navigators, Campus Crusade for Christ, Young Life, Youth for

Christ were parachurch organizations. I didn't see myself in robes at a Methodist or Lutheran or Presbyterian Church. I had nothing against those denominations; in fact, we worked with all different church groups.

I was being offered an opportunity to move and start a campus ministry, but I was debating staying in Orlando and becoming part of this local church that had captured my attention. In the end, after getting my Bachelor's degree, I took a job as an editor at an aerospace company, stayed in Orlando, and decided to work with this dynamic local church and become part of the community.

This new local church I was attending was modeled after Willow Creek Community Church in the Chicago suburbs back in the 1970's-80's. I had never seen church services like this or a church like this. They met in a school; every service was different; the bulk of the congregation was comprised of young families and singles. And the pastors didn't wear clerical garb. I began seeing these pastors as new role models; I could see myself doing what they were doing. This church was the kind of church I would want to pastor if I ever went into the local church ministry.

DEATH BLOW NUMBER ONE

I was 24 and still in college when I went home to visit my father, Charles Davis, who was in the hospital in need of a liver transplant. It was 1975, and dad's chances of survival looked bad. Typical of my parents, they had not told me how sick my father had become over the last four months. So by the time my mom told me, it was clear that dad had only weeks to live.

I stayed in New York visiting my dad and family for a few weeks. Dad was in and out of consciousness from the medications. But during the last week I was there, I was able to pray with him. I knew he never really went to church much. He wasn't against it; he just didn't have much use for it.

He knew he was dying. I asked him one day, leaning close to his face and whispering: *Did you know you could know before you die that you will go to heaven?* His eyes lit up and he cocked his head toward me, as if alert for the first time in days, and he answered: No.

So I told him about God's love and forgiveness and that the Bible says it's not by our works but by a simple acknowledgement of faith that God forgives us. I told him it was between him and God and that he didn't have to list his sins, just ask forgiveness, and ask Jesus into his heart.

He wanted me to pray for him. Looking back, if for no other reason than to give my dad hope on his deathbed, I was glad I had spent the last six years learning about the Bible, prayer, and faith. It was all worthwhile for that one prayer. I prayed a simple prayer, trying not to cry my eyes out.

The doctors said he could hang on for another few weeks, or maybe they would get a liver donor in time. I couldn't really spend indefinite time away from home. So I decided to fly back to Florida; I could easily be back in New York in a couple of hours if I needed to.

The last time I saw Dad alive, I kissed his forehead as I said good-bye. As I left the hospital room I said, "See you later, Dad."

It was a cold night; the door handle of my car was freezing cold as I gripped it and looked up at the light in the window of Dad's hospital room. Everything was blurry.

Two weeks later, my mom called to say that dad had passed away in the night. I was ruined for the next two and half years. I was not prepared for this blow. I felt cheated to have lost Dad so early in his and my life.

I upbraided myself for not staying home until his last day. I was mad at myself for not talking with him more five years earlier when I spent a week with him, mom and my two youngest brothers on a vacation. We all drove together in the family car from New York to Florida and then did sight-seeing and visiting relatives in Florida. I remember how I sat in the back seat reading a Christian book by Francis Schaeffer, lost in my religious world, being my scholarly "Christian" self, instead of really engaging with mom and dad. I try to excuse myself because I was only twenty-one and had no idea Dad would die so young. (He was 54.) But I still get angry at myself for not getting closer to him.

I was guilty of being what we'd often laughed about in the ministry: being "so heavenly minded, that I was no earthly good." It took me nearly three years to get over my cloud of sadness and grief over dad passing.

DEATH BLOW NUMBER TWO

Not long after my father's passing, another death hit home. I was helping roof one of the pastors' homes. We'd often get a crew of guys from the church and reroof someone's home. One of the guys came up to me and asked if I heard the news. He told me that one of the young ministry wives from my early years at Patrick Air Force Base had taken her own life.

I'll call her "Mary." I remember how pretty, cheerful, smiling and kind she had always been. I met her and her husband (I'll call him "Mike") the first time I went to that Bible Study when I "accepted Christ."

I remembered how her husband, an ex-military guy, was one of funnest, most upbeat, and friendliest ministry leaders. For some reason, whenever he was the team captain, he'd always select me first on his volleyball team. I wasn't the tallest, nor the best spiker, I was a decent setter, but he always chose me first. He knew I played hard, was a good team player, and wasn't afraid to dive to the ground for the ball. I think for some reason, he just wanted to give me the kudos. I'll never forget it.

Hearing of Mary taking her life really threw me. The reasons were never clear, nor did it really matter for my part. All I remember was wondering how sad, that someone so young (she was in her early thirties), vibrant, and committed to Jesus and ministry could get to that point. What brought her to such despair, such pain, shame, and guilt that she would choose to end her life?

It hit really close to home. How could this happen to such a cheerful, grounded Christian wife and ministry leader? What was really going on behind the Christian veneer?

It was another warning sign to me about the darker side of this Christianity thing that I was so committed to. I didn't know all of what it meant. It was just another red flag on the zealous road of Jesus' disciples.

Years later, in my own depression after leaving ministry I remembered Mary and understood firsthand why she wanted to end it.

Those two deaths had a huge effect on me in my mid-twenties. The contrast really hit me: Dad's eyes lighting up at being forgiven on his deathbed; and Mary, a Christian missionary, taking her own life. The same God and Jesus. Hope given, hope lost.

Some Christians and Churches believe that suicide is unforgiveable. I wasn't about to accept that view. It was during this time of two deaths that I entered a deeper questioning of my initial indoctrination and discipleship. I wanted to know more, not just go along with the theology and doctrine of the fellowship I had joined.

TURNING POINTS

Looking back at my younger self now, years later, I know I was a bit naïve, innocent, and genuinely looking to be a part of something bigger than myself, something meaningful.

I didn't completely fall into all the Evangelical theology of this new "coming to Jesus" time in my life. However, I did fall in line with the program for many years. I had experienced an awakening to Christ and a deeper, more meaningful spiritual life.

But now I was out on my own without any "contractual" or informal obligation to either the Air Force or the lay ministry I was a part of. I was able to take a breath and re-evaluate the direction of my career and life.

At what point do you heed the warning signs or inner questions? At what point do you decide to ratchet back the zeal? At what point does the authority of the group overstep its bounds in your personal life?

At what point do you recognize that you are "constructing" your own faith and can determine its hold and doctrines?

At what point do you stand up for yourself and set some personal boundaries with the group and what they say God is telling you?

CHAPTER II

THE TEAMSTERS AND THE IVORY TOWER

Go ye therefore, and teach all nations,
baptizing them in the name of the Father,
and of the Son, and of the Holy Ghost:
teaching them to observe all things
whatsoever I have commanded you.
—Jesus Christ[1]

I landed a career job as an editor at an aerospace company; nice salary and benefits. However, this job I held for two years helped me see this wasn't for me. I had the opportunity to change my career; I was only 28. My heart was in ministry. I was heavily involved in my local church and still working with para-church ministries.

One day driving home from work, I had an overwhelming sense that now was the time. I remember exactly where I was on a familiar road when it became clear. There were no voices, no angels, no opening of the skies, just a strong inner voice and sense of direction:

follow your heart, it's time, if you're going to go to seminary, now is the time. It was as close to a calling as I could have. It was a decision to make Christianity my profession, to respond to Jesus' call in the Great Commission at the end of the Gospel of Matthew.

The decision to go to Trinity Evangelical Divinity in the northern suburbs of Chicago took a few months to make. I had three pastor friends who had all gone to different seminaries. I took advice from all three and decided on Trinity, mainly because it was not so much a "denominational" school and had a more diverse faculty with a broader theological base. It allowed the seminarians to choose their theological orientation. It would provide a broader, less dogmatic approach to Scripture and Protestant Theology.

By the time I loaded up a U-Haul truck to cart our furniture to Deerfield, Illinois, we had doubled the size of our family from two to four; my wife had given birth to identical twin boys. Our home church was supportive of our move and put us on their list of "missionaries" so that people could help support us during our three-year venture.

I remember telling my mother that I was leaving a career job and going off to seminary. She thought we were crazy. To her credit, once we went off, mom was totally supportive; and once I became a pastor of a church near her home, she attended my church regularly.

The Master of Divinity degree program was a three-year intensive study. Since a lot of us worked part-time and took classes, finishing in three years was a challenge.

I took ancient Hebrew and Greek language classes in order to translate the Old and New Testaments. The professors were wonderful, and I felt in my element. For three years I was immersed in biblical studies at the deepest level. The professors often made it clear that there were different interpretations of passages. There would often be panel discussions in which three or four professors who came from different theological schools of thought would present opposing views on particular passages of Scripture or theological topics. It was refreshing and I soaked it up.

UPS TEAMSTERS

I found out right away that a lot of seminarians took part-time jobs with UPS at a nearby hub. I was hired and for three years I worked on a sort line at a huge UPS facility where trucks were unloaded and reloaded for deliveries.

It was an odd contrast to be the seminarian in the "Ivory Tower" by day and to be a Teamster working at night. UPS required their employees to be in the Teamsters Union. There was no place else at the time in 1979 to get paid over $13 an hour working only four hours a night with great medical benefits. The benefits were so good that when my daughter was born my last year in seminary, my UPS medical benefits paid nearly the whole bill.

On any given night, half of the thirty guys on the sort aisle were fellow seminary students. The huge building was a maze of conveyor belts; slides sent packages in all directions. Along with memorizing ancient Greek and Hebrew words, I had to memorize hundreds of zip codes in order to reroute packages. Lots of nights I'd be working next to a friend from seminary, and we'd have theological discussions amid all the twisting and turning of sorting packages. Twice during my three years of employment I had to go to the hospital for stitches from run-ins with boxes.

I carpooled with a couple of my fellow seminary students from our apartment complex. We would leave at ten o'clock at night and discuss seminary classes and things we were learning. Our shifts were only four hours. Many nights on the way home we stopped at Denny's for a burger at 2:30 in the morning and debated theological positions while sitting at the counter. We'd get home some nights after 3:00 and get up to go to classes by eight or nine o'clock in the morning.

There was no internet in 1979, no personal computers or laptops. We wrote papers on typewriters and spent a lot of time in the seminary library. It takes some time getting used to translating the Old Testament and going from the "back" of the book to the "front."

Hebrew is written from right to left and books start from "the back," the opposite from English. More than once I turned the page to translate a passage, went the wrong way, and wondered why the sentence made no sense.

CRITICAL THINKING

It was in seminary that I was able to feel free to re-evaluate theological positions and to question some of the things I was taught during my previous ten years. My years of training and Bible studies during the Air Force and after really helped. All that "bible college" training I went through voluntarily, and the disciplines of bible studies, devotions, bible reading, scripture memory and discipleship made seminary less daunting. I did start to learn critical thinking in my ministry days at Patrick and then in my four years in colleges. But seminary was new and welcome territory.

Many Christians do not understand the difference between "being critical" and "using "critical thinking." Critical thinking means that you are thinking logically and thinking things through, rather than just accepting what's said. That's different from just being critical in a negative way.

It was healthy having professors who were noted authors and scholars holding differing theological positions present the arguments and defense without accusing the others of heresy or error. It helped me see that beyond the roughly ten-point basic statement of faith that the seminary upheld as its core beliefs, there was a lot of difference down in the details of theology.

I was able to carve out a theological space that was less strident than both Fundamentalist and Evangelical. I was going to err on the side of grace, forgiveness, and the positive messages of Jesus. I would be less dogmatic about doctrine in general. As a pastor I would be more of a teacher than a preacher.

I made friends with a number of fellow seminarians. Some went on to be missionaries, some went back to their churches to become pastors: Presbyterians, Methodists, Lutherans, Baptists, etc. I still kept my "non-denominational" label; I made it a point not to commit to a particular denomination.

During the last year of seminary we decided to attend Willow Creek Community Church, which was a huge nontraditional church that was one of the early models for the "Community" church movement, similar to my home church in Florida. The pastor was well-known; the church sanctuary was more like a giant college auditorium; the services were not liturgical but designed to make the "unchurched" feel more comfortable. Like my home church, the services rarely had the same "order of worship." In fact, there wasn't a traditional order of worship; each service was different. There were skits, drama, no liturgy, live contemporary music, guitars, drums, no hymns from the archives of the 1700's and 1800's, but a few contemporary choruses. I felt at home and attending there for a year fueled my desire to pastor and be part of these types of churches.

"HIPPIE JESUS"

One of my fondest memories from my seminary years came during a Christmas break from seminary. My wife and I drove with our two-year old twin sons to New York to spend the holidays with my mom and family. One the way back to Chicago while driving through Ohio, our car broke down on the interstate.

It was a bright sunny day, but there was snow on the ground from the previous day and the temperature was zero degrees. I remember the temperature clearly, because the guy on the local radio station said it was zero degrees. It was Sunday morning, and we were west of Cincinnati where the NFL Bengals were getting ready for an AFC play-off game in what would become known as "The Freezer Bowl" for being the coldest game in NFL history at that time, January 10, 1981.

This was long before cell phones and laptops. There we were with two toddlers in the car in freezing weather. I figured I could fix the car problem, which I thought was a clutch adjustment on our Toyota hatchback. Unfortunately, I didn't have the right tools.

There was an overpass just up ahead, and according to our road map there was a town not too far away. Since the sun was bright, I figured my wife and boys could stay warm in the car until I got back. So I walked to the overpass and got up on a rural two-lane road to hitchhike.

There was no traffic on this rural road as I waited for a car to come by. Finally, after quite a while, a Volkswagen minivan came chugging toward me. It was one of those popular mid-1960's vans—the kind hippies used to drive—and decorated inside and out.

I stuck my thumb out and the van pulled over. I was not prepared for the encounter. I got in the van and was greeted by a long-haired, well-groomed, thirty-something Jesus-look-a-like driver. I told the Hippie Jesus that I was looking for an auto parts store and thought there may be one in town. He knew there was a Sears a few miles away and we drove off.

The van was decorated with plush carpeting and was tastefully tricked out. I don't remember all of what we said in our relatively short drive, but I knew this was an unusual encounter. The man so resembled Jesus in his appearance and demeanor I was taken aback. He was soft-spoken and gracious. He was kind and encouraging when I told him I was a seminary student. He seemed so out of place and out of time.

We arrived at the Sears and he offered to take me back to my car if I needed him to. But the Sears people said they would help. The Hippie Jesus stranger drove off in his Volkswagen van. I managed to adjust the clutch on my car, and we made our way back to Chicago without further incident.

Of all my memories in the three years of seminary in Chicago, this incident always cheers me up when I think back. I don't know who that "Hippie Jesus" look-a-like was, but he was a godsend that day.

One of those mysterious verses in the New Testament talks about how some of us may have been in the presence of an angel and not known it. Here is the verse in two different translations (the King James Version and the New Living Translation):

"Be not forgetful to entertain strangers: for thereby some have entertained angels unawares."[2]

"Don't forget to show hospitality to strangers, for some who have done this have entertained angels without realizing it![3]

Some have "entertained angels without realizing it." Let that sink in. I'm not saying that the Hippie in the VW van who came to our rescue was an angel or Jesus; but according to these verses it is possible.

You wonder how these angels decide when to appear as humans and help or intervene. They probably get a kick out of humans never suspecting. Whoever it was that day, it has remained an amusing and mysterious incident.

NOW WHAT?

When I left Florida to go to seminary, my home church had talked about starting "sister" churches and "spin-offs" around the greater Central Florida area. So I was hoping that three years later there would be a place for me.

With six months to go before finishing classes, I received a call and an offer to return and join the church staff. It was exactly what I was hoping for. I could return and mentor with the two pastors who inspired me to go into church ministry.

With two months to go before returning to Florida and my home church, I received another call.

My home church was going through an ugly split.

CHAPTER 12
CHURCH WORLD

In a religion the savior dies for you,
in a cult you die for the savior.
—Reza Aslan[1]

I hung up the phone after my conversation with Marv, one of the church elders back in Florida, and I was caught between two emotions: excitement and disillusionment. My home church, the one that inspired me to go to seminary, the one with the pastors who had inspired me to go into local church ministry, the church that had given me a whole new fresh vision for the local church and had been a breath of fresh air for me—that church had split into two congregations.

It was not quite an amicable split; it was a full-blown church conflict. One pastor was leaving with half the congregation to start services about twenty minutes up the road. The other pastor was left with the other half of the congregation. There was a lot of anger and pointing fingers.

"Are you sure you want me to come back as an intern?" I asked Marv, not wanting them to feel obligated to me.

"Yes, definitely, we need you," he said.

After we hung up, I felt a mix of emotions. Any excitement I had about my hope of going back to my home church was quenched by the sorrow. What had once been such a dynamic church was now a shadow of itself and mired in conflict.

The excitement of interning under the founding pastor, who I really admired, was quenched. The founding pastor was leaving with a chunk of the congregation going twenty minutes up the road to start another church.

A friend put it perfectly: "It's like you left a really good party to get more beer, and when you got back, the party was over." Hilarious analogy: he summed it up just right. I didn't know whether to laugh or cry.

A CRASH COURSE IN CHURCH CONFLICT

I'm going to cram my twelve years of being a pastor in full-time Christian ministry into this chapter. I'll weave in more details in later chapters.

In general, it was a wonderful time, and I would do it all again. But I'd make some wiser decisions. However, I got a good taste of pastoring full-time in three different Evangelical churches in Florida.

On my first day reporting in as the new intern, I walked into the familiar home church offices, and I could cut the tension in the air with a knife. Maybe more like a machete. Since it was only a couple of months since the sudden church split, both churches and both pastors were still using the same offices. What was once one church staff was now two. The tension was palpable. I decided not to take sides.

My home church had been meeting for years in a nearby elementary school. Without getting into too much detail, the split was over buying land and building a facility. Typical, right? As it turned out, the Elder-led original church decided to go in a direction that the founding pastor wasn't in favor of. They wanted to become a big church with a big building and a big sanctuary. There was nothing wrong with that. But that was not what the pastor wanted—no big edifice. People got upset, pointed fingers, told contradictory stories about who was to blame, and generally, things got messy and ugly.

I had the unique opportunity to come back after not being in the civil war, so I was viewed as being innocent in the conflict. I had friends who were on both sides of the argument. I heard both sides of the story. I was also able to stay close to the founding pastor when he moved out of the church offices and relocated.

For the next two and half years, I watched the waves of church conflict consume the home church where I was on staff. I plotted it on a timeline after leaving. Every three months another part of the conflict would surface or resurface.

I finally looked at those thirty months as a continuation of my training. It was as if God said, "Here, Phil, let me give you a crash course in church conflict." I learned a lot. A lot that I wish I had not had to learn so quickly and so personally.

During the continued infighting at the church: I was attacked, the other pastor and elders were attacked. It was a political mess. I watched people and friends I knew turn on each other, pull power plays, attack one another, and generally behave badly; all in the name of building a church. "Welcome to Church World, Phil."

I was 32 by the time I started my internship. I really enjoyed much of my first church position in spite of all the conflict: first as an intern, then as an assistant pastor, or co-pastor as they named it. But I left with no illusions of church and Christians being that much different from the secular world when it comes to certain issues.

Having been in the Air Force for four years, then in a professional job in the secular world for a few years, and then a Teamster in Chicago, I'd seen all types. One thing I will say is this: in my U.S. Air Force job, as well as at my editor job at Martin Marietta Aerospace, and in thirty years in the corporate world after leaving ministry—in the end, the secular jobs treated me more professionally than the churches did. It is sad to admit, but true for me personally.

I saw behind the scenes and the politics up close during my first two and half years as a pastor. I saw successful businessmen wield their undue influence on the politics of the local church all in the name of God. Many church people manage to couch their positions by "spiritualizing."

"Spiritualizing" is a carefully honed way of adding spiritual lingo to fortify one's opinion or give it more gravitas. Christians learn this as part of the indoctrination without consciously knowing it is happening. We couch our opinions with phrases like: "I believe it's God's will" or "I really believe God wants us to" or "God told me we should do this."

Even when the church managed to buy its first building (no small accomplishment), the politics behind the scenes was still at work to sabotage things, if only for the short term. My most memorable story related to this was when three wealthy businessmen came to the Elder Board and threatened to leave if the Elders did not comply with their request for staff changes (meaning firing all the staff and bringing in new staff). I was surprised when the wealthy men said they represented one quarter of the church giving. So they played the money card, spiritual blackmail, a behind-the-scenes threat.

I watched to see if the Elders would cave. The Elders stood firm and said no to those men. Those men and their families left the church. To my surprise, the church giving did not suffer one financial beat. Somehow, someway, the church never missed the financial contributions of those wealthy men who threatened and left. It was a great example to me as a young pastor.

The tension and conflict brewing were palpable at times during Sunday services. I remember that I was so nervous to be preaching on some of those Sundays, that I would take my glasses off when I got to the pulpit. That way I couldn't actually see the expressions on people's faces as I spoke, I could just see the blurry outlines of heads and shoulders. I felt the support of many of those people, but I didn't want to be thrown off by the visibly negative ones.

In the end, after two and a half years of conflict, the other pastor resigned from all the pressure. I decided not to resign, but to see how it all played out.

I was mad that there was conflict behind the scenes, yet no one wanted to talk about it. They needed Sunshine laws. So the congregation was in the dark about how a handful of men behind the scenes were disrupting things. This was exactly why the founding pastor left; there was no way for the pastors to tell the congregation what was going on behind the scenes.

In the end, they offered me a position they knew I probably didn't want. I could have accepted the position and stayed a while longer. But my heart was not in it anymore. I was ready to move on and get a fresh start somewhere else.

My first church pastoring experience was full of mostly good times; but the bad times dulled the joy of the overall experience. I left feeling wounded from the ordeal.

TWO MORE CHURCH EXPERIENCES

I was hired at a church about an hour away from Orlando. They knew about my home church and contacted me. I was hired as an assistant pastor at a growing church, and we moved to the town.

Surprisingly, within a couple of months of being there, the church suffered some financial issues and realized they couldn't pay us what they agreed to. So I took a pay cut. (I never had my pay cut in any of my "secular" jobs.) It put me on notice. I started wondering: "What's next?"

It was through this church that I entered into a loose denominational system. It was a small denomination out of the Midwest, so I got to meet other pastors and district superintendents. (More about this later.) I was able to see some more behind the scenes; this time in a denomination.

All and all, it was a fairly good experience, and I was able to leave within a year or so with that church's support and plant a church from scratch with four other families.

The church we planted was in the outer suburbs of Central Florida, not far from my original home church. Some people I knew in the area attended. It was a fun and challenging six years of trying to build a congregation.

During these years of church planting, I wrote and publish a book, and wrote and directed a summer missions video for a mission organization. For the mission video, I spent two and half weeks filming in the Venezuelan Amazon jungle. The video we produced featured a team of young people on a summer mission project to build a school. I spent time with three tribal groups of indigenous people in the Amazonas; among them were the Yanomami tribe, one of the most primitive tribes in the Western Hemisphere. It was the adventure of a lifetime and I thoroughly enjoyed working on the project.

ONE AMUSING STORY about this was when we attended the video premier. It was a Wednesday night, and the thirty-minute video was going to be shown at the mission headquarters. I knew it was an ultra-conservative group from some of the people there who attended my church. I was there, along with a friend who wrote and recorded one of the songs in the video. I had written the theme song of the video, which we professionally recorded in town.

We were sitting up front and there were probably a hundred people there. We were excited to see how the video would be received; the staff I worked with all felt really good about how the video came out.

After the video ended, I was expecting some applause. The lights went back up in the room, but there was no applause.

No applause? I was crushed; I thought they didn't like our year-long effort. After the session ended, I asked one of the leaders: "It sounded like they didn't like it. There was no applause." To which he said: "Oh, they liked it. But we don't applaud on Wednesdays."

I laughed, relieved but confused. I shook my head: "You don't applaud on Wednesdays." I wondered why we didn't have the premier on a night they did applaud. Or why couldn't you make an exception on this Wednesday?

CHURCH PLANTING WAS EXHAUSTING. After six years we had about 125 people and were meeting in a storefront that we renovated for our use.

I was hitting my stride; I was a success as a pastor. I had just published a book and I was interviewed on a few radio stations; I made an appearance on a Christian TV station; I was invited to speak at a weekend retreat about the book. The book also brought me to the attention of a church in Colorado looking for a pastor. I had written and directed a successful mission video. (I later learned they raised a lot of money selling the VHS video, which helped them buy better video equipment for future videos.)

A nice side note on this. I received a postcard almost a year after the video premiered. The postcard came from China. It was from a friend from seminary. He had watched the video in a tent in rural China where he was a missionary. He saw my name in the credits and dropped me a postcard saying he liked the video.

IT WAS around this time that I found myself at a crossroads in my career. Also, things at home were in disarray. I am not going to get into the details of my marriage and personal life in this book, out of respect for my family.

I'll just say this in general: when people are not allowed to be fully human for a long time and are put on a pedestal, a lot of personal issues go undetected and unaddressed.

After 24 years in the Evangelical movement, including seminary and now as a pastor, I didn't like who "I" was becoming and where Evangelicalism was going.

The 1980's saw the rise of the TV Evangelists and the Moral Majority. The term "evangelical" suddenly was out there in our culture. I remember that I stopped telling a lot of people I was a pastor because they would inevitably ask if I was one of "those evangelicals." I'd be getting a haircut and the stylist would ask what I did, and I'd say I was a teacher to avoid the inevitable associations and explanations I'd get sucked into. Usually, that ended the conversation. I learned this from having answered a number of times that I was a "pastor" and then having to explain how I was not like those TV Evangelists and the rising "Moral Majority" of Christian politics.

In an opening chapter of this book, I recounted three scenes from my time of "leaving." They fit here. If I was going to make a change in my career and life, it was going to be now.

- I didn't like the voice of God in my head (it had become too negative and harsh);
- I didn't like who I was becoming in this "Evangelical" world I was in, and
- I wanted to find out what I missed in my spiritual journey to know God.

PART THREE
DECONSTRUCTING MY FAITH

CHAPTER 13

1 HAD TO LEAVE MY FATHER'S HOUSE

He will do his very utmost
to get away from you.
He will turn himself
into every kind of creature
that goes upon the earth.
—Homer, *The Odyssey*[1]

WRESTLING THE ANGEL

One of the most visceral and human encounters between God and man in the Old Testament is the episode where Jacob wrestles "the Angel of the Lord" in Genesis. It is "visceral" because the text makes clear that this is an actual wrestling match that goes on throughout the night. It's not a dream or a vision. It is "human" because it's not an apparition Jacob encounters, it is clearly a man. It is God in the form of a human being rolling around in the dust and dirt with Jacob in what was apparently a no-holds-barred, one-on-one wrestling match. Here's how the scripture states it:

"That night Jacob got up and took his two wives, his two female servants and his eleven sons and crossed the ford of the Jabbok. After he had sent them across the stream, he sent over all his possessions. So Jacob was left alone, and a man wrestled with him till daybreak. When the man saw that he could not overpower him, he touched the socket of Jacob's hip so that his hip was wrenched as he wrestled with the man. Then the man said, "Let me go, for it is daybreak."

But Jacob replied, "I will not let you go unless you bless me."

The man asked him, "What is your name?"

"Jacob," he answered.

Then the man said, "Your name will no longer be Jacob, but Israel, because you have struggled with God and with humans and have overcome."

Jacob said, "Please tell me your name."

But he replied, "Why do you ask my name?" Then he blessed him there.

So Jacob called the place Peniel, saying, "It is because I saw God face to face, and yet my life was spared."

The sun rose above him as he passed Peniel, and he was limping because of his hip."[2]

The passage says it was "a man," yet Jacob says he was "face to face" with God. Some translations say it was an angel of the Lord. Jacob knew that this was no ordinary man or angel, this was God himself choosing to engage physically with Jacob. It is also fascinating that God wrestled in Jacob's weight-class. In other words, God let it be a fair fight by not doing what he could easily have done: overpower Jacob with supernatural powers.

Regardless of all the various theological takes one might have on this episode in Genesis, it stands as a powerful metaphor for engaging with God. Wrestling with God is one metaphor for our struggle to engage, debate, take on, grapple, and try to make some sense out of this perplexing connection with an unseen deity.

By nature, as a Christian I was taught to submit, to obey, to please, to listen, to trust, and to follow. I tended to downplay and repress whatever doubts I may have had during my early years as a Christian. I didn't want to be the "doubting Thomas." Doubts were to be overcome by faith. Who was I to question the Almighty? Who was I to second-guess the all-knowing, all-perfect, all-Holy Supreme Being?

Jacob's wrestling with God shows me God can handle our spiritual angst. Instead of crushing Jacob with his size, or knocking him out with one punch, or presenting himself as so immoveable that Jacob couldn't even make a wrestling move, God comes as man and allows Jacob to get the better of him. It's important to notice that Jacob pinned the man. Jacob won the wrestling match.

It shows both the tenderness of God and his willingness to get down on our level. It shows that this Divine Being is not above rolling up his sleeves, taking off his shirt, and going to the mat with us to wrestle something we need to wrestle out. It shows that this Superior Being will roll around in the dust and dirt all night long if that's what it takes. God meets us face-to-face, one-on-one, away from all the crowds, the temples, the sacred places, the audiences.

That night there was no referee, no umpire, no corner men, and no official ring. It shows me that God is man enough to take his lumps, to get driven to the mat, to set aside his title, his glory, and to let himself get beaten and pinned by someone his own size.

Yet it is more than a wrestling match. It's beyond words, beyond dialogue and talk. At some point in the hours-long match both Jacob and God knew this was what Jacob needed.

I believe this was the point at which we might say, to put it in human terms, that both Jacob and God reached a new respect for each other. The way an underdog gains the respect of a champion after a tough match. The way Rocky earned Apollo Creed's respect.

TRANSFORMATIVE EXPERIENCES

For Jacob, wrestling God was a transformative experience. A transformative experience is an experience (or event or moment) that may not seem full of deep instruction and meaningful messages, but carries so much import, so much that can't simply be put into words, yet it is clearly life-changing.

Maria Popova writes about transformational experiences in the lives of a selection of historical women in her book *Figuring*. She points out:

> This is the paradox of the transformational experience: Because our imagination is bound by our existing templates of how the world as we know it works, we fail to anticipate the greatest transformations—the events and encounters so unmoored from the familiar that they transfigure our map of reality and propel us into a wholly novel mode of being.[3]

For me it would be the "events and encounters" outside my normal tribe, "unmoored from the familiar," and beyond the range of my church and dogma, discovering new maps of the world, that would propel me into a new sense of being.

I imagined Jacob wrestling and wondered during that long night what words or sounds were shared between him and the man? Wrestling is a highly physical, strenuous activity. It's not boxing, it's wrapping your arms around someone, forcing them to the ground, twisting and contorting arms and legs and torso.

In Homer's *The Odyssey*, we have another story of man wrestling with a God. Menelaus (The King of Sparta) tells Telemachus, Odysseus' son, the story of how he and three of his best men wrestled Proteus to get information on how to return home after the war with Troy. Menelaus is given aid by Idothea, a sea Goddess and daughter of Proteus, who Menelaus said "she had taken a great fancy to me." Idothea tells him:

"...he will do his very utmost to get away from you. He will turn himself into every kind of creature that goes upon the earth, and will become also both fire and water; but you must hold him fast and grip him tighter and tighter."[4]

In this ancient Greek classic, we see a variation on wrestling God motif. Menelaus gives us more details about his strenuous match than the writer of Genesis gives us on Jacob's bout. Menelaus and his three best men took on Proteus:

"We rushed upon him with a shout and seized him; on which he began at once with his old tricks, and changed himself first into a lion with a great mane; then all of a sudden he became a dragon, a leopard, a wild boar; the next moment he was running water, and then again directly he was a tree, but we stuck to him and never lost hold."[5]

A lion, a dragon, a leopard, a wild boar...water and a tree! The Greeks were used to their gods and goddesses taking on our earthly forms to interact with humans. For Jacob it was one-on-one. This God could feel the muscles and sinews of his creation. I wonder what came through to God viscerally in that grappling with Jacob's sweaty, determined, impassioned, willful, powerful, and muscular humanity. They wrestled—they didn't debate! I wonder what nonverbal language, what intangibles God came away with from that match.

I believe that in a human transactional way, Jacob earned God's respect that night and there was a mutual understanding forged. Jacob went onto become the father of the Israelites.

I have wondered as a Christian if God respects us; it doesn't seem like it from the theology I learned. In my world it was the other way around: God doesn't respect us; we're supposed to respect him. Whatever respect comes from God towards humans, in my Evangelical theological worldview, it is usually connected to performance.

THE LONGING AND THE PRESENCE

The longing and the presence have been the two consistent parts of my spiritual pursuit. A longing for connection with the divine and the unshakeable sense I've had since I was a kid that there is a Presence, a personal presence that knows us. I realize this is a spiritual construct that I chose: God is present and personal.

I've been driven by a longing to discover if I can connect on a personal, experiential level with the Divine Presence. Is God real? Or just a scholastic exercise in believing things about God? Is it nothing more than a "when you wish upon a star" Disney fantasy faith? Or is there real substance to the Presence? I wanted to get behind and beyond theology and dogma.

For most of my life, it had been real. I had studied it as a layman and as a seminarian and as an ordained pastor. So much of my Christianity had been based upon scholasticism: reading, studying, believing in doctrines and teachings. In other words, head knowledge that eventually sank down into the heart.

In my heart I knew that if this Supreme Being was as great and powerful as I believed a supreme being should be, then my little detour and experimental challenge would not threaten the relationship we had forged when I was a young man; this was just a new stage of it.

In some ways it can be likened to a father and son relationship, in which the son knows it's time to leave Dad's house and become his own person. Like the son who loves his father dearly, but needs some space, distance, time, and air to breath, so he can figure some things out. Like the son who is so overshadowed by his father that he feels invisible or unable to rise in his own right into manhood and be his own person. There is a time to leave the nest, the fold, the comfy bedroom in mom and dad's house. There is a time to leave the tribe.

After tearing my Bible in half that day, I began a new journey of spiritual discoveries that I hoped would lead me to greater truth and freedom. In place of reading the Bible, I read other spiritual books.

For the next several years I read regularly from *Leaves of Grass*, the poetry of Walt Whitman, along with the poetry of Rainer Maria Rilke.

DECONSTRUCTION AND RECONSTRUCTION

I had constructed my faith over many years, and even though I was leaving many assumptions behind when I left the ministry, I held on to three basics:

1. *God is personal.* This was a choice, but it had been confirmed for me over the years.
2. *God is good.* It is also a choice to believe this. I do believe the Divine Presence is not indifferent, but is the essence of goodness.[6]
3. *God is Love.* I look no further than John's verse, where he says, "God is love." The very essence of the Divine is goodness and love.[7]

My Christian training provided a basis of Biblical knowledge and a good spiritual foundation. During my Air Force discipleship days, I had memorized this obscure verse from one of the Minor Prophets of the Old Testament in the book of Nahum:

"The Lord is good, a stronghold in the day of trouble and he knoweth them that trust in him."[8]

As I struck out on my own in leaving the church and Evangelicalism, this verse was all I needed to remember. It hits on the most important aspects of spirituality that I hoped to expand on:

1. *"The Lord is good."* I believe The Presence is good and not malicious. If there is not this to hold on to, then there is only darkness and nihilism.

2. *"A stronghold in the day of trouble."* Whatever characteristics The Presence consists of aside from goodness, The Presence is not absent, but is present and helpful.

3. *"He knows them."* The Presence is personal. This is one of the great hallmarks of Christianity, the faith I was drawn to because of a Jesus who was a person, not just an amorphous, nebulous God energy, but one who knows and can be known. That God, both the he and she and them, whatever pronoun you prefer to use, personally knows me, and all those who trust and seek and knock. I had experienced the Spirit, the Presence of God enough times to know there was something behind my faith.

4. *"That trust."* Ultimately, whatever religion you choose, it comes down to trust, faith that in some senses is more than belief. We are flying by the seat of our pants. There are as many religious paths as you can imagine. We can't all be right, but we can all be wrong. Nobody has definitive proof; it's by faith, not sight.

I didn't know all of what would be ahead of me and where the journey would lead, but I was looking to build upon those three things and find a greater spirituality that included these things:

- A more expansive and inclusive faith. One that does not claim it's the only way, but appreciates and respects the wisdom and practices of all the other great religions.
- A more human and humane faith. One that respected the dignity of the individual and our shared humanity.
- A faith that celebrates all of creation and the wonder of this world. One that didn't dismiss, curse, and deride this world and the great diversity of human experience.
- A more honest and real connection with the Divine Presence. One that is beyond the trappings, ceremonies,

and traditions of one particular faith; one that is beyond mere scholastic and pious assent to its own dogma.

- A faith that is based more in an inner personal connection than in doctrine. One that has its strength in a soul connection, not in a specific religious creed, a doctrine, a dogma or statement of faith.

As Christians we read about people in the Old and New Testaments who had direct encounters with God. But that's history; and we don't expect to be afforded the same relational experiences. But why not? Are we just left with millennia-old stories and doctrinal boundaries that we are supposed to be satisfied with by faith?

I wanted to get beyond all the filters that are put between me and the Presence. Strip it down and get back to the simple basics of Jacob wrestling God through the night.

I would no longer be bound by the main pillars of my evangelicalism: the inerrancy of the Bible, Jesus as the only way to God, the original sinful nature of man, mankind bound for Hell without Jesus, the literal interpretation and historicity of the Bible.

OKAY, IT'S BOTH OF US

If you've ever been in one of those relationships where you come to that point of feeling it's time to break up, usually it's a combination of both partners. But sometimes it's easier to say: *It's not you, it's me.*

My uncomfortable relationship, however, was with the Almighty. I basically told God: I'm tired of always saying *it's not you, it's me.* Truthfully, it was both of us. My image of God was too small, too Christian, too Evangelical.

Deconstruction was already in full swing, and I was swinging a wrecking ball. I was going to take the building apart and decide how to put it back together again in a more suitable fashion. My "Pillars of Evangelicalism" were crumbling, and I was hoping for a clear vista.

Ralph Waldo Emerson is a good counterpoint to the fiery Jonathan Edwards. Emerson was one of the leading spiritual lights in New England in the 1800's. He was invited to deliver the Divinity School Address at Harvard in 1838.

It was the speech that got him banned from Harvard for thirty years. What did he say that got him in so much trouble? Emerson spoke about being truthful and genuine. He said, "Dare to love God without mediator or veil." Institutional religion does not like that kind of talk. It's heretical to them.

CHAPTER 14

THE BALLAD OF FELIX MANZ AND PASTOR Z

By this shall all men know that ye are my disciples,
if ye have love one to another.
—Jesus Christ[1]

O ne of the more disturbing historical anecdotes I heard in seminary really hit home for me. I'll put it in context.

In my earliest days of Christian zeal, while stationed at Patrick Air Force Base when I was a nineteen-year-old Airman crossing into my twenties, I was heavily involved in bible studies with a local military base ministry and later in home bible studies. So years later when I went to seminary and heard the story of two bible study mates that ended with one of them being executed for a theological disagreement, I was appalled.

So I put the story in a song. I'm calling it "a ballad" because I prefer that type of intimate song rather than a long explanation of what went down between the two historic characters.

"THE BALLAD OF FELIX MANZ AND PASTOR Z"

Bob Dylan wrote a memorable song on his *"John Wesley Harding"* album titled: *"The Ballad of Frankie Lee and Judas Priest."* Dylan's song has the feel of an old country tune. You just know the song is going to have a sad ending. Here's my Dylanesque *ballad* penned by yours truly and sung to the tune of Dylan's song mentioned above. It's a light-hearted way to tell a sad story.

"The Ballad of Felix Manz and Pastor Z"

Now Felix Manz and Pastor Z
were churchmates in the sixteenth century,
living in view of the snowcapped Alps.
meeting together in prayer and Bible study

Now these were not such peaceful days
as the setting might suggest,
for these were the days of religious zeal
and persecution of heretics.

Now Felix Manz was not a common man
by any means, why, he could read and write,
and had a sharp inquisitive mind,
not the kind to shy away from a theological fight.

And Pastor Z, well he was once a rebel himself,
defied the Holy Catholic Church and Lent
by eating sausage during a Holy Day Fast.
It was around this time the two men met.

Felix watched his mentor and Bible Study mate,
as Pastor Z took up with a widow and did cohabitate.
Z was not a priest who would remain celibate—

114

He married that woman when she was six months'
pregnant.

So Z's child and the Swiss Church were both born,
with Felix urging his mentor on...
'til one day, Felix had a change of heart
But for Pastor Z, adult baptism was a reform too far.

"Why are you defying me, Felix?" Pastor Z asked.
"I'm baptizing believers like John the Baptist," Felix did
reply,
"Don't speak of such heresy," Z to no avail cried.
Felix went on baptizing as he thought was right...

It ended one day when they tracked him down,
Felix was arrested and sentenced to death
in the cold River Limmat where hands and knees bound
there before the whole town, Pastor Z had Felix drowned.

Ah, Pastor Z would go on to reap what he sowed...
dissent, division, fighting Holy Norms...
silencing men like Felix for their reforms... until
Pastor Z died violently by the sword in another Holy War.

The moral of the story, if there must be one,
Is let your zeal be measured, don't let it run on and on.
'Cause that dogma that consumes you to a flaw today,
is but the Letter not the Spirit of the law... as they say.

So if it's Jesus you wish to emulate...
remember the Gospel words he said
"Greater love hath no man than this.... for his friends
"Than to lay down his life for" them.

I can't imagine living in a time when the mode and theology of Baptism would drive someone to drown a close friend, a spiritual brother, over such a thing. But zeal can consume us in all the wrong ways. Zeal for dogmas and doctrines that Christians declare non-negotiable...and yet both sides use the *same Bible* to defend these dogmas to the death.

A HISTORY OF LEARNED ABUSE OF SELF AND OTHERS

Serious Christians can't avoid reckoning with our collective, sordid church history. However, many still do. Many manage to live in a Christian bubble inside their holy huddles. They turn a blind eye to the atrocities committed in the name of our religion, the church and God.

The truth is that Christianity and Judaism grew out of a heritage of wars and conflict—from the Old Testament and the wars for land and territory, to Christianity's early struggles to survive persecution while at the same time battling for its identity as a cult in a hostile world, then to the first couple of centuries of internal battles for doctrine and structure, and finally to its official recognition as the religion of the Empire. After that, Inquisitions, Crusades, heresies, the Protestant Reformation, all the many roots of its divergent and competing tangents and schools of thought—Christianity fought for its place and ruthlessly branded anything and anyone threatening its hold as heretical and unorthodox. Today there are innumerable Christian denominations, all to suit the innumerable interpretations and preferred applications from the same book.

Joseph Campbell put it directly:

"Christianity and Judaism are religions of exile. Man was thrown out of the Garden."[2]

God and man got off to a bad start from the beginning. We have a murderous history, and not just with others, with heretics and infidels. Yahweh in the Old Testament is quite the murderous God, a national deity of the Jews who frequently orders the killing of whole tribes by his Chosen People.

The church has a long history of teaching its own people a form of holy sanctioned war, sadism, and masochism. Self-discipline can turn into a kind of punishment of ourselves on God's behalf. Since we have Christ and the Holy Spirit in us—and the whole Godhead for that matter—they become a sort of internal disciplining and governing authority to keep us on the straight and narrow.

But within many of us, this inner governing voice of God can become an overbearing disciplinarian. This is where the church's history of believers' self-abuse produced some strange things. Today we talk about the problems of emotional abuse in relationships. There is emotional and psychological self-abuse that Christians put themselves through in the name of devotion and commitment to God, their dogma, and their church. I am among those who allowed myself to abuse myself silently and psychologically. You might say that figuratively, my internal Pastor Z was on a mission to repress and silence my Felix Manz...not over modes of baptism, but in the sense of the older and the younger brothers.

Church history is replete with stories of self-flagellation, castration, self-torture, burning at the stake, drowning, and on and on. There is a dark side to romancing the faith. You can gloss over it and put a coat of white paint on it, you can feel all cozy and uplifted in the beautiful sanctuaries and warm glow of morning worship, with everyone dressed in their Sunday best, but our heritage is one of war and power struggles.

Our heritage is one of shaming, of manipulating an individual into feeling guilt, purportedly so she will be as holy and obedient to God and church as possible. When people get out of line they are often shunned, disciplined, asked to leave, punished, or excommunicated. The term *heretic* was soon used to brand anyone who disagreed with the teachings and dictates of a particular church or fellowship. The individual was sacrificed for the dogma, the doctrine, the decree.

I WOULD COME to discover that in me there was both a Felix Manz and a Pastor Z. Not precisely them, but their archetypes: the rebel purist (Felix) calling believers back to the Gospel and taking scripture seriously and personally; and the professional cleric (Pastor Z) trying to maintain some sanctioned authority to build church theology upon. They are different versions of the same person at different times in life.

The battle between Felix Manz and Pastor Zwingli would play out in me as I grappled with internal and external battles of theologies, theological arguments, opposite positions on the same point, and changing viewpoints on my beliefs, as I argued with myself over divisive doctrinal positions.

However, I yearned to lean toward love and grace when it came to people. But I know many times dogma and doctrine won out. I was taught to defend the faith, which I did for many years before growing uncomfortable with doctrines I no longer believed were important enough to "drown a brother" who disagreed.

Seminary taught me many things. One of the most important things it taught me is that there are a variety of interpretations of scripture and schools of theology that defend their positions using the same Bible. Not all interpretations are equally tenable or valid. Sometimes people misuse, misinterpret and misapply scripture and principles of interpretation. Sometimes the interpretation is based upon a predetermined theological position or system.

Seminary helped demystify much of the dogma and doctrine that accounts for the internal conflicts, squabbles, and divisions within the Christian community. By the end of my three years of seminary, I was so tired of the predictable theological debates over doctrines that people never would solve or agree on. Some theological conundrums will never be satisfactorily solved. We have a Divine Presence who often operates with mystery.

I would hear two guys at the next table in the White Horse Grill on the seminary campus arguing about free will versus predestination and I would have to get up and move. I so wanted to say before leaving: "Guys, get over it."

Felix Manz and Ulrich Zwingli were two guys stuck in time. If you were to pluck them out of their time and set them down today, it wouldn't end in the death of one of them. You could simply direct one of them to this denominational church and the other to this other denominational church. Today they could argue it out on social media. Today we have churches to suit every fine line of your theological preferences. And after church we could all meet at my place for the Sunday football game and have a couple of beers or cokes, depending on your church's prescribed guidelines. Nobody gets killed over the method of baptism today in our country. You could perhaps get killed over the NFL team you cheer for, however.

The proliferation of churches, denominations and religions shows me that ultimately, each individual chooses the belief structure that he or she prefers. That doesn't necessarily mean all belief systems are accurate or true. What it shows is that the individual makes the choice in the construction of his or her faith.

Ulrich Zwingli was a leader of the Protestant Reformation in Switzerland. Felix Manz was an Anabaptist and co-founder of the Swiss Brethren in Zürich, Switzerland, and an early martyr of the Radical Reformation—martyrdom bestowed upon him by an erstwhile mentor, a Christian brother, and Bible study mate. Nonsense.

What was the main issue that brought about such an extreme reaction? It was infant baptism versus adult baptism. Felix Manz and others refused to have their infant children baptized and chose to baptize adults only, meaning that baptism was reserved for adult believers who professed faith in Christ for salvation. That theological stuff could get you executed a few hundred years ago. Fundamentalists and Evangelicals would have been executed back then for adult baptism.

When you mix the complications of church membership and national citizenship, you wind up in a tangle of theological explanations and national pride.

FELIX AND PASTOR Z BEFORE THE REFEREE

I try to image these two men coming before God like two dirtied, bruised, and bloodied schoolboys who got in a scuffle in the yard – Felix and Ulrich. In my imagination it goes something like this:

"Now what drove you two boys to this ruckus?" the Lord asks. (Of course he already knows, and they know he knows.)

The two boys can't look up because they are both embarrassed. They mumble a barely audible reply.

"Speak up, boys, and look at me," the Lord asks calmly. (Of course he knows what they said; he's not hard of hearing.)

"Baptism," they simultaneously respond, and each starts his defense.

"And sausage," Felix mumbles. "Pastor Z left the Roman Catholic Church over sausage. Then he drowns me because of baptism." The two argue some more.

The Lord leans back and lets them further embarrass themselves. Their voices eventually fade, silenced by a single look.

Then the Lord speaks: "Thankfully for both of you, my forgiveness extends beyond all your lunacies and shortsightedness, beyond all your hopelessly confining doctrines and creeds, beyond baptism modes, and even beyond sausage."

The Lord looks over at one of the Arch Angels, Michael, and one of the Cherubim, and with a sigh born of millennia of grief and the well-worn patience of the original Saint, asks: "Michael, how many deaths have resulted from theological dissent over the mode of baptism?"

Michael flips through some pages of a huge ledger. (Of course, they don't really need books or ledgers here. It's just for the drama of it.)

The Lord knows the number (just like he knows the numbers of hairs on our heads). It was a rhetorical question, "Never mind, Michael, it's an embarrassingly ridiculous number." Michael exchanges a look with the Cherubim that says, "Why do we even keep these books? The numbers are all in Hashem's head." (They have many names for the Him-She.)

Felix and Ulrich look down sheepishly, each feeling the burn of shame rising on their necks and reddening their cheeks.

The Lord, Hashem, then seems to drift off into a moment of self-reflection and speaks quietly, knowing they are listening. "I suppose we should take the blame for all this, shouldn't we? But we thought it was clear enough when John the Baptist was baptizing adults, and even an adult Jesus, in the Jordan. Did we ever or did Jesus ever tell them to baptize infants? Did we ever somehow connect it in their minds that it had to do with citizenship in a state or country?" Rhetorical again.

Hashem paused, as she often did. It was then that Felix and Ulrich looked up again at the Lord and were surprised to see a beautiful Goddess in flowing, glowing garments like a prism of rainbow blends. Neither Felix nor Ulrich ever imagined that Hashem, Yahweh, their Lord, was female as well as male. Surprise, surprise.

It was then, as if involuntarily, they bowed and slowly knelt in awe.

Hashem leaned forward, her face so beautiful that Felix and Ulrich had to look down. "Boys," she said with warmth that was beyond words. "You may stand now, and do not turn away from me, but look me in the eyes."

Felix and Ulrich stood and gazed into her eyes and without another word their shame was replaced with a knowing and a realization. All their doctrines, dogmas and creeds faded, escaped their memory. All their reasons for fighting evaporated. Their need for discussion and clarification between each other and with

Hashem were like a bad nightmare one cannot remember upon waking.

NEEDING A REFEREE

Seminary gave me a chance to debate theology and to validate some of my own doubts and questions about what I had been taught in those first ten years of Evangelical discipleship.

However, since I am not able to literally stand before The Presence with the veil removed and all revealed and known, my internal battle of warring beliefs, opposing sides, of wrestling with the Angel of the Lord through the night would need a referee or two.

Where do you find an internal referee? Where and how could I find an internal parental self who could step in and break up these schoolyard scuffles between the Felix and Ulrich, both vying to be the theological alpha male within? Which one of these combatants is the Angel of the Lord and which one is me? What if there is no referee? What if the internal parent or the referee is asleep or just absent?

CHAPTER 15

DECONSTRUCTING MINDSETS

*The quest for the warm and cherishing God
and the warm and cherishing self
is the essence of spirituality.*
—Fr. Andrew M. Greeley[1]

So let me explain how it came about for me. The Gospel was and is often presented at first with the verse from Revelation 3:10, conveniently lifted right out of context from the Vision of Saint John on the Isla of Patmos when he was divining messages to the early churches in the first century of Christianity. You've probably seen the famous painting of Jesus literally standing at a big wooden door of a house.

A BRIEF PROFILE OF A "NEW CREATION IN CHRIST"

So Jesus is at the door of your heart, my heart, and you invite him in and you are agreeing to become a believer and have him forgive your sins. The verse in Revelations says if you invite him in, he will have a meal with you (he will have fellowship).

> "Behold, I stand at the door, and knock: if any man hear my voice, and open the door, I will come in to him, and will sup with him, and he with me."[2]

So you "pray the prayer," as I did. There are a number of versions of "the prayer" so you don't have to make up the words yourself. The prayer simply includes: forgive my sins, come into my heart, and I trust you for my salvation. The wording varies, but it's usually as simple as that. Some people go forward at a crusade or at church, some people pray with someone one-on-one, like I did with Ray in Eau Gallie.

Jesus forgives your sins and he brings gifts, eternal life being the biggest wrapped box under the Christmas Cross. So now what?

"Oh," you say in a slow drawl that betrays your uncertain surprise after it is explained to you that "Jesus just moved in." He is now within you (via the Holy Spirit) and all that metaphysical mumbo-jumbo suddenly becomes literal (even though it was a figurative "door" and a figurative "heart" that we invited him into). Then after an uncomfortable silence you say, "Ah, I see."

So now the Good News is that Jesus forgave your sins, gave you eternal life and now you're in God's Family. It's all free and by grace through your faith.

"So, let me get this straight," you say, "I'm in God's family, but Jesus is moving in with me for good. That means he's in my head, my spirit, my personal life, my mind." Correct. "Oh."

I grew up feeling like God was always watching me. But now the Watcher is inside me, in my head, my heart, and my soul. Now he not only knows when I am sleeping and knows when I've been bad or good, but he knows when I'm thinking bad and good thoughts.

I'm not only a new believer, but I am also a "new creation."

"Therefore, if any man be in Christ, he is a new creature: old things are passed away; behold, all things are become new."[3]

It's a lot of existential, cosmological, metaphysical, theological, psychological stuff happening just by opening a "figurative" door to one's heart. But this was not just any door and not just any solicitor knocking; this is Jesus Christ, the Son of God, the Messiah, the Savior, the one who died on the cross.

As an Evangelical, I adopted the beliefs of what is often referred to as "conversionism" or "decisionism," the belief that individuals must make a personal decision and invite Christ into one's heart, which constitutes a conversion, or a "born again" moment that in turn transforms the believer into a "new creation" in Christ.

In this brand of Christianity, an emphasis is placed on praying that prayer that puts action to one's "belief" and "trust" in Christ. I grew up as a Protestant and as far as I knew I always believed in Jesus, but that was not good enough. According to Evangelicals, belief alone isn't enough—you have to decide and pray the prayer.

In the Evangelical camp, I was taught from scripture that Jesus and the Holy Spirit are not just concepts for us to embody, but that they are literally "within" me and one with me. "Christ in you" is the wonderful mystery. It is very "literal" and very personal. Christians are to be "Spirit-filled," which means that the Holy Spirit is active in each of us as a presence, the Comforter.

Where this gets tricky is in each person's head, in our inner mind and spirit where we process life, interpret the Bible, and apply the truths.

LEARNING THE CHRISTIAN LINGO

There's a lingo in these Christian circles. You learn to talk about spiritual things in a certain way. I began hearing people say things like, "I was talking to the Lord today," and "The Lord said to me today" when such and such happened. I was not used to this lingo, so it took a while to get used to it.

"Fundamental Christianity constitutes a full-blown subculture with a common language, belief system, and behavioral code."[4]

Before long I was speaking the lingo. There are feelings of inspiration and fillings of the Spirit. Again, these words are all very subjective. However, I was now aware of The Presence in a personal way. John Wesley, the famous evangelist and theologian, described that in his moment of conversion he felt his heart "strangely warmed." Not a very precise nor necessarily spiritual description, and yet, I know what he meant. I felt my heart strangely warmed many times.

The language is not totally descriptive or accurate. It's figurative, not literal—but don't tell the Evangelicals that. No one ever stopped anyone and asked: "You heard a voice? You really heard Jesus out loud?"

Of course, none of us heard an actual audible voice. I never heard a voice in all those years. You have a strong feeling or leaning. You read your Bible and reflect and conclude. Many Christians develop this merger with the Lord and they sense when their thoughts are coming to them as if the Lord is revealing directly to them. Everyone in the fellowship is talking in this language, so I wound up using the same Christianspeak.

What this lingo jump does is to immediately create a "personal authority" within the individual. How can anyone really challenge what Ray just said if he prefaces it with "the Lord told me" or "the Holy Spirit told me?" How can I challenge my friend's relationship with God if he says, "I was praying and reading my Bible this morning and God told me....."

Nobody really asks, "God told you?"

This "unaccountable" personal authority is one of the foundations of Evangelical Christianity. It's unaccountable in the sense that, if Joe says God told him so and so, who can challenge that? Suddenly, everyone feels they have a direct line with the Almighty.

"Authority" becomes a key pillar of the Evangelical life. The Authority of Scripture—that the Bible is the Word of God, that it is not only divinely inspired but also inerrant and infallible—is perhaps the most important foundation of Evangelicalism.

So a Christian might be reading their Bible or devotions and they reflect on the reading and will say, "The Lord was telling me this morning that I need to" and you fill in the blank. The truth of it is that no one hears an audible voice, and we know we don't, but we still say, "the Lord spoke to me." What we really mean to say is "this is what I took from the verses for myself personally." But we tend to skip that.

This is the Protestant Reformation's "priesthood of believers" doctrine: you don't need a priest to mediate between you and your God. But that same doctrine has opened a huge can of worms.

So Christians automatically leap to the conclusion that the more devout and Christian they are, the more often their thoughts are from God. These personal messages come through Bible readings, study, sermons, devotionals, prayer time, and meditation. And as a young new Christian I began to talk like the other Christians I was around.

Along with conversionism, as an Evangelical I was taught that the Bible (our Protestant one) is our primary "authority." The Bible was the infallible, inerrant word of God. We became Biblicists, schooled in a distinct "literal" interpretation of scripture. Biblical literalism was what we defended. However, the position that the Bible is inerrant and infallible is not really defensible. It's untenable, because all the translations have errors and contradictions. The history and study of how we got our translations is a whole story in itself.

The danger is the assumption that your spiritual thoughts, leanings and inclinations are mostly, or all, from God. We understand this in the extremes, as is in the case of cult leaders believing they are the Messiah. But the pastor who wields a prophetic hold over his tribe of believers? That is still extreme, though to a lesser degree. So when is a cult a cult? So when have I crossed the line and become a cult member? When did I drink the Kool-Aid and go too far?

The personal relationship aspect of Evangelicalism is one of its main draws. We are invited to a relationship with Jesus. This is a good thing; it's a personal relationship, not just a list of beliefs and dogma.

There's a more subtle danger that pervades the church. Individual believers can assume that whatever they get out of the Bible is just as valid as any other believer. It leads to a lot of clashing "authorities," like Felix and Pastor Z. Let's just say, I have heard a lot of whacky ideas come from people thinking they heard the voice of God from their scriptures and Bible Studies.

Too many believers, ministers, ministry leaders, and preachers no longer know where Jesus leaves off and they themselves pick up. That line can get blurred, and it is usually where errors and extremes come in. It's because this two-headed person has tried to be both Jesus and himself or herself, and the schizophrenic nature of the beast often leads to some strange psychological-religious imbalances.

You may have a "personal relationship with Jesus," as we put it, but that doesn't excuse the fact that the Bible might be misappropriated.

DECONSTRUCTING THREE INITIAL MONOLITHS

So that's the milieu and the school of thought that I was trained in as an avid, zealous, sincere new believer and new creation in Christ. Whatever was going on in my head, the whole Trinity was right there hearing it in real time.

There were no longer any private moments; there would be no time off the clock, alone with myself. From that moment on, I was being watched, listened to, scrutinized, tested, catalogued, and disciplined by my new cosmic Jesus, His Father and the Holy Spirit. I was saved, born again, and a new creation in Christ ready to live a Spirit-filled life and the "wonderful plan" God had for my life.

Eventually, the "I," the Self, the Me, within whom Jesus has come to reside, becomes the Shrinking Man. In that old classic sci-fi movie, *The Incredible Shrinking Man* becomes the size of an ant, but it doesn't end there. He is doomed to forever be shrinking, infinitesimal, invisible to the naked eye. We had a verse to justify this. We memorized John the Baptist's words "He (Christ) must increase, but I must decrease" (John 3:30).

Woven into all of this "starter religion" that I began training into as a new "disciple" were three topics that became mental monoliths before I knew it:

1. Literalism – Literal interpretation of the Bible is the primary approach to scripture among Evangelicals and Fundamentalists.
2. Dualism – The paradoxical nature of opposites (good-evil; the church-the world, etc.)
3. Man's Depravity and Sin Nature – Man, even the believer, is forever saddled with a sin nature; there is no good thing in man (Romans 7:18).

Literalism is Evangelicalism's primary and preferred Biblical interpretation approach. Literalism stands on the principle of taking the scriptures literally first, unless it clearly indicates an analogy or some metaphor. So if it says God created the earth in "seven days" then it was literally seven days. If the numbers in the Bible are taken literally, then the earth is only about 6,000 years old; never mind what science may uncover revealing a much, much older earth.

Much of our Western Christianity is built on dualism; Evangelicalism and Fundamentalism are steeped in dualism. Dualism is the idea that there are scores of opposite forces and dynamics that control our world and worldview.

DUALISMS

God / Satan
Good / Evil
Light / Dark
Angels / Demons
Heaven / Earth (The World)
Eternal / Temporal
The Spirit / The Flesh
Holiness / Sin
Sacred / Profane
Incorruptible / Corruptible
Godly / Worldly
Blessings / Cursings

This two-sided mindset has a way of oversimplifying and categorizing the Christians' world view. It's "Either-Or" and "This or That" labeling leaves little room for discussion, elucidation, shades of meaning, and nuance. Its hard-cast categories become concretized in the believer's mind.

PARADIGM SHIFTS

One of the helpful books I read after leaving ministry was Father Andrew M. Greeley's autobiographical *"Confessions of a Parish Priest."* Father Greeley was a Roman Catholic priest, novelist, and author. Hearing his "Roman Catholic" side of things helped me see some of my "Protestant" differences more clearly.

In comparing his Catholicism to Protestantism, he points out that the two view "the world" differently. Protestants tend to view the World as Satan's realm, it's a scary, fearful place; whereas Greeley's Roman Catholic view was that this World is God's creation, it is to be welcomed and enjoyed. "The Catholic experience is sacramental," Greeley writes, "it sees God disclosing Himself/Herself through the people, objects and events of ordinary life." [5] The Protestant view is that God is dissimilar from the World, which is a "bleak and unsacred place." Protestantism "tends to assert God is radically unlike the world."[6]

He was right, I thought. This was a paradigm shift for my mindset. Greeley rejoices: "All is grace....Everything is capable of being a sacrament."[7] This was one of the first steps toward "deconstructing" the dualistic thinking that had been imbedded in my mind.

The third initial monolith in my mindset that rose up like the rectangular slab in the movie "2001 Space Odyssey" would be harder to label, harder to name and harder to grasp. The theology is often referred to as Man's "Sin Nature" or "Original Sin" and in some doctrines it's called "the total Depravity of Man." It is one of the pillars of John Calvin's Calvinism, but it is a major belief of Evangelicalism as well.

I will talk more about this later. But I personally believe that the "original sin" theology of Christianity has spawned much of Evangelicalism's tendency to dismiss and deny the true value and God-given wonder of our humanity and human beingness.

Man's "original sin" in the Garden of Eden and man's "sin nature" are pillars of Fundamental and Evangelical Christianity. In this theology, man is hopelessly helpless in redeeming himself. God cast man out of the Garden of Eden and our sin nature permeates every human baby, child, adult from henceforth. Man's sin nature permeates and sabotages our best efforts. Christ may be in you, but you are still saddled with this sin nature.

This is why Jonathan Edwards tells us God "abhors" man in his sermon "Sinners in the Hand of an Angry God." This is why we're told again and again "God hates sin" but he loves the Sinner. Really? After many years in the church, all I heard again and again was that man, his humanity, his very existence was an affront to God.

I recommend Marlene Winell's book *Leaving the Fold* to anyone needing more details about leaving their church. She has counseled scores of people going through the process. Her book contains many personal accounts of people wrestling with this very dilemma. She writes this on the opening page of her book:

"In conservative Christianity you are told you are unacceptable. You are judged with regard to your relationship to God. Thus you can only be loved *positionally*, not *essentially*. And contrary to any assumed ideal of Christian love, you cannot love others for their essence either. This is the horrible cost of the doctrine of original sin."[8]

I believe that the doctrine of original sin, how it is taught, and how it permeates the mindset of Fundamentalism and Evangelicalism, is at the root of so much spiritual turmoil and angst for many of us. It was one of the main pillars of my first faith that I had to topple. The debasing of man and woman and our human beingness is at the root of much of Evangelicalism's problems.

Again and again, I saw the church be anti-humanity, anti-man, anti-woman, anti-human being. Along with their anti-science, anti-intellectualism, anti-higher education, anti-psychology this basic stance fuels their underlying anger; it adds up to an "anti-human being" bias that runs through much of their theological rhetoric. It's so ingrained in their theology and attitudes that they don't quite see how much it colors their thinking. It is so foundational to their overall theology that they can't get away from it. They are actually closer to Anti-Christianity because of it.

I understand that the injunctions to crucify yourself, deny yourself, lose yourself are primarily meant to help us rid ourselves of the self-centeredness that can be the opposite of Christianity. The dissolution of the self is a key step in most major spiritual and religious paths. But the messaging extended beyond just that. There was a deep strain of self-hatred that was being fostered.

In seminary, I remember asking why we don't have a healthy

theology of what it means to be human, to be a homo sapiens human being, to be a human being and a believer?

I was ready to unlearn some of what never sat right with me; to be deprogrammed from my indoctrination and education. I was ready to enroll in an independent study, to hear and learn from another collection of mentors and teachers.

FATHER ANDREW GREELEY

In my second call to adventure, I would not read my Bible for many years as part of my therapy. I had enough verses and passages memorized to both comfort, admonish and torture myself for the rest of my life. I was looking for new voices and guides.

Joseph Campbell points out that in the Hero's Journey, when you respond to the call and set out on the adventure, a surprising thing happens. As you set out, you run into mentors, guides, and helpers.

I had already found a couple of guides in Walt Whitman and Father Andrew Greeley. Whitman's poetry compilation, "*Leaves of Grass*," would prove a lifelong companion. Father Greeley's autobiography would be one I returned to here and there to remind myself of important details. Both of these writers would often bring the sunshine and humor into any of my dark thoughts about The Presence. Greeley says that his novels are "comedies of grace" and writes in his *Confessions of a Parish Priest:*

> "All my novels are about God's love. They are stories of 'epiphanies' of the 'breaking in' of God to the ordinary events of human life."[9]

I read several of Father Greeley novels; he calls them comedies of Grace. I noticed how he'd weave an intriguing story and just when you thought things were really bad for the main characters there was what I came to call his "Ah-Ha of Grace," the surprise of Grace. He saw the journey of faith as a "pilgrimage toward the Tenderness of God"[10] and believed that "the quest for the warm and cherishing

God and the warm and cherishing self is the essence of spirituality."[11]

One of my favorite Father Greeley comments has to do with how he imagines God:

"My own image of God is that She is a Comedienne—and an Irish one at that. Life is finally either Comedy or Absurdity and I opt for the former alternative."[12]

Father Greeley constructed a faith that seemed much healthier than the one I had constructed. I do not want to take anything away from the first half of my journey as a Christian initiate and seeker. I had been at it a long time and it had all been worthwhile. I was not rejecting the first decades of the journey; it was the journey that made me who I was, and I couldn't change that part of the story.

Nonetheless, it did not take me all the way up the mountain. It took me part way and I could have stayed there below the clouds and been comfortable for the rest of my life as a well-paid professional, full-time minister with good benefits.

But it was time to proceed up the mountain, through the clouds and beyond, or maybe the trail needed to go back down the mountain and around and up another trail. Whichever way the journey would go, this time I was going into it without blinders, without a muzzle, without fear. and without a straightjacket.

I could have been more graceful and careful in my leaving. Sometimes when life was spinning out of control, I was just trying to stay alive. No one but my first wife and I knows the behind-the-scenes story of how too many things came to a head over the last couple of years together. The wrecking ball seemed to be swaying without much help from me at times. I was ducking under cover from the rubble at times, not knowing exactly what the ruins would look like when it was over.

CHAPTER 16
FRANKENSTEIN AND ME

Listen to me, Frankenstein.
You accuse me of murder; and yet you would,
with a satisfied conscience,
destroy your own creature.
—The Monster[1]

Sometimes I think my Christian Evangelical story is part Frankenstein tale and part Frog Prince fairy tale. There is tragedy, fairy tale and comedy for sure and all the talk of demons and angels, powers of evil, the "new creation" in Christ and the dark, wicked, sin nature of man.

Joseph Campbell, the author of many books about mythology and comparative religions, talks about how he was raised Roman Catholic. He makes a telling comment when he says that he got out of it at age twenty-five before it "concretized" in him. He appreciated the faith and rich symbolism of his Catholicism. But he warns that we can find ourselves "blocked by a concretized" religious symbol or image.[2]

He goes on to explain that when our images of God, the doctrines, dogmas, and biblical stories get "concretized:"

"You can't get rid of them, because the symbols that are taken concretely are put right into you. They are internalized and can't be dismissed."[3]

For me, the images and doctrines had concretized after decades in the Evangelical church movement.

DR. FRANKENSTEIN AND HIS MONSTER

In Mary Shelley's original novel, *Frankenstein*, the comparison of the Monster (created by Dr. Frankenstein) to that of "Man," the first Adam, is directly made by the Monster himself. In the novel, the Monster is never given a name; only the doctor who created him is referred to as Frankenstein. But through time and popular imagination, the monster became known as Frankenstein, the monster.

In the novel, a scientist, Dr. Victor Frankenstein, creates or animates a "being" – a man – but he is horrified by his creation, which he decides is a "monster." Ultimately, Victor Frankenstein is tormented by what he's created and decides the creature must be destroyed. In the original story, his "monster" learns to read and write and becomes intelligent. The "monster" variously compares himself to Satan and to Adam, God's first "human" creation. He rails at the doctor for bringing him to life.

"I ought to be thy Adam, but I am rather the fallen angel...."[4]

Dr. Frankenstein addresses his creation:

"Begone vile insect! ...Abhorred monster! Fiend that thou art! The tortures of hell are too mild a vengeance for thy crimes. Wretched devil!"[5]

"Abhorred monster" reminds me of flashes of Jonathan Edwards. I recently listened to an excellent audio version of Shelley's novel that brings to life the humanity of the Monster. When the Monster speaks to Dr. Frankenstein, I couldn't help but relate to the monster. The monster feels rejected by his creator. Here is the monster speaking to Dr. Frankenstein:

"Hateful day when I received life! ...Accursed creator! Why did you form a monster so hideous that even you turned from me in disgust? ...my form is a filthy type of yours, more horrid even from the very resemblance. Satan had his companions, fellow-devils, to admire and encourage him; but I am solitary and abhorred."[6]

The Frankenstein story strikes some all too familiar chords for me with God's creation of man and the subsequent fall and expulsion from the Garden. By Chapter 6 of Genesis, the very first book of the Bible, the Creator is so horrified by his creation that he decides to destroy mankind and sends a Flood to wipe out all but a handful of his creatures.

It says in Genesis 6:6, "it repented the Lord that he had made man on earth and it grieved him." Basically, we are told right up front that God was sad that he made man: the Creator turned away in shame at the sight of his creation: Frankenstein and me.

"You're no good, you're no good, you're no good, baby you're no good,"[7] the pop song goes (written by Clint Ballard Jr.). Linda Ronstadt sang her version of the hit song to the Tennessee State Prison inmates live as part of Johnny *Cash's "A Concert Behind Prison Walls"* in 1974. The audience cheered. They cheered because it's what they'd heard their whole lives: You're no good: You won't amount to

anything. I'm sure all the negative reinforcement these men received in their lives didn't help their criminal inclinations.

Somehow, amid all the talk of Jesus' grace and love, the message that took root deeper in me was that God hated the sinner in me, God would always be dissatisfied. I read many of those pious Christian devotionals and sermons of the great preachers over the years. There is a whole genre of what can be classified as motivational Christian devotional writings. "You're just not holy or perfect enough" was often the underlying message. "Work harder and maybe God will be pleased." Looking back on them I see how they influenced the melancholy spirit in me.

From the monster in Frankenstein, to the darkness of Jonathan Edwards' imagery, to Calvinism's total depravity of man theology, to the New England Puritan roots in my family DNA, there is a dark alienation at the core of the God-and-man relationship in much of my Christianity. And it's not without its melodramatic Biblical stories to back it up. Churches and evangelists are quick to remind us "it is a fearful thing to fall into the hands of the living God" (Hebrew 10:31). They like to keep us in fear and trembling.

The opening chapters of the Bible are the original "modern" filmmaker's template: start your movie with a dramatic action scene. Grab their attention in the first five minutes. We're only in chapter six of the Bible and God is already tired of man. Is this really who God is? Did he not see all this coming? Is this really what God wants us to think of him? How is it that this "great" God was outfoxed by a serpent in a perfect Garden?

By Chapter 11 of Genesis, God is angry again and decides to "scatter" his creatures after they have grand designs in mind and are building the Tower of Babel.

Whether you believe these stories are literal or mythological "origin stories" that explain why things are the way they are, I find it difficult to escape the image of God that comes across: short-tempered, capricious, angry, vengeful, and short-sighted. This God seems to be perpetually angry and not really up to the complicated task of managing his creation.

Apparently, God was as disappointed in his creation as Victor Frankenstein was in the "monster" he created. And God was ready and willing to destroy mankind a second time after he sent the Flood to do it the first time. It's rather disconcerting that God had so little patience with these creatures he created.

I spent many years accepting this as the definitive attitude of God toward man without really being honest with myself about how this affected my whole mindset. It was another mindset that was changing. My old "Evangelical Discipleship Liturgy," as I've come to call it, had to go.

MY EVANGELICAL DISCIPLESHIP LITURGY

You will not find this "liturgy" or "creed" written any other place. But you can find all the verses in the Bible. It is a liturgy that I wrote or one that was composed in my head. It's the tape that played in my mind in various forms and order of verses.

It is the "liturgy" or hardcore mantra that became the "voice of God in my head" that led me to finally want to change the tape and the church, to replace that voice in my head with something more representative of a loving, tender God, instead of the drill sergeant, hard-line voice that took root.

This series of verses from scripture was drummed into my head like a code through memorized verses, bible study and the hardcore discipleship program I enlisted into. This became the voice of God in my head, the God who expects me to always be about the Mission, the Great Commission, his great plan. The following lines are all from the Bible.

"My Evangelical Discipleship Liturgy"

I know that in me (that is the flesh) there dwells no good
thing...
He (Jesus) must increase and I must decrease...
I am crucified with Christ, nevertheless I live, yet not I,
Christ lives in me... I am a new creation in Christ...
You are the temple of the Holy Spirit,
you are not your own, you are bought with a price...
Be ye Holy even as I am Holy. Crucify yourself. Deny yourself.
Lose yourself. Reckon yourself dead.
Trust not in thine own understanding, but trust in the Lord.
Without me (Jesus) you can do nothing.
Study to show thyself approved unto Christ.
Work out your own salvation in fear and trembling.
To whom much is given, much is required.
I press toward the mark for the prize of the
high calling of God in Christ Jesus.
Let us therefore, as many as be perfect, be thus minded.
Be ye perfect even as your heavenly father is perfect.[8]

I'll take the blame for the voice that became the voice of God in
my head. Admittedly, this was an extreme. These were the marching
orders, the mission, and the ministry. It's no wonder I got tired of
being in the military and working for this Commanding Officer. It's
no wonder I wound up feeling like I wanted out of this army. I was
ready to retire and get away from that Voice.

I don't want to have my God regard me mainly as a servant, a
worker in the field, just another cog in the wheel of His Glorious
Plan. I don't want a distorted view or voice of God to persist in my
mind and spirit. I do not believe that God abhors man, or that he
views his creations as monsters. That Evangelical pillar of theology
was toppled. I was officially a heretic to that tribe. So be it. I think
I'm in some good company.

"BATTER MY HEART THREE-PERSON'D GOD"

Perhaps the part of the creed that became the most problematic for me was the denigration of the "Self" and the repeated message that there's nothing good in myself. This is the underlining message that took deep roots in my soul and mind, the message that there is something inherently bad and wrong with me as a human being— that is the tenor of the message.

Whether you dress it up by explaining that Paul's use of "the flesh" is just a term for the sinful tendency of man and downplay the harsh dualities of Christianity in the Bible, there is no getting around the message that man is always sinful. Redeemed or not, a human is a human, fallen and born in sin, as the creed goes.

Lines from classical Christian poetry also drove me as well during those early years. John Donne's lines from his poem *"Batter My Heart Three-Person'd God"*[9] was a mantra for the pious, devoted believers like myself who wanted God to drive all forms of sin from our lives in order to show God how sincere we were. "Be ye Holy... as I am Holy" was God's call to perfection. After all, we had to show ourselves "approved unto God." There was a good dose of self-hatred mixed with some Holy-sanctioned masochism in our pursuit of being "approved unto God."[10]

Of course, I knew the message of God's grace and love that I preached to others, but I no longer believed that message was for me. The deeper I went into my Christianity, the more it seemed that God didn't like me. He may have "so loved the world" (John 3:16) but it sure seems like he doesn't really like people. "You're no good, you're no good, you're no good" rang in my ears. Is it really just transactional for this "Yahweh-Jesus" God: "to whom much is given, much is required?"

CHAPTER 17

ENCOUNTER ON THE BEACH

I am larger, better than I thought
I did not know I held so much goodness.
—Walt Whitman[1]

I was sitting on the beach in New Smyrna, Florida, on a chilly winter day. It was about a year before I would leave ministry. I would often go to the beach on Monday, my day off as a pastor. I'd go on overcast, chilly days as well as sunny, hot tropical days. It was my time to get alone and decompress, read, meditate, and relax. On this particular day I had Whitman's *Leaves of Grass* with me and my study Bible.

Sitting in my beach chair with my sweatshirt hood pulled up to block the wind, I first picked up my Bible and read a passage that did nothing for me. So I switched to Whitman's *Leaves of Grass* and chose his poem, *"Crossing Brooklyn Ferry."*

My roots go back to Brooklyn, on Long Island, New York. The East River separates Manhattan from Brooklyn. My German grandparents lived there, and we visited often. My parents' first apartment was there, where I lived the first two years of my life.

Whitman toiled in Brooklyn as a writer and his birthplace is on Long Island, in Huntington, a town near my hometown. I used to pass his historic birthplace when I drove to my job as a teenager at the Big Apple Supermarket. I felt a kinship with Whitman.

Whitman wrote as if he knew people would be reading him years after he was gone, much like a timeless Spirit, a compassionate lesser angel, a herald of a new era. In his poem *"Crossing Brooklyn Ferry"* we go with Whitman as he rides the ferry across the East River to Manhattan and takes in the sights and sounds of the city and the great, swelling populace of humanity in the mid-1800's.

That overcast day, I was alone and there were only a few people on the beach when I read these words from Whitman...as if he turned to me:

> *"Closer yet I approach you,*
> *What thought you have of me now, I had as much*
>   *of you—*
> *I laid in my stores in advance,*
> *I consider'd long and seriously of you before you were*
>   *born.*
> *Who was to know what should come home to me?*
> *Who knows but I am enjoying this?*
> *Who knows, for all the distance, but I am as good as*
>   *looking at you now,*
> *for all you cannot see me?"[2]*

When I read those lines I literally had chill bumps on my neck. I looked around as if feeling someone's eyes on me. There was no one around or nearby. I had similar experiences at times reading Scripture; times when you feel the Presence of the voice behind the words. I admit, I looked around to see if Walt was really there.

Reading Whitman that day was transformative: his voice, his

words, his celebratory love of all humanity in all its grandness, beauty, pain, and darkness. That was the voice of a grand, magnanimous, loving creator, one who knows our humanity better than anyone.

Whitman continued:

> *"We understand then do we not?*
> *What the study could not teach—what the preaching*
> *   could not accomplish is accomplish'd, is it not?"[3]*

I also read that day his poem "To You," which has since become one of my favorites. If you only read one Whitman poem, read this one.

> *"You have not known what you are*
> *   you have slumber'd upon yourself all your life."[4]*

I had been slumbering upon myself. Whitman's words that day brought me to tears:

> *"I am larger, better than I thought*
> *   I did not know I held so much goodness."[5]*

These are not words I ever heard in a church or Bible study. My Christianity was not a celebration of man, it was a celebration of God. Most Evangelical and Fundamental Christians I've known won't touch Walt Whitman's *Leaves of Grass*. Not only is it "secular poetry," there's the talk of Whitman being gay. One strike and you're out.

It didn't matter to me that Walt may have been gay. If you actually read Whitman you will find that he loved women and men. There are a few mildly erotic passages in Whitman, but you'll see more eroticism on nightly television. Whitman is writing more with an expression of wonder and beauty, not some seedy creepiness.

Christianity has never seemed to know how to handle sexuality; even though the Old Testament book of *The Song of Solomon* is a celebration of romantic love. (To deal with that, many Evangelicals drop their "literalist" approach and adopt a "figurative" approach to the *Song of Solomon*, saying it is an extended analogy of God's love for his people.)

I remember quoting Walt Whitman in a sermon once during my last year in ministry and you would have thought I had invoked Satan. Most of those who responded with disapproval I can guarantee never read any of Whitman. It was the typical Evangelical/Fundamentalist narrow-minded, uninformed judgment. It was another sign to me that I was in the wrong pulpit in the wrong church.

I cannot stress enough how important Whitman was for me during this time. Whitman wrote as if he knew he was a Herald, an angel, a messenger of the divine ("angel" literally means messenger). He wrote as if he knew he was a voice from on high. No one champions the dignity, the uniqueness, the beauty, and the wonder of human beings as much as Whitman.

THE POETS

It was when I got back to reading the poets and Walt Whitman in particular that I heard another voice. I had read many of the classics over the years, both before being an English major and after. I found more kinship in the classics and the poets when it came to understanding what it meant to be human than I did in most of my Christian education. Writers like Dostoevsky, Tolstoy, Steinbeck, Hemingway, Graham Greene, Isaac Bashevis Singer, Victor Hugo, Bernard Malamud, Mark Twain, Aleksandr Solzhenitsyn—I could go on and on.

But it was Walt Whitman who through his single volume of poems *Leaves of Grass* became my private tutor, my revival tent preacher, my John the Baptist, my voice in the wilderness, proclaiming the wonders of humanity, the Creator's highest achievement: man.

In Whitman I heard the voice of a magnanimous "God" who is thrilled by and marvels at the wonders of humanity. Whitman woke me up. Here was a voice of a creator in love with his creation, not angry and displeased. I felt I had in some ways become like Rip Van Winkle, sleeping long and comfortably in my Christian solace, salvation, sanctification, and slumber. Whitman's poetry was part of my coming to consciousness.

I have read passages of Whitman in tears and wondered why I have not heard such a celebration of humanity in the church or in the Scripture. Well, actually, I know why. The church is all about Jesus and worshipping God. Whitman turns it all on its head. He knew that the innate goodness and dignity of men and women was not a message you would hear in most churches.

In fact, there is a bias against saying there is anything good in men and women in the church. We're the sinners; only Jesus and God are good. Actually, you can cross Jesus off the list because he said only God was good (Mark 10:17-22). It's one of those "Come on, Jesus!" moments. I can imagine one of the disciples whispering, "Did he really just say that? Then how can he be the "sinless lamb of God" who takes away the sins of the world?"

I did not believe the theological reasoning I was taught about man's sin nature any longer. That mindset was changing.

CHAPTER 18
YOU GOT NO SALSA

Christianity and Judaism are religions of exile:
Man was thrown out of the Garden.
—Joseph Campbell[1]

In that initial time of transition after leaving the church, My Jesus Doppelganger and my Christian Pious Self would gang up on my Once Ignored Self, who was no longer being the wall flower... and I'd get beat up in the name of Yahweh-Jesus and have to go to Father Walsh to get some patching up.

I knew I was on the right track and figured I'd been beat up in the name of Jesus at other times in my life. I guessed it was my turn to feel what it's like to be on the outside of the church. At the same time, I knew it was mostly a mind game: changing my mindset from that war within to finding peace with myself, becoming a more honest self, and finding peace with who the real God is.

There is the "Frankenstein and Me" analogy of being the alien-ated, abhorred monster that God can accept only because of Jesus.

But then a different analogy hit me: Once I am a "Christian," I am expected to divest myself of "self" and become an instrument, a vessel or a host that God works in and through. It's the whole "he (Jesus) must increase, but I must decrease" (John 3:30) ordeal that reminds me of a couple of sci-fi movies—*The Invasion of the Body Snatchers* and *The Stepford Wives*. There is a sense in which one can feel he has become merely a "host" to another entity that has over-taken him. In both of those sci-fi movies, individuals are taken over and their individual identities and personalities are eradicated as they are possessed by foreign or alien life forms. It's creepy and eerie. In these movies, we watch as people appear the same outwardly to their family and friends, but they are no longer themselves. They have been taken over and replaced by some Giant Borg or Alien Presence.

I have witnessed this in my years in the church. After a while it seems that Christians in their tribes and churches start to look and sound the same, as if they have become homogenized, pasteurized, and processed so that individuality and personality have been white-washed. It's as if "in the name of Jesus" we piously conform to a stereotype of a saint—at least, when we're with the tribe.

How much of that had happened to me?

NO SALSA

Within a couple of months of leaving ministry I had picked up a free-lance writing job for a video company. Interestingly, the Amazon mission video I wrote and directed helped land me the job. I was no longer Pastor Phil, but I was just a regular guy helping write a medical script and I was on a road trip to Miami with the director and video production crew who worked full-time for the company.

We were all sitting at a breakfast place along Miami's Art Deco strip. I had worked with this camera guy and another assistant for only a couple of weeks, so they didn't really know me. I was really going through the emotional wringer of my leaving ministry, changing careers, and trying to re-build my life. My wife and I were also separated. I was preoccupied with personal issues, and I was wondering if the freelance job would lead to something more permanent.

At lunch, this brash, foul-mouthed cameraman said to me: "You know what your problem is? You got no salsa."

I was feeling emotional enough to want to reach across the table, grab him by his yellow collar, pull him nose-to-nose, and say: "You want some salsa… here, have some salsa." And pour some salsa from the bottle sitting on the table on his face. That would have been my old New Yorker response. But I needed this job. So that day, I just sat back a bit and said: "I got some salsa. I just save it for who I want to share it with." We all laughed.

But he was right. I had no salsa; it had been buried. I knew he was right. He was referring to my subdued personality and my near "zombie-like" state. I was going through a major transition in my life, and I wasn't sure who I was once I left the ministry. Who was I without my title, my mission, and my theology? Who was I without Yahweh-Jesus in my corner?

WHERE'S PHIL???

A few months later I started working for a Church Directory company that had me covering a territory of about 700 churches. How poetic. Over the next 18 months, I walked into about 700 churches and talked with people about a product the company was selling—a photo album of church members. It was a wonderful job placement strategy by The Presence; my independent study course had its Divine Professor working behind the scenes. It was as if The Presence said, "Let me show you how big my kingdom really is, Phil. I have some people for you to meet."

I met and struck up relationships with a few ministers who were lights and messengers along the way: an Episcopal priest, a Presbyterian minister, and a few other denominational pastors.

One day en route to churches in another county, I was driving along and spotted a huge billboard with a simple yellow background and big black letters that said, "Where's Phil?"

It was the weirdest thing because there was no product or business associated with it, no phone number, branding or logo. I saw the sign once and I saw only one other in that county. Then I never saw them again. It was both humorous and a bit odd. I thought maybe the billboard was part of an advertising reveal and a follow-up message would appear. I even went back along the highway to see, but there was no follow-up. It was, however, another perfect little wake-up: "Where's Phil?"

An Episcopal Priest, Father Bob, was especially helpful; he and his wife reached out and had me in their home. He had been divorced while in ministry and his second wife had been like his saint. They were gracious and loving. We spent a few lunches together and Father Bob was another light along the way. He met his wife when she had cancer and was healed by prayer. He recounted how the doctors were in disbelief. "Real miracles can happen, even to Episcopalians," he joked.

An older Presbyterian Minister was genuinely pastoral and said, "If you had been in our system, you could have been divorced and stayed in ministry." Another local pastor had the first book I'd authored on his shelf (*The Father I Never Knew*, NavPress). He recognized my name as I was talking to him in his office, and he got up and pulled my book off his shelf. He had read it and had me sign it. Another pastor offered to help me get back into ministry if I wanted to.

It helped me see what a bubble I had lived in. I was also convicted of my years of spiritual arrogance as an Evangelical in thinking how we were the only ones who had it right. Coming to terms with one's spiritual arrogance is a critical step toward growth.

Though these few ministers were all sympathetic to my challenge in leaving ministry, none of them really heard the dark side of my need to sort things out and how I was avoiding going back into church for a reason. The last thing I wanted was another Christian church.

SEEING COLORS AGAIN

There was another little awakening during that time. I remember exactly where I was when it happened. I know the exact spot on the exact road, about an hour from where I live today, when it happened. I still can't explain it empirically, medically or physiologically. But it was as real as any eureka moment in my life.

The road dips down between two hills outside the town of Mount Dora. I have to preface this by saying I am not color blind, I do wear glasses, but my eyesight isn't that bad. I was driving along on that sunny spring morning and all of a sudden, it was as if I was seeing colors for the first time in a long time. It was literally as if I had gone from viewing a black and white television to viewing a big widescreen color TV. What was happening to me? How could this be?

There is a difference between being in a cult and having a cultic mindset. However, some of the deprogramming steps and milestones are similar. I want to make this clear. My first nine years of early Christian discipleship and being involved in the parachurch ministry was a wonderful few years for me. I have the utmost respect for the ministry leaders I had during that time. In the ministry group I was involved with, I never saw or heard anything untoward or the least bit off-color. It was a great group of men and women. I don't think I'd change any of it; I think I would just try to be a bit more balanced, less one-track.

But sometimes, how we internalize an experience is where the problem takes root. For some of us who are more sensitive souls, we experience things at a level that can sometimes hurt us deeply even though we are not aware of what's going on psychologically. Can religious training, vows of devotion, and ordination damage some of us?

Karen Armstrong, a famous religious author, apparently says yes. In her autobiographical *The Spiral Staircase,* she writes from her experience of having enthusiastically become a nun at a young age only to feel after seven years of training that she was damaged and needed to get out. Her story has been another inspirational example of someone leaving ministry and the church and moving on to a different stage of their spiritual journey. She writes:

"If you want to preserve your faith, the trick clearly was to keep practicing. If you stopped and looked at those rites and stories from the outside, they seemed absurd. Ludicrous, in fact."[2]

In his autobiographical *The Dance of a Fallen Monk,* George Fowler tells his story about training as a Trappist monk and serving in ministry for many years before leaving the order.

"The regimen of the monastery got inside of young men's hearts and minds and seeded an explicit religious motivation for conscious self-abjection. I spent my first fifty years in self-hatred, and all of that turned out to be silly."[3]

The spiritual step of the "dissolution of the self" can become a quagmire for many devotees. Yes, we need to step outside ourselves and see that we are part of something much bigger and eternal. But it is not supposed to be the complete negation, elimination, or rejection of self. I will discuss this more as we go. Fowler's self-hatred is common in many Christians, whether they are conscious of it or not.

Pastor Michael Walrond Jr. at the First Corinthian Baptist Church in Harlem, NY, talked about the "religious trauma syndrome" in an article in the New York Times. He says for some people, "religion has been more bruising and damaging than healing and transformative." He goes on to explain that too often churches "weaponize scripture and religion to do very deep damage on the psyche."[4]

Weaponizing scripture is a great way to put it. In my Evangelical discipleship training, scripture was weaponized against the self and others. Damage to the psyche? Where is the psyche exactly? It's a central part of the self. The very "self" I was taught is bad and needs to be crucified.

The Christianity I was drawn to as a nineteen-year-old was not a cult. It was the meat-and-potatoes, basic core of Christian Evangelical message that drew me. It was not that different theologically from the churches I grew up in. It was not some odd-ball sect of snake handlers or crazies. But I was finally standing up for my "battered" self and psyche. I was finally willing to change some of my beliefs and reclaim slumbering parts of my personhood.

CHAPTER 19
THE ALIENATED SELF

*In the fundamentalist system,
the self must be rejected
because it is essentially bad
and cannot be trusted.*
—Marlene Winell[1]

The real question that I have asked again and again in one fashion or another was simply this: Is there a place for the "Self" in Christianity? Mostly, the answer came back "not really." Mainly because how "they" understand "self" and how it should be understood in a holistic, healthy sense are two different things.

What I am asking relates to a Biblical view of the Self, my humanity, my personhood; all that comprises the core self, my individual psychological make-up of consciousness, ego, psyche, and essential core being, soul, spirit or whatever you want to call it. The human "self" is comprised of many pieces and parts. We have a whole collection of words that constitute the "self"—personality, individuality, mind, soul, heart, spirit, memories, motives, critical thinking, reasoning, ego, psyche, body, etc.

"Self" and "Ego" were always "four-letter words" in my Christian circles. Self and ego were equated, which is the root of the problem. It's amazing to me how Evangelicals will carefully parse and define their theological words, but can't take the time to differentiate words that are not convenient for them to deal with. Some of it is willful ignorance; some of it is just laziness.

Ego was sinful; it was self-centeredness; it was narcissism according to our Evangelical-Fundamentalist party line. But there's a big difference between the words and meanings of ego and egotism. The oversimplification and misuse of words like ego and egotism is another example of the lack of a more well-informed and sound approach by many well-meaning believers who are just not careful enough about messaging and meaning.

These same people make things synonymous that are not synonymous: like Self and Ego, like ego and egotism. Words and meanings matter. The Self is comprised of so much more than the ego. The willful ignorance and decision to be uninformed about the complexity of the human condition and psychology by Christians is embarrassing and inexcusable. It's often driven by theology, not intelligence.

THE WAR AGAINST THE SELF

There are two diagrams that are used by many Christians to teach the importance of "the Lordship" of Christ, a major teaching point in being a committed disciple of Christ. Versions of these diagrams have been around for decades. I was taught the Lordship of Jesus by others who used these diagrams with me. I, in turn, was guilty of oversimplification and taught others using the diagrams myself. I have long-since abandoned these types of diagrams, but I am using them here to explain why I find them inadequate.

The questions typically used to introduce the subject usually go something like this: *Who is on the throne of your life? Is Jesus the Lord of your life? Or is your "Self" or your "Ego" or "I" on the throne of your life?*

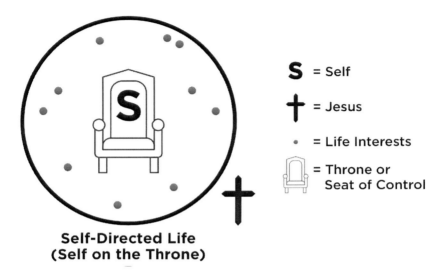

S = Self

✝ = Jesus

• = Life Interests

= Throne or Seat of Control

**Self-Directed Life
(Self on the Throne)**

In Diagram 1, "Self" has become the enemy. The self-directed life has no real place for Christ; he is outside the circle. Unfortunately, this is what is taught about the Self in many Evangelical circles. In some diagrams Self is replaced by Ego. Either way it reveals what that theological school of thought thinks about the human person-hood, the individual, the self. The comment is usually made that the self-directed life is full of discord and frustration (another oversim-plified and unsubstantiated claim).

According to this Evangelical reasoning and Diagram 2, the goal of the Christian is to put Christ on the throne of your life so that everything will work out properly. Get rid of your "self" and life will be wonderful. Being Christ-centered is a good thing; but just what happens to the Self in this scenario?

**Christ-Directed Life
(Jesus on the Throne)**

Put Christ first, not yourself, and according to this diagram everything will line up just dandy. But are there only two options: either Self/Ego or Christ on the throne?

I have seen a third diagram, that of the Carnal Christian (Diagram 3). It is similar to the Self Directed (or Natural Man) diagram, except the Cross or Jesus is inside the circle. So you get something like this trio of diagrams where Self is replaced with Ego. This is yet another misrepresentation of both the Self and the Ego; but these diagrams are geared more toward simplifying the guilt message than worrying about the semantics of the psychology and what constitutes the Self, or the ego for that matter. But some Christian groups love their simplistic illustrations.

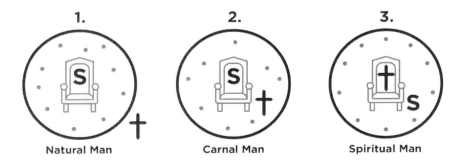

So here we have only three types of "Man" according to these diagrams: the Natural (i.e., unsaved man), the Carnal (i.e., a believer who is controlled by sin not Jesus) and the ideal Spiritual person (i.e., Christ-controlled man).

As long as we're narrowing life down to simple pictures, I have imagined another diagram, Diagram 4. In this one "Self" winds up outside the circle, alienated from the circle of self that Jesus rules.

That's how I began to see myself: the alienated self of the Christian who has exiled his or her self in the name of Jesus. My diagram would look like this:

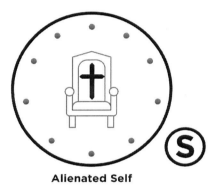

Alienated Self

In this version, Christ is on the throne and Self has been completely alienated and "kicked to the curb," you might say; life appears in order from the outside, the believer is doing all the right things, but has essentially ceased being a free human agent; he is playing a role, playing a part, going through the motions.

How about another couple of ways the Throne can be portrayed:

 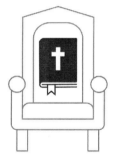

The Church on Throne   **The Bible on the Throne**

For some believers, the Church (or "their" church or Preacher/Pastor) is on the throne instead of Jesus (Diagram 5). Their Church has set the doctrine, the lifestyle, the boundaries of behavior, the sacraments, and the path. The believer doesn't need to think about too much, just follow the program.

For other believers, their Bible is on the throne instead of Jesus (Diagram 6). For too many believers, the Bible (the Word) has become the Fourth Person of the Trinity and their interpretation is the ONLY interpretation. Their Bible and "their Doctrine" take priority over Jesus. But they get around that by equating the Bible with Jesus (the Word).

Evangelicals love their diagrams and simple acrostics. I grew weary of them. Take, for example, the "JOY" acrostic: Jesus first, Others second, You last. It's virtually impossible to not be guilty every day with this one acrostic hung around your neck like an albatross.

Then there is their illustration of a railroad train with its engine (or locomotive), a passenger car, and caboose. They label it "Facts, Faith, and Feelings." The "Facts" of our religion are the locomotive; our "Faith" is the passenger car being pulled, the caboose is the last car and represents "Feelings." The first problem with this is labeling the locomotive as Facts; the other problem is always putting Feelings last.

I find these types of oversimplified diagrams more harmful than good. They have a way of trivializing both man and God, the complexities of faith, and the mystery of our connection with the transcendent. They continue the war on the "self," the individual. They are part of the war that includes their anti-science bias, anti-intellectual bias, anti-higher education bias, and their anti-psychology bias, which extends to their anti-humanity, anti-human-beings mindset and theological slants.

Let's be clear, the Self and the ego are not the same. Nor are the ego and egotism the same. For me, understanding the complexity of my "self" as a sentient human being apart from God was a central part of my journey toward health. I will return to this Self and ego topic in another chapter.

THE ROOTS OF SELF-ALIENATION

When we cast off all of the "Self" as a single entity and then make ourselves our own enemy, an alienation process is set up that makes it hard to disentangle the good from the not so good and the bad. Ego alienation (or disconnection) is a major psychological struggle that carries a complexity of internal repercussions. Swinging the pendulum from the extremes of ego inflation to ego alienation only confuses the internal center of control within a person. This was at the heart of what Father Walsh explained in his diagram about my condition when we first met.

The verse that long perplexed me as I started looking at things more closely was:

"I am crucified with Christ, nevertheless I live, yet not I, Christ liveth in me."[2]

Paul says he is "crucified with Christ," but then right away says "nevertheless I live." For years the "nevertheless I live" just kind of slipped past, almost said under our breath. Then, the big "YET NOT I, Christ liveth in me."

Wait a minute, Paul. Where did YOU or your "I" go? Clearly, you are still a living, breathing, and thinking person. So where did your "I" or your "Self" go? You didn't literally crucify yourself or execute yourself. So where did your "self" go?

It seems that Paul, who talked about being crucified with Christ and his "self" being crucified and dead, was an awfully opinionated and dogmatic person.

Too many Christians gave up the throne of their lives to Jesus in the wrong ways; myself included. All of these religions that call for abandoning the Self, getting beyond the Self to some super-spiritual "egolessness" are not helping. These many forms of self-denial, self-crucifixion, and self-abnegation do not clearly delineate the balance.

We are not helping ourselves when we obliterate "Self" or Ego. We are supposed to be maturing adults. Where's the locus of control? Where's the strong sense of self—the *healthy* sense of self—supposed to come from if we are obliterating the self on some extreme spiritual-diet of egolessness?

I like the way Joseph Campbell put it in one of his lectures:

"You've got to have your ego in play. We hear so much talk now, particularly from the Orient, about egolessness. You are trying to smash this thing which is the only thing that keeps you in play. There's got to be somebody up there; otherwise you're not oriented to anything. The self, that's the great circle, the ship, and the ego is the little captain on the bridge."[3]

OLD JOURNALS

I have kept journals since the start of my Jesus moment. I remember around this time in the course of moving that I dug out some of my earliest journals. I had three or four boxes from above the garage that I had not looked at in years. So I chose a couple at random and read what I wrote. I read entries from 1970, 1971, 1974, 1979 (when I was in my twenties).

My early journals were finely printed in my compact clear penmanship on thin-lined pages. After reading some of my old journals over a span of ten years of my younger self I was struck by the melancholy tone of my inner spirit. I could feel my soul going dark, melancholic from the hyper-zealous pursuit of holiness by my pious, young monkish boy Self.

As I read my own writings from my own journals, I felt sad for myself. I could see it now, reading decades later. But then I was being as genuine a follower as I could with the light I had at the time.

What would I have said to myself, if I could have had a minute with my twenty-year-old self? Perhaps I'd say, "You're on a good path, just lighten up and ask bolder questions. Enjoy your youth!"

We often hear about the challenges of young adulthood and how people were coming to grips with their "inner demons." For me, in ministry and Christian service as I look back, my conflict was that I needed to face my "inner angel" and wrestle that Angel.

I am reminded of Henry David Thoreau's line from Walden:

"What demon possessed me that I behaved so well."[4]

The war is set up theologically as: the "New Man" (the new believer) must defeat the "Old Man" (the old self). The way of the cross becomes an ongoing spiritual battle to conquer and defeat self and Satan and the dark powers. "Get thee behind me, Satan!" was a favorite line repeated.

The Self in my theology had become the embodiment of all that God opposes: "the heart is deceitful above all things, And desperately wicked."[5] What a negative outlook on life. I didn't resort to alcohol or drugs in response to being loathed by my creator. I was at war with me, myself, and I on God's behalf.

When religion subordinates the dignity of human beings in support of its dogma and authority, beware. When our humanity is denigrated by religious doctrine, it leads the way to the justification of abuse, mistreatment and devaluation of the individual.

I threw out the boxes of my early journals. More recently I gathered up another few boxes of old journals and made a ritual of burning them at night in a fire pit in my backyard. Nobody, including me, should read these. They represented part of this war on me, myself, and I.

I was now wrestling the Angel to get myself back.

CHAPTER 20
A FUNERAL AND A DIVORCE

I had gone very far, as far as the angels,
And high, where light thins into nothing,
But deep in the darkness of God.
—Rainer Maria Rilke[1]

I had not seen people from the old Patrick Air Force Base ministry group in many years when I went to a funeral for one of the women I knew from that ministry fellowship. She and her husband had always been sweet and supportive toward me. I'll call her Martha. The funeral was in Orlando, so it was easy for me to attend. I knew I would probably see a lot of people that I had not seen in years. Both of my first Christian mentors were there. It was a strange event for me to see so many people who were such a part of my life for a decade.

But I had left that fellowship sixteen years earlier. I was on a different trajectory and wasn't sure what I would say to them. Some people I had not seen for nearly twenty years. I was sad about

Martha's passing and I felt bad for her husband, who was so disconsolate about her death. They were one of the couples I met that first day at the Bible Study when I made a decision for Christ.

One of my mentors, whose home I lived in for almost two years, was surprised that I was heading toward divorce and had left ministry. In our few short minutes together at the funeral, he empathized: "I wish I could have been there for you," he said. I choked back a few tears as I thought, "I don't think you would understand or agree with me on my journey."

The first mentor I had during those initial two years at Patrick AFB flew in from halfway across the country and needed to catch a flight home after the funeral. I offered to drive him to the airport so we could talk.

I had not seen him in a number of years. I'd only talked to him a handful of times. He was a wonderful human being, husband, father, family man and leader. I'll never forget the kindness that he and his wife showed me as a nineteen-year-old Airman and new Christian. His confidence in me during those years in the military ministry moved me toward wanting to be in full-time ministry.

We grabbed a coffee in the airport before his flight. I felt uncomfortable, because there was no way to convey in a short amount of time why I was both leaving the pastorate and getting a divorce. By this time, I felt we spoke different languages.

I don't remember all I said or all he said. Time was too short and we felt rushed. I felt too much like the disappointing son, unable to adequately describe the "logic" in my spiritual mind to a dad who couldn't really accept what had happened.

But I do remember what he said that made me want to give him a Dirty Harry reply. I know he intended no harm or insensitivity, so it was not totally his fault. It's just what he said underscored the problem I had with the thinking and mindset of the tribe.

At one point my friend said, "Do you think it was God's will that you go into the pastorate?" I knew all the caveats and mental constructs behind his question. Essentially, he was implying that I had missed the will of God for my life.

I had to suppress my inner urge to pound the table hard enough to spill his coffee and say, "What you just said is exactly why I am leaving the tribe! All the mindsets and theological presuppositions couched, implied, and referenced in your simple question would take way more than the ten minutes we have before your plane leaves for me to dissect, vivisect, and clarify to my own satisfaction."

In a lot of my old Evangelical discipleship training, God's "perfect will" was like a single door; like the game show where there are three doors and the contestant has to choose the right door to get the big prize. If you choose the wrong door you may only get a year's supply of paper towels; if you guess the right door you'll get that all-expense-paid vacation to Tahiti. Likewise, if the believer picks the wrong door, then he missed the perfect will of God. You're left wondering why you screwed up.

I suppressed my initial response as his words reverberated in my head: "Do you think it was God's will that you go into the pastorate?" How could he say such a disrespectful thing? What a contrast to what my ten-year old daughter, Kim, said when I left ministry. She said, "Jesus lost a good pastor when Daddy left the church."

I wanted to at least show some emotion and say: "Do you really think I went into ministry so lightly? Do you really have so little respect for my spiritual sincerity and the last decades of my Christian service? Do we really still believe it's a single door? God must be endlessly disappointed and throwing away "perfect plans" for our lives *ad nauseam* if we must always discern the "perfect" plan like we're reading some handwriting on a wall or tea leaves in a cup or waiting for stars to align perfectly."

I silenced my abrasive Dirty Harry, and I thought to myself, "We are speaking two different languages. I don't know that he would ever accept how my beliefs are changing. This is exactly why I am leaving the Evangelical tent."

Here again was another example of that Catch-22, or the "double bind" as Marlene Winell so clearly identified it. In that Christian thinking: It's always the believer's fault or mistake or sin, never God's fault.

The "double bind" is simply this: If the believer does the right thing, that's because it was God doing it through the believer; if the believer does the "wrong" thing, it is the believer's fault. God always gets the credit, the glory; man always gets the blame. It's on you, man. It's your fault, it's never God's fault.

The double bind works like this:

1. "I can do all things through Christ who strengthens me," the verse tells us. God is our source of power and goodness. To God be the glory. You can't take credit for the good things you do. (Notice the athlete who is interviewed after he wins and says "To god be the glory" or some such nod to the divine.)
2. But if you sin, screw up, or go off-script in any orthodox way, well, that's your fault, not God's. (I don't think I've ever heard a guy from the losing team say, "To God be the Glory.")

Marlene Winell summarizes it as: "You are responsible for your sins, but you can't take credit for the good things you do." She goes on to point out that the double bind is one of "responsibility without ability." Jesus has all the ability; the believer has all the responsibility. It's the double bind.[2]

There are a number of presuppositions that fuel this double bind as it pertains to my airport conversation with my old friend, teacher and mentor:

THE PRESUPPOSITIONS

1. God has a perfect plan for our lives. Jesus promises "abundant" life (John 10:10)

2. If something goes wrong in your life plan or somehow you make a left turn instead of a right turn, or you make a decision that leads to difficult circumstances: It was probably your fault, not God's. The thinking is: Christians fall, stumble, sin, and make bad decisions because we are sinners. We can't help that.

3. The other thing underlying this "mindset" of theology is: since you are leaving ministry, the pastorate, it must be a mistake and you must have missed God's call to begin with.[3]

4. So that opens the whole can of worms about "what's wrong with me?" I know these traps that are set up in Evangelicalism. We look to label and profile people. Is he backslider? Has he become a "carnal Christian"? Has he fallen prey to bad theology and error? Is he a wash-out (someone who couldn't handle the rigors of a higher calling)?

5. Remember, someone has to be blamed and it's not God, so you must have screwed up, missed something, sinned or have unconfessed sin in your life. God is perfect; he never has to ask for forgiveness from us.

It's the whole "If God feels distant, guess who moved?" rhetoric. The question makes it clear that it was your fault, not God's. Always.

It's hard to explain how the very language used by some believers can drive many others of us crazy. I felt the utmost respect for my friend who had been so instrumental in my early days away from home in the Air Force. I didn't want him to think I was a heretic or wash-out. I didn't want to disrespect his theology, especially after he taught me mine and we agreed on a number of things.

That first fellowship of monkish boys at Patrick Air Force Base when I was 19 became my family. As their ranks grew and I committed myself more and more deeply to the ministry of Jesus, it was this Christian fellowship in its many forms and communities that gave me so much of what I first needed in my twenties:

- A sense of belonging
- A fraternity, a fellowship
- A part of something bigger than myself, a cause
- An enduring spiritual and moral tradition and foundation
- Guidance and support
- Safety, a haven
- A desire for transcendence

These are things many young people are looking for and hope to find in churches, clubs, fellowships, and cults. Sadly, some groups that provide them wind up hurting people.

I wanted to be more strident with my friend. But my defenses and emotions were running low after this difficult funeral and after seeing so many of the early Christian mentors and leaders who had been a part of my life. I didn't want to end our visit with a debate or on an unsavory note.

In the end my response to my friend's question was to off-handedly dismiss his notion. I said, "Of course I believe I was called. And I believe I am still being called. It's just a different path."

WHERE DO I TURN?

It was the early 1990's when I left ministry. I didn't know where to turn for help. There was no talk of post religious stress syndrome back then that I knew about. I couldn't talk to most of my ministry friends about the faith issues or about the issues in my marriage that had brought us to separation and divorce. Some things are private and should remain private unless discussed with a counselor.

I couldn't talk about what I was going through because of all the judgment and labeling that goes on in the church and among church leaders. To this day I have only spoken to a couple of these folks about some of these issues.

How could I explain how, after many years of delving deeper into the light, one becomes disenchanted by the Evangelical façade? Telling someone in the Evangelical movement that you are leaving only confuses them more. They usually think you are an apostate, a backslider, or a heretic.

I didn't know it at the time, but today there's a name for my condition. I didn't discover Dr. Marlene Winell's book *Leaving the Fold* until twenty-five years after its date of publication. She defines "religious trauma syndrome" or "the shattered-faith syndrome" as a condition experienced by people who are struggling with leaving an authoritarian dogmatic religion and coping with the damage of indoctrination.

Call it what you like, religious trauma syndrome, post-traumatic pastor's syndrome, abused Christians syndrome, obsessive-compulsive guilt disorder, or just time to get a new perspective... maybe finally some people are getting help.

MANY CHRISTIAN CIRCLES treat emotional and psychological issues with out-and-out ignorance and cruelty. In some tribes there is complete denial of any legitimate struggle that can't simply be fixed by the believer just praying and reading the Bible more. I had seen and heard enough of that.

When my wife and I first discussed our issues with our elder board, we were met with exactly what I anticipated. *Going to a psychologist wasn't going to help*, was the general consensus. Half of them said, you both need to "read your Bibles and pray more."

Literally, and to my utter disappointment, those are the words that rang in my ear: "Read your bible and pray more." It's just willful ignorance and primitive superstition. You might as well tell someone with a broken arm: "Here, go home and rub this rabbit's foot twenty-five times."

My wife and I were hurting in different ways at the same time, and neither of us quite had the inner strength to help each other—or even want to help each other at times. You've got your pain and I've got mine. You need to get your help as you need to. I need to get my help as I need to.

I couldn't, at that point in my life, find enough strength to give her what she needed. It was a combination of burn-out, ministry fatigue, years of stifling inner conflict, and then a meltdown. I was also feeling that I had taken her on my spiritual journey for nineteen years and I wasn't sure where this new phase would end. Why should she have to go through another one of my crazy spiritual adventures? I'll take my share of the blame. But I'm beyond assessing degrees of blame.

I am not going to get into the details of my divorce from the mother of my three children out of respect for our privacy. But suffice it to say, during the past two-plus years of ministry, things had begun to unravel between us. She had been seeing a counselor to help deal with the death of her father and all that had been dredged up in her family history. I was glad she was getting the help she needed. But I was drowning. I was dealing with complete disillusionment with the local church and my own changing beliefs.

Though the funeral I attended that day was for a dear friend who passed away, in another sense, it served as a moment of closure on the old ministry gang from my first years as a believer. In many ways, I was saying good-bye to one phase of my life as I was moving into completely uncharted territory.

CHAPTER 21
NEW VOICES AND MENTORS

Why, what have you thought of yourself?
Is it you then that thought of yourself less?
—Walt Whitman[1]

THREE "BROTHERS"

Several months after leaving ministry, I was on the phone one day talking with a friend I'd known from bible study and church for 18 years. He was, in fact, someone I had discipled as a young believer. He was part of a singles' ministry I led, and he had been in our home and over for dinner many times over the years. I told him how I wasn't doing very well. I was being honest and thinking I could be vulnerable with him, as I always had been. I told him I was feeling suicidal. His response nearly floored me. He said: "Well, maybe you should."

I don't know what I said in response; I was so enraged at the time. Imagine someone, a "Christian brother," telling you "maybe you should" commit suicide. Looking back, it was another sign that leaving the church and that brand of Christianity was the right move. I thought of Felix Manz and Pastor Zwingli and their falling out, with one sentencing the other to death. Insanity, I thought.

I told two others that same week that I was feeling suicidal. One was my younger brother, Glenn. He is not particularly churchgoing, but he is a good person and has always been a great brother and friend. When I told Glenn, he told me that if I did that, "I will kick your ass!" when he saw me again in the great beyond. He was dead serious. I needed to hear that.

The other person I told was my good Christian friend John, who is gay. We had been friends through the church for ten years at that time. We knew each other's wives and children from church. We were good friends and were going through a lot of the same things at this time. He had been an elder in the church.

John left the church a little while after I did. He came out as gay and there was no place for him in the Evangelical church. I had been the first person he came out to, and I had accepted him without reservations. He was my friend and good brother.

John and I were sitting in a little café in Winter Park one afternoon. I can still see the setting: by the window, small table, sun streaming in. I told John that I was feeling suicidal and by the time I looked up at him after explaining, he had tears in his eyes. He reached over, tapped my hand, and said, "If you did that, it would make me very sad." His response brought tears to my eyes.

Three different close friends: an Evangelical Christian brother, my blood brother, and a gay, divorced, Christian friend and brother.

NEW VOICES

I grew up with stories of magic and adventure; stories of epic journeys and heroic characters. Joseph Campbell writes in his classic scholarly and popular book *The Hero with a Thousand Faces*, that there is a pattern to the journey with some expected stages and characters.

The hero's journey typically begins with a call to adventure. Luke Skywalker is called away from his routine at home to become a Jedi and realize his destiny, and then he meets Obi-wan Kenobi, his guide, mentor, and wizard. Frodo Baggins is invited to leave his peaceful, comfortable shire and go on a great adventure with Gandalf, who becomes his guide and wizard. Fresh off his victory in the Trojan War, Ulysses starts his Odyssey home, and he is aided by Athena, the Goddess Guardian of Heroes. The journey is similar in many of these stories.

There are two common aspects of the early stages of the journey paradigm: the call, and the mentors and guides who come alongside.

> "If what you are following, however, is your own true adventure, if it is something appropriate to your deep spiritual need or readiness, then magical guides will appear to help you."[2]

Two of our most enduring hero journeys are J.R.R. Tolkien's *The Fellowship of the Ring* and *The Hobbit.* In Tolkien's Middle Earth, choosing Hobbits doesn't exactly seem like the best strategy, considering Hobbits are small and not really given to adventures or battles.

Hobbits prefer staying at home in their comfortable shire; an adventure holds no interest to them. Why would Gandalf choose Hobbits for such a wild and crazy adventure? When Gandalf first comes to Bilbo their exchange goes like this:

> (Gandalf:) "I am looking for someone to share in an adventure that I am arranging, and it's very difficult to find anyone."
>
> (Bilbo:) "I should think so—in these parts! We are plain quiet folk and have no use for adventures. Nasty disturbing uncomfortable things! Make you late for dinner!" [3]

Gandalf knew that the main reason he chose Hobbits was because there was an essential goodness of heart in Hobbits. They were not easily tempted by power or prestige. Hobbits were less likely to be tempted by the dark powers of the Ring (which he will be entrusted to carry on their journey). He needed someone (like Bilbo and Frodo) for what we might call their essential goodness. Gandalf explains:

> "There is more in you of good than you know, child of the kindly West. Some courage and some wisdom, blended in measure. If more of us valued food and cheer and song above hoarded gold, it would be a merrier world."[4]

I don't ever remember anyone in my Christian circles tell me that there was goodness in me. I never had that sense from my Christianity, that God saw an essential goodness in me. If anything, I was reminded at every turn that I had "original sin." The whole negative reinforcement of my faith left no room for any sort of human nobility, or human heroic action. Instead, it was all "to God be the Glory" and remember all that Jesus did for you.

One might expect that J.R.R. Tolkien was far from a Christian: he created wizards and a world of magic and spells. But it's just the opposite. Tolkien was a devout Roman Catholic. He was orphaned as a pre-teen: his father died when he was three and his mother died when he was just entering his teens. It was a Roman Catholic priest, Father Francis Morgan of the Birmingham Oratory, who became Tolkien's legal guardian. I wonder how much of Gandalf may have been inspired by Father Francis Morgan.

But as I began my journey out... my journey beyond the holy huddle and comforts of my church shire, I felt very much alone in my spiritual journey. I was hoping to find some of my own Gandalfs and Merlins.

MEETING FATHER WALSH

As I stated in an earlier chapter, I had gone to three different Christian counselors in the year since leaving ministry hoping to find someone to help me make sense of what I was going through.

I realized that the three counselors I'd gone to were all from the same general conservative Evangelical Christian schools of theology and practice that as I was from. They couldn't really help me because they were in the same tribe I was leaving.

That's when I met Father Walsh—just when I needed a "magical guide." Father Walsh did have a certain twinkle in his eyes, like he had some magic. Father Walsh explained that "the Church" (my belief system, theology, church, Evangelicalism) had become "God" within me. Like an overbearing, cruel, abusive parent, that "God" had crushed the Me (the Self) within me.

"You have deified the Church," Fr. Walsh said calmly. "And it has become this giant superparent within you that has diminished and squashed the very core of your individual self. "

Fr. Walsh continued to explain that there's a good parent within, the adult, mature Phil who needs to stand up, stop being silent while watching the "abusive," cold, dogmatic, unloving parent crush the life out of you. It's like the mother who silently knows the father is abusing the child, but does nothing.

Fr. Walsh's assessment was essentially: "You – Phil – have stood silent while you allowed your zealous self (in the name of your God, the church and your doctrine) to be overly cruel to yourself; all in the name of serving God and the mission." Father Walsh drew a rough diagram on the board (see diagram below). First, he pointed out that Self and Ego are two different things.

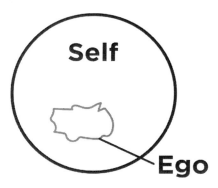

Finally, I met someone with a wise spirituality and a broader education who had a deeper understanding clinically and psychologically about the Self and the complexity of its components. Then he explained what was going on inside me with two other diagrams.

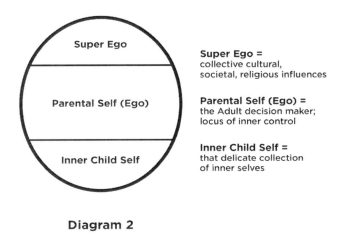

Diagram 2

In Diagram 2 (above), the healthy Self is balanced and taking care of itself. Different psychological schools of thought may name these aspects of the Self differently, but the point is the same. It was Diagram 3 that Fr. Walsh sketched out that really hit home.

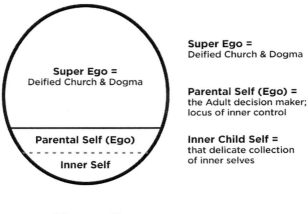

Super Ego =
Deified Church & Dogma

Parental Self (Ego) =
the Adult decision maker;
locus of inner control

Inner Child Self =
that delicate collection
of inner selves

Diagram 3

In Diagram 3, Fr. Walsh explained that I had deified the Church and its dogma and I had abandoned my Parental Self, whose role it is to protect myself from being run over, abused and used. By abandoning my Inner Parental Self, I had allowed my Inner Child Self to be crushed under the weight of an oversized, deified church and dogma.

Light bulbs were going off in my "figurative" head and soul.

The Super Ego is not GOD. But when I had equated the Super Ego with God (my theology, the church, the tribal liturgy), I had allowed it to crush both my Parental Self and my Inner Self. Fr. Walsh was a Jungian counselor, but regardless of what you call these various "monitoring" selves within, the truth is there.

We are supposed to be in control of this collection of selves and personas within. We have a complex Self, comprised of different roles we perform for ourselves as we mature. It's more complicated than the simple diagram Fr. Walsh drew, and he would be the first to say that. However, his straightforward explanation to me that day was a revelation.

We have a sovereign self, an inner locus of control, but it can be crushed, absent, asleep or silent if completely crucified. Even mentioning a sovereign self to the wrong Evangelical crowd would have earned me a Bible sermon rebuke on God's Sovereignty and Christ's Lordship.

This was when I stood up and asked: "Why haven't I heard this before?" It was one of those transformational moments when the brighter lights came on and another big shift of tectonic plates moved in my head. It was like the prism turned just enough to reveal colors I had not seen before.

It was during these sessions with Fr. Walsh over the next two years that I began to reconstruct my inner self with a wise guide, mentor, and friend.

Fr. Walsh was also the one who sent me to a psychiatrist who prescribed anti-depressants to help with my nearly depleted serotonin levels. Fr. Walsh saved my life: physically, spiritually, and psychologically. Depression can be caused by circumstances. Depression can also be caused by a chemical deficiency. Just reading the Bible and praying won't solve a chemical deficiency.

When my depression became circumstantial and chemical, my body wasn't producing enough serotonin, which helps the body maintain a balanced emotional level. So anti-depressants helped me in the overall battle to get healthy.

It was time to stop fighting with God, the church and myself. It was another critical shift in my thinking. It was time to stop fighting with myself and to fight *for* myself for a change.

OTHER LIGHTS

I walked into Ms. Hamilton's group session for divorced people that met weekly at a local church fellowship hall (though it was not affiliated with the church). I was now single again and divorced.

Though the group was a bit intimidating, I felt immediately comfortable with Diane as a person and counselor. There were about 15 people in the group and when it was my turn to introduce myself, I briefly explained my situation.

I'm not sure what I said, but when I finished Diane must have sized me up well, because she asked: "But what does Phil want?"

I couldn't answer that question. As weird as it sounds, her asking it so bluntly and directly really hit me. I didn't know what to say. Her point was clear: it's time you allow yourself to say what you want, what you need.

I eventually started seeing Diane Hamilton in monthly sessions individually at her counseling office. Both Diane and Fr. Walsh were godsends who helped me navigate some rough waters.

Another thing I started doing was listening to music again, old favorites, things I missed, and new music. Not Christian music, but secular, classical, and pop music. I specifically started listening to more female singers, as another way of changing the voice of God in my head. I was tired of the old Christian Boys Club of the Patriarchal Holy Trinity (God the Father, God the Son, and God the Holy Spirit). I knew The Presence was more than male, but the Presence had become too male in my Evangelical world. I wanted to get in touch with the Goddess side of the Presence for a change.

I had been out of ministry for a couple of years when a parishioner from my last church called me. Marvin Chamberlain was almost thirty years older than me, but we became close friends when I was his pastor. We became closer friends once I was no longer a minister.

He called me and said he missed me and that I should come by his house to visit. For the next few years, I would see Marvin about once a month. I'd go by his home and we'd take walks. He was already in his mid-eighties by this time. But he was still sharp and mobile. He probably had no idea how much he helped me during those walks. He had grown children and I got to know them during these years; they were all around my age.

My mother, who knew Marvin from church, said at one time, "You know he's about the age your dad would have been. And he is a lot like dad."

When I first stepped in to Marvin's home after not seeing him for two years, he opened the door and gave me a big hug and said, "I love you, Phil."

I nearly melted. That was something I never heard my dad say to me. Marvin told me some of his own personal secrets. We read poetry together, selecting some of our favorites and sharing them. I'll never forget a few things he told me.

When I was still the pastor of the church, Marvin had asked me to do his funeral when he passed away. He told me after I left ministry that he still wanted me to do his funeral. When he passed away, at the age of 95, his wife and grown family honored his request.

Over those next few years and continuing up until the present, I witnessed a string of relationships, encounters, experiences and eureka moments that showed me again and again that this God, this Presence, didn't need the church, doctrine, dogma, or the Bible to engage with me. There was a whole host of fellow travelers who had taken similar off ramps as I had. I slowly realized that The Presence clearly knew Whitman's *Leaves of Grass* and Rainer Maria Rilke's poems better than I did.

I look back now and see that leaving the ministry was the start of another Call to Adventure, as in Joseph Campbell's stages of a hero's journey.

I have continued to read Whitman. His words have become the banner, the flag on my ship:

> *"Sail Forth—steer for the deep waters only.*
> *Reckless O soul, exploring. I with thee and thou with me.*
> *For we are bound where mariner has not yet dared go.*
> *And we will risk the ship, ourselves, and all."*
> *O my brave soul!*
> *O farther farther sail!*
> *O daring joy, but safe! Are they not all the seas of God?"*[5]

I have held that passage as my guide for nearly thirty years now.

Sail forth! Whitman is inviting his soul: "Reckless O Soul... I with thee and thou with me." I love Whitman's line, "Are they not *all* the seas of God?" The church directories job had been a way of showing me how big the kingdom of God was. Father Walsh had helped clarify my struggle within. The world outside the Evangelical bubble started to look more colorful and welcoming to me. And I was starting to see that this Supreme Being, this Presence, this God/Goddess was well-read, a student of and comfortable with all the great religions, thinkers, philosophers, poets, musicians, songwriters, and novelists. I remember one of my English literature professors in college giving the best definition of literature's value: "Literature teaches us what it means to be human."

I knew the Bible and Christian theology. But my first faith was dismissive of my human beingness and my humanity. That was finally changing.

Jesus talked about the straight and narrow road.

I was discovering that the narrow road widens out.

CHAPTER 22

NEVERTHELESS ME, MY SELF AND I... LIVE

I now felt distaste for the whole churchy experience...
Conventional religion had worn me out
and I wanted nothing more to do with it.
—Karen Armstrong[1]

As a young woman, Karen Armstrong decided to join a convent and become a nun in the Roman Catholic Church. After seven years she left and wrote about that time of leaving in her autobiography.

"I now felt distaste for the whole churchy experience... The word "God" or "Jesus" or "church" filled me with a lassitude akin to nausea. Conventional religion had worn me out and I wanted nothing more to do with it."[2]

Shifting mental constructs is not as easy as closing one file on your laptop and opening another. Theological beliefs that had concretized and become pillars of my faith were being toppled; some I would never rebuild.

Joseph Campbell, in his book *The Hero's Journey*, says this about leaving one's first faith:

"And the problem is when you're deeply built into the system of the church and you're losing your faith. It's no fun."[3]

It wasn't fun, but it wasn't all "gloom, despair and agony on me" either, as the Buck Owens and Roy Clark recording goes.[4]

There were enough times that I had the "Ah-Ha" moments, the Eureka lights coming on, the prism turning slightly, and I'd see new colors. Or sometimes a major shift in the tectonic plates deep under the surface would move. There would be enough of them to keep me going.

In Native American Navajo folklore there is the belief that if you find a bird feather it's a sign you are on the right trail. I found some literal as well as figurative bird feathers during these transition years.

THE DAMAGED CHRISTIAN SELF

Karen Armstrong, after leaving her life as a nun, went on to become a well-known and successful author of books on Christianity and comparative religions. Though she was from a Roman Catholic background, and I was from an Evangelical Protestant Christian one, the details and particulars didn't matter that much, because so many of the experiences of training and leaving were similar.

I could relate to her anticipation when she entered her training as a seventeen-year-old. I knew that same religious enthusiasm and idealism and her hope of finding God, discovering some secrets of the universe, and feeling a part of something enduring—that whole romancing the faith. She describes in her book how difficult she found the Jesuit order of training and indoctrination.

She recounts how she would hear other girls in the other convent rooms crying themselves to sleep at night. She felt so much of the training was counter to her natural instincts. She describes how they were expected to be dead to themselves, they were warriors and soldiers of God, and they were trained to not need human love, affection, or approval.

Finally, after seven years of training, she left the program and went back into the secular world. She left the order feeling that it wasn't for her, that she wasn't cut out for it. She felt that in the training she had "become less than human":

> I had wanted to become transformed and enlightened; instead I was diminished. Instead of becoming strong, I was simply hard....The training was designed to make us transcend ourselves, and go beyond egotism and selfishness.... But no, I felt stuck inside myself.[5]

Then, after leaving the order and going back into her old world, she realizes that she "was inhabiting a world that I had been trained, at a profound level, to reject."[6]

I was particularly moved by her description of coming back to her family home and her bedroom that she left seven years earlier:

> At every turn I kept meeting my former self—the undamaged, seventeen-year-old Karen, who had been vital and full of hope. In my bedroom, I remembered how I had sat in this very chair and lain on that very bed, full of excitement about the great adventure I was about to begin. When I took a book down from my shelves, I remembered my wonder and delight when I had first read that novel or poem.... That person had gone; she had indeed died under the funeral pall. I felt bereaved—full of grief as if for a dead friend.[7]

I didn't go through the rigors of her Jesuit Order training, but I could relate to the feelings she described and the trauma she felt when she left her church and returned to her once familiar world. I, too, felt a part of me had died—and not necessarily the part that Jesus intended. I remembered the books I, too, loved from my youth that were deemed secular, unchristian, or liberal.

I remembered how I had wanted to go to Los Angeles, California, and become songwriter and music producer, but had decided that it was not God's will. I remembered how I had toyed with the idea of becoming a novelist, journalist, or writer after college, and how that idea had been ridiculed by a church leader who was my ministry leader at the time. So I turned toward full-time ministry.

Karen's terms hit home: she felt "less than human" and "that person was gone" and her younger, idealistic, enthusiastic self had "died." She describes her condition upon leaving the church as "damaged."

But she didn't blame her superiors or the training. She took responsibility and felt she just wasn't strong enough.

I believe there are sensitive souls, like Karen and myself, who readily take things to heart in a more personal way and wind up damaged, run roughshod over by certain religious rigors and excessive discipline. I don't think Karen was too feeble to stay with her training; I think she needed to leave to write the books she wrote from first-hand experience.

Again, I am indebted to Marlene Winell, her story of leaving, and all the meticulous research for her book *Leaving the Fold*. She writes:

> ...Some people are more prone to struggle with their Christian lives than others who are less sensitive by nature.[8]
>
> ...Leaving a cherished faith is much like the end of a marriage. The symptoms of separation are quite similar—grief, anger, guilt, depression, lowered self-esteem, and social isolation.[9]
>
> People from a wide variety of religious groups were struggling with self-esteem and needed to reclaim the ability to think for themselves, to understand and accept their own feelings, and to take more responsibility for their own lives.[10]

She hits the nail on the head—believers "needed to reclaim the ability to think for themselves." It's part of critical thinking—maintaining a locus of control within oneself. But it was drilled into me as a believer: "Trust not in thine own understanding" (Prov. 3:5-6). The learned (or indoctrinated) helplessness of many believers is a major problem in the church.

Think for ourselves? Wait a minute. Are we allowed to do that? I thought the Christian life was mainly letting Jesus take over and believing in the Bible. Who am I to question our doctrine and practice?

You start thinking too much and you'll have some questions, then you'll have some doubts and then there goes your faith. It's a slippery slope.

In her book, *Pure: Inside the Evangelical Movement that Shamed a Generation of young women and I how I broke free,*[11] Linda Kay Klein recounts her painful story of leaving a Christian sexual purity movement that damaged hundreds of women. More and more people have come out over the years and are recounting their religious "war stories." Many of these stories of recovery reveal the same issues.

How is it that this religion that advertises grace, forgiveness, and the loving Jesus, can wind up damaging so many?

CHALLENGING THE AUTHORITY OF THE CULT OR TRIBE

Leaving the fold of your first religion requires some fortitude and honest soul searching. I had to be willing to challenge the "Authorities" that I had been living under for over twenty years. Marlene Winell points out the key grip that the Evangelical/Fundamentalist movement rules with:

"One chief characteristic is a mood of militant opposition to secular culture, liberal theology, higher criticism, and scientific views that challenge the Bible."[12] The church is built on its "authorities." It starts with their necessary authority of Scriptures. Their Scriptures are not only inspired by God, but rather they are the inerrant, infallible Word of God. Most everything then proceeds from that. But if your religious constructs can't withstand honest questions, then something is amiss.

CHALLENGING THE AUTHORITIES

1. Challenging the Authority of Their Church, the Evangelical Movement, the Cult, the Tribe Itself. This is the over-arching power and mindset that disapproves of higher education, science, intellectualism, and secularism. For the most part, right-wing Christianity (Fundamentalists and Evangelicals) views most "liberal Christian theology," Roman Catholicism, and their writers/thinkers as the enemy, so they will avoid them like the plague. Though I had an undergraduate Bachelor of Arts degree and a Master of Divinity degree and had personally not been opposed to higher education, I still had to be careful who I quoted from the pulpit or what books I told people I was reading.

Mind control in the church is not consistent with "the truth will set you free."

Challenging the Authority of the Tribe means reading and learning from those outside the Tribe. Many church groups have their list of "acceptable" authorities (writers, speakers, leaders) and "unacceptable" authorities. They have their own list of "banned" books and writers.

Paul writes to Timothy that we have not been given a spirit of fear but of "a sound mind" that we need to use.[13] Any real or substantial faith or religion would be able to withstand interrogation and critical review.

I was no longer going to pretend to be part of any religion that is anti-intellectual, or anti-science, anti-higher education, or anti-humanity. If your faith and church's theology is so fragile that it cannot stand up to doubt, interrogation, reasoning, and challenge, then why is that? What are you afraid of?

2. Challenging the Authority of Their Interpretation of Scripture. Evangelicals and Fundamentalists should just go ahead and do away with the Holy Trinity and admit that it's a Holy Quaternity (or Quartet) because their Bible really is the fourth person of their Trinity. It's more important what the "Bible" says and what their leaders say it says, than what Jesus or anyone else says.

The inerrancy or infallibility of the Bible is the main pillar of Evangelicalism's authority. All else depends upon this. It is why "authority" is so essential for their structure. It's why they believe they are the only ones who have the truth of the Bible. The reality is that the inerrancy/infallibly position is not defensible.

Do the Scriptures need to be inerrant for them to be inspirational and helpful? Which "Scriptures" are they? The Protestant Bible has 66 books (Old and New Testament); the Roman Catholic Bible has 73 (Old and New Testaments and the Apocrypha); the Ethiopian Bible (the oldest Bible known) has 81 to 88 books, depending on who is counting. Why did some groups omit some books? Who decided and when? What are we missing?

I'm not going to get into the formation of the Canon of Scripture, but it is important and significant to explore as a believer. There was a battle in the early church as to what books would be in the canon of the Bible. Let's just say, the institutional Christians won after a couple of centuries and many books got banned, listed as heretical, or buried. The Bible and whichever number of books your church approves of was curated by an assembly of men, councils of men with political and cultural agendas.

Many of those "lost books" would be discovered in 1947, in clay jars in the Qumran caves. They would be called the Dead Sea Scrolls. Some of those books tell us things that the "accepted texts" didn't. In these books, among other things, we find a little different Jesus than the Jesus in the canonical Gospels (Mathew, Mark, Luke, John). We read that Jesus laughed, danced, and even kissed. Sounds like a more human Jesus than the institution would allow.

3. Challenging the Authority of Their Dualistic Mindset and World-view. I never totally bought into the strict dualistic thinking that plagues Evangelicals and Fundamentalists, but it's hard to avoid the problems it produces that infect that worldview.

The "this or that" of dualism is overly simplistic and misses so much of the beauty and nuance of the world around us. The church sets up so many taboos that it fails to recognize that in labeling them taboos it only makes them more attractive to inquiring minds. It was important for me to be vigilant in diagnosing all the strains of that mindset that wrap their tentacles around the believer's mind. It's definitely a head trip.

We see the results of it today in the way wholesale labels are grouped into one or the other side: the Christian and the World. In dualistic thinking there are only two sides: this or that, good or bad, Godly or Ungodly, truth and lies, righteous and evil, etc.

So much of our Christianity gets touchy and narrow-minded when it comes to applying its theology. The whole injunction to be "in the world" but not "of the world" has led to a myriad of fine lines and hard lines about which things are socially acceptable and unacceptable behaviors for Christians.

I have run up against these things many times. One case in point was a social event. The church at which I interned would have an annual Barn Dance. It was a fun event where people invited friends and family and there would be a big square dance at a local center rather than at the church. I can't think of a more innocent dance than a square dance. That is, until I decided to have one at the church I was planting a few years later.

Some folks from my church who were missionaries said that if their supporters back home saw that our church was having a square dance in our church bulletin they would cut off their financial support. It wouldn't matter if they didn't go to the dance themselves; what would be a deal killer is to be a *member* of a church that sponsored a square dance. That's misapplying theology to an extreme.

4. Challenging the Authority of Their Holy War Against This World. It amazes me how much of my Evangelical/Fundamentalist thinking was shaped by the mindset that we are always in a Spiritual War, the battle against the powers of darkness. So much of the Movement's mindset depends upon the need for an enemy. I heard just as much talk about Satan and demons in the Evangelical church as I did about

Jesus and angels. The Fundamentalist/Evangelical religious right cannot function without their enemies; it's why it winds up becoming militant and legalistic.

In recent church history, the term "militant fundamentalists" was often used of the right wing of the Church. Lots of sermons preaching *against* something. Fundamentalist religions of all kinds usually need a good Enemy. Satan is the standard go-to Enemy, but depending on the times, the contemporary Enemy shifts. Sometimes the Enemy is the social culture itself. Most religions have their militant fundamentalist extremists. And today's militant Christians can be as dangerous as any "foreign terrorist." It breeds hate, violence, intolerance, bigotry, discrimination. It breeds all the things that are anti-Jesus.... All "in Jesus name."

Today, looking back on my leaving in 1993, I feel more clearly than ever about why I left the Evangelical movement and church.

I could see it coming through the late 1970's and building steam in the 1980's. The temptation to political power has corrupted most of right-wing, conservative Christianity in the United States. They have honed their authority into a weapon by standing on the Authority of Their Interpretation of the Bible Alone, on the Authority of their Dualistic Worldview, and the Authority of their Holy War against all who do not share their viewpoint and mindset.

5. *Challenging Their View of the Self and What It Means to Be Human.* When I left the church, a handful of good friends kept in touch with me. We had all been in the church for twenty years or so and half of us were going through a crisis in faith and changing churches or rethinking our part in it.

Fortitude and separation were critical for rebuilding my Self. I would occasionally run into people from the old church circles. I slowly realized we now spoke different languages, though we were speaking English. I discovered that as long as I spoke their lingo they would think I was okay. I threw in a couple of "The Lord has been good," and "Jesus" this or "Jesus' that. At least we'd part company without any recriminations; no sense getting lambasted as a heretic right there in the Publix produce department where I might have to duck a tomato thrown in haste. I was still on a spiritual path, so I wasn't being disingenuous. I was just using the lingo they were used to.

Truthfully, though, I didn't know where to begin to tell them what I was going through and I knew it would only register to them as: He's a heretic, or a backslider, or a carnal Christian.

ALMS OF MY OWN KINDNESS

In his autobiography *Memories, Dreams Reflections*, Carl Jung tells the story of his emerging spiritual path. He references Jesus' comment in Matthew 25:40-45 about how what we do "unto the least of these" (the poor, unfortunate, needy) is as if we did it unto Jesus himself. It is the essence of the "do unto others as you would have them do unto you" ethic at the heart of Christianity. Jung realizes: what if these unfortunate ones are all "within me"?

> But what if I should discover that the least among them all, the poorest of all the beggars, the most impudent of all the offenders, the very enemy himself—that these are within me, and that I myself stand in need of the alms of my own kindness—that I myself am the enemy who must be loved—what then?[14]

This alienated self, the self I was taught to lose, to not trust, to crucify, this self who is now called my "old man" within, this inner self was my enemy, according to my old theology.

I had a well-practiced discipline as a disciple of Christ; I was harder on myself than I'd ever thought of being toward others. I had a well-developed "biblically sanctioned" self-abuse that I had developed as a "gung-ho" young, zealous disciple. It was "Biblically sanctioned" because "my Evangelical Discipleship Liturgy" of verses permitted a pious self-abuse, a kind of spiritual masochistic treatment of my "self" on behalf of the "Yahweh-Jesus" mission-driven God I had cultivated in my head.

Carl Jung had a dream in which Christ appeared to him. It helped him realize that "something essential was missing from my 'Christian' view ... my traditional Christ-image was somehow inadequate."[15]

The real Presence, the real Great Spirit, the one beyond all our names and religions was making itself known to me all during this time outside the insulated church world of my previous twenty-plus years. Alms of my own kindness would be me welcoming back a once enemy self.

Rainer Maria Rilke was not a particularly "Christian" poet, but he did write deeply spiritual poems. He was a devout seeker, one trying to connect with the Presence in a deeply personal way. Yet he did not care for the spiritual monopolies of the institutional churches. The words from his poem "Autumn" spoke to me:

> *And yet there is One who holds this falling*
> *With infinite softness in his hands.*[16]

When I left the church and ministry, I was not looking for another "better" church or denomination or movement to join. I was leaving the institutional church and religion. I wanted to be on the outside looking out and around for a change.

Walt Whitman, the herald, the pioneer, a fellow traveler, calls me:

> *"You shall no longer take things at second or third hand,*
> *nor look through the eyes of the dead, nor feed on the spec-*
> *   tres in books,*
> *You shall not look through my eyes either, nor take things*
> *   from me,*
> *You shall listen to all sides and filter them from your self.*[17]

CHAPTER 23
ALCHEMY OF THE SELF

Do I contradict myself?
Very well then I contradict myself,
(I am large, I contain multitudes.)
—Walt Whitman, *"Song of Myself"*[1]

I was changing my views about who God was and who I was. George Fowler, in his wonderful autobiography *The Dance of a Fallen Monk*, also went through this process of leaving and changing his theological views. He put it in simple terms:

"But if God is not what I've been taught,
  then neither am I."[2]

He talked about his process of recovering himself as "coming home to one's self" (p. 304).

When it comes right down to it, when we talk about the Self, the individual, so many of the words we use are figurative terms for intangible things: the heart, the soul, the spirit, the unconscious, the inner drives and motives that we don't always acknowledge.

THE COMPLEXITY OF THE HUMAN "SELF"

Being the father of twin boys gave me a front row seat to the mystery of human identity and individuality. My sons are identical twins; even now in their forties they still look alike. But they are each distinctly different individuals.

One day when the boys were about eight years old, Scott came home from school upset. I asked him what was bothering him, and he said, "Everyone keeps confusing me with Steve."

I asked him the obvious question, rather than reminding him, "Why do you think that is?"

He said, "I don't know. I don't look anything like Steve."

In his mind, he was uniquely himself and thought people should see that.

Brought up in the same loving family and environment, my identical twin sons, Scott and Steve, have always had their own unique personalities. Personalities, talents, individual minds, thoughts, and motivations all seem to come innately as part of the Self's essential makeup and soul.

What constitutes the Self? What comprises the I, me, myself? We have a lot of words that express various aspects of the Self. We do not know where "the soul" is, where "heart" comes from within the anatomy of the person; these are not organs in our physical bodies. We have a tangible brain that can be weighed, yet the mind and memory cannot be easily weighed or measured. We use words to delineate functions that the Self performs or feels. If we were to list them all, the list is long. Here's some:

- personality
- individuality
- heart

- soul
- spirit
- mind
- brain
- Intelligence
- ego
- psyche
- memories
- emotions/feelings
- critical thinking
- creativity
- motives
- reasoning
- self-control
- self-worth
- conviction
- belief/faith
- dreams
- unconscious
- subconscious,
- passions/drive
- imagination
- talents/gifts
- charisma
- attitudes

I'm not going to pretend to delineate or build a complex under-standing of the human self in this book; I am primarily pointing out that when we talk about the person, the human "self," there is a lot that constitutes the individual.

When we oversimplify or trivialize or simply "theologize" the human individual identity, we are denying people the dignity and respect they deserve as God's unique creations.

In most of my Christianity, the "self" was viewed as some

holdover malcontent rebel from our old sin nature. The self was primarily viewed as a negative thing in my theological training and mental constructs. We would quote: "The heart is deceitful above all things, and desperately wicked, who can know it?"[3] What a horrible foundation upon which to construct a healthy self-image.

After leaving the convent, Karen Armstrong found it difficult to know how to live, how to be. She writes in her autobiography: "We did not know how to live anymore. We had somehow lost the knack."[4]

George Fowler writes about his adventure as a Trappist monk: "I had come to the abbey to find myself, and I immediately set to work to make sure I never would."[5]

Fowler spent over twenty years in the ministry. The main thing he said he would do differently is that he would have left much sooner.

Catholic priest, writer and novelist, Father Andrew Greeley, writes about how he was instructed: "We should repress and suppress our talents and abilities for reasons of obedience and humility and concern for the feelings of others who might not be so gifted."[6] Greeley had the fortitude to say that he "never took such nonsense seriously."

Joseph Campbell, whose pioneering work in mythology and comparative spiritualities contributed so much to popular interest in those fields, wrote:

> Until I was twenty-five-years old I took Christianity concretely. And I must say I'm grateful to having been exposed to such rich symbolism.... Yet, there's also some great strength to be gained by giving up that religion, by going beyond it. If you really do.[7]

CHIPPING AWAY AT THE CONCRETE

I first read Rainer Maria Rilke's poetry during these years. I came upon a copy of selected Rilke poems translated by Robert Bly in a used bookstore. One of the passages in Rilke's poem "Moving Forward" became a goal for me to strive toward.

> *The deep parts of my life pour onward,*
> *As if the river were opening out.*
> *It seems that things are more like me now,*
> *I can see farther into paintings.*
> *I felt closer to what language can't reach.*[8]

It was tough during those first couple of years after leaving the ministry and going into the real world. I was scrambling to find a new career path, to get back on my feet again, while trying to rebuild my soul and self.

Those few lines from Rilke's poem became a goal for me... the deep parts of my real life should be like a river opening out rather than narrowing... to have a new way of seeing... like seeing deeper into paintings and closer to what is beyond language. Poetry and music became the first doors through which I could make this happen for me.

RECLAIMING SOUL

Before science and religion became distinctly separate fields of study, there was alchemy. The Alchemists were trying to transform one material into another. It was essentially the process of taking ordinary things and transforming them into something extraordinary (like turning lead into gold). It was an early form of chemistry, but it also included a degree of magic. Many of these alchemists were intelligent, scientific people looking for cures and solutions for humanities problems. It was an ancient practice in China, India, Egypt, Greece, Rome, and Europe.

While it became clear that the alchemist could not turn lead into gold, at the heart of alchemy was the search for spirit in matter.

Today, alchemy is often thought of in terms of the spiritual transformation process. I am using the term as it relates to the idea that spirit and matter are related in the healing and health processes of human beings. There is a deep connection between our spirit, soul, and body. Spiritual alchemy seeks to restore the inner balance and wholeness that will allow us to heal and transform.

Spiritual alchemy is not an exact discipline: it's a combination of art, spirituality and psychology. Since the main ingredient is the person (body, soul, and spirit) you can't throw out the self.

This whole eradication of the "self" is taught in so many religions. I get the point, but why do they all wind up throwing the baby out with the bathwater?

What constitutes the "Self?" More importantly for me: What does it mean to be a person, a human being? What does it mean to be a human being, a homo sapiens human being, AND to be a spiritual being?

Carl Jung has a uniquely expansive view of the Self: "the self encompasses all the possibilities of your life, the energies, the potentialities—everything that you are capable of becoming."[9]

Campbell talks about this issue of religions pushing for an "egoless" state, the rejection of this world, and going deeper that way. I like his straightforward matter-of-factness about steering your own ship. Your ego is a central part of who you are, the decisions you make, your inner locus of control. *"You've got to have your ego in play."*[10]

What does it mean to rid yourself of your "I, me, myself?" I get that it is basically a call to not be self-centered. I get that I can be my own worst enemy. But why all the negativity about the person, the human being, *Me*? Why this perpetual war on self?

Obviously, you really can't rid yourself of your "self," but you can lose enough of yourself to lose your locus of control, your clear identity, your self-confidence, your strong sense of who you are. You can wind up with no salsa.

"YOU ARE A PERSON"

Fred Rogers, known as Mister Rogers, the creator and star of his popular children's television show *Mister Rogers' Neighborhood* (which ran from 1968 – 2001), said it simple: "You are a person."

Many may not know that Mr. Rogers was also a Presbyterian minister. He received over 40 honorary degrees and numerous awards for his work with children. Mister Rogers was dedicated to helping children develop a positive view of themselves as individuals, unique human beings:

> As human beings, our job in life is to help people realize how rare and valuable each one of us really is, that each of us has something that no one else has - or ever will have - something inside that is unique to all time. It's our job to encourage each other to discover that uniqueness and to provide ways of developing its expression.
>
> It's not the honors and the prizes and the fancy outsides of life which ultimately nourish our souls. It's the knowing that we can be trusted, that we never have to fear the truth, that the bedrock of our very being is good stuff.[11]

Both of these above lines are not what I heard in church. The "just as I am"...ok, sure, in the hymn, but if you don't come to the altar, you'll be sent to the fiery pit. The idea that "the bedrock of our very being is good stuff" is not something I heard in church or from my discipleship training.

It's horrifying that the Church routinely burned people at the stake. How soulless, heartless, and *un*-Jesus is that? Can you see Jesus standing by, lighting the match and then watching? It's a reflection on how theology has inured the Church into devaluing and debasing the human being. Their thinking is this callous and perverted: *"If they are going to Hell anyway, let's help them on their way by getting the fire going."*

Who made them God's judge? (Oh! That's another theological story I'll avoid.)

Perhaps the greatest deficiency in Evangelical Christianity is its lack of a unified, coherent, and realistic understanding of the person, the human being and what it means to be human. It's not just a lack of respect for our humanity, it is a debasing of man, woman and our *in-the-image-and-likeness* humanity.

In my time as an Evangelical, I don't remember ever hearing things like: "believe in yourself" or "trust yourself"—certainly not "be true to yourself."

The Christian Church (Protestant and Catholic) needs a Human Manifesto, a new theological stake in the ground, a new pillar of the faith that declares its commitment to honoring our humanity and properly valuing our human beingness.

We shouldn't even have to say that. It was Jesus' number one theme. Jesus gave us one commandment: love one another.

SINS AGAINST ONE'S SELF

In the Jewish traditions, there are three types of sins: sins against others, sins against God, and sins against one's self. I believe I have sinned a lot against my Self. I once felt free to abuse, deride and bully myself on behalf of God; free to devalue myself because I was born with a sin nature.

I believe that the soul (my soul and your soul) is divine; my whole being is "the temple of the Holy Spirit," and I mean that in the sense of the sanctity of the human being. We are created and still "in the image and likeness" of God. We have the divine spark of God in our soul, our being.

James Hillman describes the complexity of this thing we call our human, homo sapiens Self. Hillman writes:

> "We have lost the third, middle position which earlier in our tradi-
> tion, and in others, too, was the place of the soul: a world of imagi-

nation, passion, fantasy, reflection that is neither physical or material on one hand, nor spiritually abstract on the other, yet bound by both."[12]

Hillman writes as though the Spirit were masculine, and that it deals in ultimates and absolutes in religion. It is this type of Spirit that leads our religions to form official doctrine, dogma, liturgies.

Then we formulate disciplines to train our spirit: devotions, bible reading and study, church, prayer, meditation. These are all good things. Our clergy goes to school to train our spirits in our beliefs and intense spiritual disciplines daily. Church services become routines with orders of worship, liturgies, recited creeds, and memorized prayers. These are all good things for our spirit in our spiritual life. These are all good things, but sometimes they can lull us to sleep or breed dead orthodoxy.

We resist dead orthodoxy, but do we know and feel any longer when our church and spirituality is soulless?

That's when people go through the motions, but their heart and real self aren't in it. The soul, Hillman says, is something very different from spirit.

> The soul is vulnerable and suffers, it is passive and remembers...it is water to the spirit's fire... Soul is imagination, a cavernous treasury —to use a phrase from St. Augustine—a confusion and richness, both.[13]

I had a spirited faith; but I found my soul was no longer in it. I could talk all the theology; I knew the seminary debates on the finer points of theology; I had memorized hundreds of verses; I had led people to Christ, I had discipled, taught, preached, and ministered.

Eventually the spirit couldn't crusade any longer. Something had disengaged, my soul wasn't in it anymore. The soul is more the real me. The spirit can go through the motions. If I've denied, lost, crucified, dismissed, and warred with my Self, then it's like the guy said, "You got no salsa."

The spirit tends toward doctrine, sermons, and studies; the soul tends toward wonder and art, music, and poetry. Soul needs to come up against and feel the experience of the divine, the transcendent—the Presence. When my soul was forced into imitating my spirit, something was wrong with the picture.

The soul needs the arts, poets, painters, writers, and storytellers. Soul needs the romance of myth and mythology, the wonder of the earth and nature, the fascination of the imagination of artists and poets.

MONKISH BOYS

I was sitting at a performance of the cantata *"Carmina Burana,"* written in the 1930's by Carl Orff. The cantata is based upon 24 poems that were found hidden in the medieval Benedictine monastery in Beuren, Bavaria, dating back to about 1280 AD. Carl Orff used the monks' manuscripts to write what is called *"Carmina Burana" ("Songs of Beuren")*.

Though I didn't understand the Latin being sung at the performance, I could feel what language couldn't reach in the emotion coming through the music and sounds. I was intrigued that these cloistered monastic monks had to hide these private songs. Clearly, it was not material the Holy Order would look kindly upon.

The subtitle of the original Latin title translates as: "Secular songs for singers and choruses to be sung together with instruments and magical images."[14] These were "secular songs" that the monks could never perform either in public or in the monastery.

These were private songs of longings, lust, love, dance, and romance. These were their rock and roll songs, their "bar" and shanty songs, their protest songs.

I sat there in the theater and was thoroughly caught up in the performance of *"Carmina Burana."* I could feel all the colors of the monks' passion. This was something they needed to express, but it couldn't be safely expressed in their cold, religiously formal monastic life.

I could feel the yearning, the longing, the angst, the beauty, the spirituality, the humanity, the desire, the love of life in these monks who could never share these emotions and these "selves" that looked for expression.

The church has forever sought to divide the secular and the spiritual, to our loss. Believers become schizophrenic and divided against our very souls.

How sad, I thought, that these human needs and desires had to be hidden and repressed. These monks may have taken vows, may have submitted to the strict regimen of their monastic order, may have been young, sincerely devoted souls. But secretly, privately, they had a passionate humanity, a humanity that could not be contained by the narrowness of what their "church" said was permitted by God.

I was moved to tears by the musical presentation of their sacred hidden selves.

CHAPTER 24

ROOMMATES TOO LONG

*Honest spirituality
always provides enough security
to let one react spontaneously, and
not infrequently spurs one to act outrageously.*
—George Fowler, *Dance of a Fallen Monk*[1]

Salvador Dali's painting "The Ship" is a jarring freeze frame image of a transformation process: a big clipper ship becoming a human being. The painting depicts what appears to be a man (or androgynous human) stepping on a sandy shore from out of the ocean where his body is partly morphed with a big clipper ship and its tiers of white billowing sails. It looks painful.

I stared at the painting the first time I saw it and felt the agony of this half man/half woman person trying to emerge from an inanimate wooden ship. The head of this androgynous human is covered with what looks like the bow of the ship, but also with a warrior's helmet. The human is emerging and we are seeing a freeze frame of the process. I felt the pain.

Before I noticed the title of Dali's painting, I gave it my own title: "The Vessel." The Bible taught me as an Evangelical that as a believer I was analogous to a vessel—something that God can use; Mary is the most vivid example of a vessel because she gave birth to Jesus. Ships are often called vessels. There are other analogies of who I was: a branch (with Jesus as the vine), a sheep, a clay jar, the salt of the earth, soldiers, students, and stones being used to build a house.

Dali's painting captures my morphing, a snapshot transformation from one stage of life into a more human stage of being. I thought of it as Jung's coming to consciousness and Whitman's call to wake up from slumbering upon myself.

When I "prayed the prayer" with Ray that day sitting by the canal to the Indian River Lagoon in Eau Gallie, Florida, and "figuratively" opened "the door" and let Jesus into my "heart," everything that was presented in a metaphorical, figurative way became "literal" in my spirit. Thus began a very long, genuine, and close "relationship" with the Christ above and within.

THE PERPETUAL HOUSE GUEST

For all the use of "figurative" language by Evangelicals in their gospel message, they insist upon a strict "literal" interpretation of Scripture. It's rather baffling.

Allow me to continue and extend the metaphor or figurative use of the door and house I "literally" invited Jesus into. It's kind of like this...

So Jesus comes into "my house," my soul, my heart, my being and life. And as time goes on, He is kind of the elephant in the room and the house. He brings the Holy Spirit with him, and of course His Dad, Yahweh. They all move in.

So here I am and Jesus takes the Throne (again it's figurative) and chooses the best living room chair, and, of course, he takes the

"Master Bedroom." I don't protest. Who am I to tell the Messiah what he can and can't do? It's Jesus, after all. I trust him.

Gradually, Jesus winds up taking over the TV and the whole stereo system—his music, his favorite shows. He replaces all my books on the bookshelves with his books. (Yeah, he knows you keep a few hidden. His Father knows, too. They have been doing a sweep, cleaning house.)

And the whole place has cameras monitoring everything. It's not "Big Brother" watching, it's "Big Daddy" watching. There is no privacy. He sees you when you're sleeping, he knows when you're awake.... and we know the rest. We are always "on."

In the beginning Jesus is always kind of cool, so you don't realize he's slowly taking over your whole house. For a while, you don't notice, because you and Jesus kind of like the same things at first.

But I start to feel like I miss that book and that album that isn't around anymore. I'm going through some changes. I realize that I've been relegated to the back bedroom while Jesus and company have literally taken over my whole house—the whole *"he must increase and I must decrease"* routine.

Is it time for me to move out? Should I find a new place? It's crowded in here. But this is *my* house, *my* home—why should *I* have to move out?

How do I ask Jesus for my house back?

I'd like some privacy for a change. Even though I know there is no privacy, no private life, their cameras are always watching and recording. There are no secrets.

I begin to feel like my private life is dead, like in those sci-fi movies. It doesn't even have to be sci-fi. I think of the movie *"Doctor Zhivago,"* from Pasternak's novel, and how the Russian State took over people's lives, took over Zhivago's family home. How they ordered him into military service and outlawed his poetry. The private life was dead in that state.

Look, I didn't think that inviting Jesus into my heart would mean He would become the perpetual house guest who took over my home and turned it into a temple, a shrine, along with his Dad and the ever nosy Holy Ghost.

Look, I'm not trying to live some devilishly secret life; I just want a personal life without being watched, spied on, reported on for every action and thought.

I want my house back. I don't want to live in Notre Dame Cathedral; I don't care how "sacred" or beautiful they say it is. It's creepy at night. I invited him into my heart and Jesus and his "Trinity" have taken over the whole place.

There are no authorities to go to in order to plead my case or ask for an eviction or some livable arrangement or settlement. I have slowly given up rooms of the house as "Yahweh-Jesus" spread out and took over. I now live in a back bedroom and the common areas are not really common anymore. I can't really go to an exorcist because of the obvious.

Go ahead, laugh. I do. It took me a while to get beyond the crying to lighten up. But it's not really a laughing matter, when I think about how hard it's been getting my house back.

What's the saying? "Possession is nine-tenths of the law"?

Possession? It's more like Possessed!

I never thought that possession by the Holy Family could be so creepy and oppressive. Working through the whole schizophrenic nature of Christianity is not an easy thing. It's probably been my primary and proverbial "cross to bear." My Jesus Doppelgänger. My Yahweh-Jesus.

"WE'VE BEEN ROOMMATES TOO LONG"

To be frank, the whole concept of "inviting Jesus into your heart" is both a "nice" way to phrase the "figurative" entry into the personal nature of Christian faith as well as a double-edged sword to those of us who have taken it too seriously and too literally.

The Bible talks about "Christ in you" as one of the great "mysteries" of our faith. Mysteries can be both fascinating and scary as Hell.

It came down to this: Jesus and I had been roommates too long. I needed some space.

It's most troubling when individuals lack the ability to discern where Christ in them leaves off and their individual "Self" picks up. When the line is too blurred between God and self, Christianity breeds strange cult leaders, strange believers, and kooky ideas. We've all seen these types of characters in movies, on TV, in the news and in our towns. I've run into my share of them. You don't have to fly off to South American jungles with the Jim Jones zealots and unknowingly drink the poison Kool-Aid to be in danger of being whisked away on the crazy train.

A man sat on my couch one night while I was a pastor and said vehemently: "If God told me to kill my son, I would. Just like Abraham."

I cringed, knowing that I couldn't reason with this man. But I had to try. I said, "But Abraham didn't kill Isaac." The man persisted: "If God told me..."

I tried again, "How would you know if it was God telling you? Maybe you heard wrong. Have you ever heard a literal "voice?"

It was useless. Sadly, I would hear many years later that the man's son walked out into the Florida wilderness and sat down under a tree. His badly decomposed body was eventually found.

A woman sent my wife a letter when we were in the pastorate. The woman prefaced the letter by saying that this was a prophecy that God spoke to her and she dictated what God said. Here we go again, I thought.

Her (or God's) letter droned on and eventually told us we were to name our soon-to-be born daughter "Sarah." Nonsense, I thought.

First of all, how is it that God has such bad grammar, poor sentence structure, and broken English when he dictates these things? Second, the person who sent this is clearly confused and deluded. Third, even if Sarah was the favorite name we had already chosen for our soon-to-be born daughter, we would change her name because of this letter. We already knew we would name her Kimberly.

Another man comes to me and prefaces his comments with the reminder that he has the gift of prophecy. Right away I brace myself. That usually means I'm in trouble.

He proceeds to tell me, "God told me to tell you that you are not broken before God." I listen while he elaborates. I honestly want to know what indications he has that I am not broken. He has no clear examples. My real question is: "Why can't God tell me himself? Why did he tell you to tell me?" It's always some secret handshake I got wrong or some spurious motive they detected in something I said. Profiling. They are always profiling those around them; sizing people up with their theological litmus tests. Judging "righteous judgment," of course, they would say. *As iron sharpens iron, so one person sharpens another.*" They quote Proverbs 27:17 with all the self-righteousness they can muster.

I'M at New Smyrna Beach one summer day when I stroll over to the food truck to grab a snack. While the man is fixing my hot dog, he hands me a brochure he published, a Christian tract titled: "88 Reasons why Jesus will return in 1988." It was 1988, so Jesus only had about six months left, according to his tract. I perused the tract while he cooked. Nonsense, I thought.

It was my day off and I was not in the mood for a lengthy theological discussion that I could not win with this guy. So as he handed me the hot dog, I casually said, "You know, even if you are right that he's going to return this year, Jesus would change the year."

He stopped for a minute. I continued, "Because in Matthew 24:36 Jesus himself says, 'But of that day and hour knoweth no man, no, not the angels of heaven, but my Father only.' So even if you actually did miraculously decipher the exact day, God would change it. Because it says nobody knows."

He had no good comeback for that.

It seems in America, the ranks of the crazy Christians grow in number year by year. Most of it comes from a predicable combination of willful ignorance and not remembering the admonitions of their own scriptures that say to be of a "sound mind" (II Tim. 1:7) and to "test the spirits" (I John 4:1-5).

Then there are the ever-persistent Christian Nationalists and political power mongers in America determined to make this a Christian nation. They forget that Israel's pursuit of theocracy ended badly in the Old Testament. These Christians will wind up making everyone mad at their churches and their religion.

People use the Bible to justify a lot of untenable theological positions. The truth is, you can't always get "that" from the verses they use. The "you can't get there from here" reasoning doesn't work on them. There are sound principles of biblical interpretation; some people do not use or even understand the principles properly. Some use the Bible errantly. They can claim their Bible is inerrant; but that doesn't make their interpretation inerrant.

BREAKING UP IS HARD TO DO

How do I tell Jesus to move out? Or even just: I need my house back?

How do I tell Yahweh-Jesus I'd like to renegotiate the terms of this relationship?

How do I tell God that I need some space, my space? Or that I am tired of his constant, perpetual, and never-ending invasion of my privacy?

How do I tell them that I'd like to see other people?

"Look, it's fine if you're next door, but just please knock when you want to visit, or at least call ahead."

But then, maybe next door was too close also. Maybe I needed to be a drive away or a town away. "Look, maybe we'd be better friends if we just hung out once in awhile."

"I know it's not in the Bible, but someone once said — dare I quote anyone but You? — but here goes. There are two much-quoted opposites, no

doubt you've heard: "Absence makes the heart grow fonder" and "Familiarity breeds contempt."

My "Yahweh-Jesus" had worn out their welcome.

So I say to Them (all three of them), *"Remember this passage?"*

"To everything there is a season, and a time to every purpose under the heaven:

A time to be born, and a time to die; a time to plant, and a time to pluck up that which is planted;

A time to kill, and a time to heal; a time to break down, and a time to build up;

A time to weep, and a time to laugh; a time to mourn, and a time to dance."

Of course they remember it. So I don't have to read it all.

I say, *"Look, keeping in that spirit of turn, turn, turn in this list of (insert air quotes) "wisdom" writings, I would add: A time to move in and a time to move out, a time to live with your parents and a time to get your own place, a season to live with your college buddies and a season to move on into actual adulthood..."*

Yahweh and Jesus understand. It's not the first time this has happened, and they are used to having their feathers ruffled, their cage rattled. They don't get offended easily anymore.

I'd like to somehow still be friends, but if we stay roommates, I think we might all wind up hating each other.

This "literal" world of my metaphorical Christianity bred this kind of extended analogy of what was going on in my psychology.

I would look over and see my "figurative" self (the one crucified, denied, reckoned dead) sitting with my knees curled up to my chest and having outgrown the cage. The cage was where I put my crucified self, who wouldn't just go away. So by now I'm in a back room of my house with my caged self, who now I can't even get to stand up—it's a disturbing site. I'm the "Incredible Shrinking Man." Meanwhile, out in the living room Jesus and Yahweh are playing their music too loud.

I have often had dreams where I was carried off by some crazy group of religious fanatics who were preparing to do dastardly things to me. I always manage to escape, thankfully.

It wasn't a pretty break-up. Jesus and I didn't really talk it out. He got the message one day when I took all his stuff and put it out by the curb.

I knew Jesus and I were still family, but we needed a break, a long break. As Father Walsh said to me, "You need to not go to church for a long time."

Often our relationships take a turn. Life changes a bit, seasons change, and maybe you're not as close to some friends as you used to be. Or sometimes you feel you've outgrown some friend, or perhaps you or they have changed and it's not as cozy and comfortable as it once was. Or maybe you don't like who you are when you're with them. Or maybe your relationship has hit a different stage altogether.

Jesus and I had been roommates too long.

PART FOUR
RECONSTRUCTING MY FAITH

CHAPTER 25

A SECOND CALL TO ADVENTURE

Look, you are in sleepy land. Wake.
Come on a trip. There is a whole aspect
of your consciousness, your being,
that's not been touched.
—Joseph Campbell[1]

I was camping alone near the summit of Mount Mitchell, North Carolina, the highest point east of the Mississippi River. I was on a week-long sabbatical from my church, reading, praying, studying, and debating. It was about six months before I left ministry, though I didn't know it at the time.

My campsite was in the clouds for two days as some nasty weather passed. It was a fitting image of me in my own clouds of uncertainty.

I drove up from Florida along the east coast and made a few stops on what I viewed as a bit of a pilgrimage. I stopped at St. Simon's Island in Georgia and visited an old, historic church I remember passing back when I went to a Christian conference nearby twenty years earlier. I stopped and spent a night in the Outer Banks of North Carolina, watched an outdoor drama presentation, walked the beach at night, visited the dunes where the Wright Brothers first flew. Then I went inland and wound my way along the Blue Ridge Parkway from Blowing Rock to Mount Mitchell.

DO I DARE?

Hollywood director George Lucas structured his first three Star Wars movies on the stages of the hero's journey from Joseph Campbell's book *The Hero with a Thousand Faces*. In his book, Campbell used his studies on comparative religion and mythology to show the pattern that is consistent in many hero stories.

In one of his lectures, Campbell recounts how George Lucas invited him and his wife to Lucas' home for a personal viewing of the first Star Wars movie trilogy. They watched all three movies in one day; *Star Wars* in the morning, *The Empires Strikes Back* in the afternoon, and *The Return on the Jedi* in the evening. Campbell admitted that he ended up becoming a fan of the movie series.

Lucas used the archetypal journey and mythic characters based upon Campbell's book to guide the movie trilogy. Campbell points out that the series is like a three-act play. In the first movie, *Star Wars*, the hero, Luke Skywalker, responds to the call to adventure and leaves the safety of his home. In *The Empire Strikes Back* the hero faces tests and trials and faces his enemy, which he discovers is his father. In the third movie, *The Return of the Jedi*, the hero faces his reconciliation with his father and returns across the threshold. Campbell explains how the second and third movies show the "father-atonement motif" that the hero works through.

> "In *The Empire Strikes Back*, Luke Skywalker confronts what he thinks is Darth Vader, the shadow-father figure [while training

with Yoda on Dagobah]. He kills the figure and then sees that the face of the machine man is actually his own."[2]

Luke Skywalker is making peace with his past, his own shadow-figure. His atonement with the father is deeply connected to his inner psyche. In the film *The Return of the Jedi*, Luke risks his life to redeem the life of his father, Darth Vader—this is the father-atonement motif played out on a grand scale: the son saves the father and father saves the son."[3]

Campbell goes on to say:

"What I think is that a good life is one hero journey after another. Over and over again we are called to the realm of adventure; you are called to new horizons. Each time, there is the same problem: do I dare?"[4]

I'M ON A JOURNEY, not unlike the classic journeys in literature, history, and film. Like Luke Skywalker in Star Wars, Ulysses in Homer's *The Odyssey*, Christian in Bunyan's *The Pilgrim's Progress*, Parsifal in search of the Holy Grail, Lewis and Clark crossing the Continent, Magellan circumnavigating the globe, or Frodo in Tolkien's *The Lord of the Rings* Trilogy. In all these tales, the journey is epic, arduous, and rewarding; you wouldn't want to miss it. These are all archetypal journeys with archetypal heroes.

The personal spiritual journey is a little bit of all these journeys in the archetypal sense, though perhaps not as far flung or dramatic. My journey shares similar longings, callings, and phases. It's getting back home, it's finding something that was lost, it's discovering some Promise Land, a place we've longed for but have not yet seen. Sometimes it's conquering an enemy; sometimes it's discovering a new land. People are counting on you to come through, to prevail. Sometimes there's a trail, sometimes a road less travelled, sometimes no trail at all. Maybe there's a map, maybe not. Sometimes the map is incomplete or simply marked, "Here be dragons."

I've known I was on a journey for a long time. I'm closing in on the last leg; a good portion of the journey is behind me now that I'm in my seventh decade. There was my conversion and zealous early days, wrestling with callings and finally being called, my seminary years blending into my ordination and first full-time pastoral position, my years of pastoring, preaching and church planting, publishing a book and directing a mission video before changing careers and leaving the church.

There was another adventure around the next bend.

There's romanticism to the journey, maybe even honor, and there are hardships to be sure. There are those days you're not sure how you'll get by the giant Cyclops or the ghostly Ring Wraiths or the lure of Vanity Fair. There are plenty of reasons not to continue along the way. Why not just stay here in this lush valley or linger longer with the Elves in a wispy, dreamy place? And there are surprising twists and unexpected paths that take us where we never quite imagined we'd be.

Sometimes it seems the journey has been postponed or had to be abandoned for unforeseen reasons. I think of Sir Ernest Shackleton, whose expedition to cross the Antarctic had to be abandoned when his ship was stuck in the ice and crushed before ever reaching the Antarctic coast. It turned into a rescue mission. Shackleton was determined to get all his men home safely. The story of how he and his crew of 29 men survived became his most famous exploit – his most memorable journey was not the one he planned when he left home.

Some journeys may not seem that consequential or that momentous, but it's the telling of them that becomes iconic for others. Like the two aging Texas Rangers in Larry McMurtry's novel, *Lonesome Dove,* on a grueling cattle drive and trail-blazing their own "helluva vision."

In the classic Holiday movie *It's a Wonderful Life,* our hero, George

Bailey (played by Jimmy Stewart) never leaves his home town. It's a deceptively dark story of a man getting to see what life would be like in Bedford Falls if he had not been born. George Bailey's alternate universe journey is him getting his life back after seeing the nightmare of a "what if" he was never born and realizing *It's a Wonderful Life* after all.

In Wes Anderson's movie *The Darjeeling Limited,* three brothers set out on a train to find their mother who has gone off to be a nun in a convent in the mountains of India. The eldest brother, played by Owen Wilson, has a detailed itinerary planned for their trip. But when they are kicked off the train in the middle of nowhere and their itinerary is shot, the real journey and the real transformations begin. Sometimes our plans have to go off the rails before we can surrender to something higher. The journey can transform our lives at the deepest levels.

Today, in the modern "built-out" world we live in there are very few "undiscovered lands" waiting for Magellan's ships to discover. There is no Mordor somewhere off in Middle Earth that Frodo and his Fellowship need to reach to free the world from its curse. There is no giant Cyclops or seductive Sirens threatening my commute home on the Interstate after work. Or are there?

We are drawn to these stories, myths, fantasies, and histories because they speak truths that generation after generation can relate to. If you only escape into the Journey stories to marvel at the escapades of Ulysses or Frodo or Luke Skywalker, you may be missing the point.

I am aware that I am all of them in some way or another: Frodo, Bilbo, Ulysses, Luke Skywalker, Magellan, Shackleton. I have been them at particular points in my journey.

For me all of these tales provide an archetypal journey, which is ultimately about a spiritual quest of some kind. Their lessons go beyond the particular terrain and particular destination of the story.

The poet Rudyard Kipling said it simply in his poem "The Explorer":

*"Something hidden. Go and find it. Go and look behind
the Ranges—
Something lost behind the Ranges. Lost and waiting for
you. Go!"*[5]

JOSEPH CAMPBELL AND ME

I was reminded of my first encounter with Joseph Campbell back in my nascent Christian convert days. In 1975, while I was in community college as a writer for the campus newspaper, I was assigned to cover one of Joseph Campbell's lectures on campus. I didn't know who Campbell was at the time.

After attending his lecture, I wrote an editorial in which I took the Christian point of view opposing some of his points. I look back now and realize how little I really knew about his books or studies at that time. I had taken offense at his view of Christianity (which I didn't fully understand either). It was because of my typical Christian blinders and zeal of the time.

Twenty years later I was reading and devouring his books because of the breadth and insights of his research on world religions and mythologies. Twenty years later I became a fan of Joseph Campbell's books. I felt I owed him an apology for my short-sightedness twenty years earlier. But by then he had passed on.

"LEAVING GOD FOR GOD"

We tend to think that we labor to get to a stage in midlife where we can sit back and coast a bit, or at least relax some. We think our career path has taken us to a good place, we have a family and a nice house, perhaps we have our church and our faith, we have our investments and retirement plans lined up, and we can cruise peacefully for a change. Plenty of people, of course, do just that. For some, however, something deep within is calling us. Maybe that still small voice couldn't be heard before over all the churning of our wheels and the hum of the treadmill.

It was Campbell's stages of the journey that was instructive for me. The hero is called to set out on a journey; along the way mentors and guides come alongside and help. Campbell also views the "curve of a lifetime" in two halves: "the first half is a time of relationships, and the second half is the time of finding a sense of life within."[6] He further breaks the span into four quarters:

The first quarter of life is that of a student, and the ideal there is obedience.

The second quarter in that of a householder...you have moved into the responsibilities of adult life.[7]

Obedience and responsibility. There are numerous books about the passages and stages of life that men and women go through in life. They have contributed to our understanding of the common phases we go through as people. What I find most interesting is how Campbell categorizes the second two quarters of life. Of the third quarter Campbell says: "Midlife is typically the period, not of achievement, but of realization, and it should be the period of fulfillment."[8]

This is where many people wind up as Thoreau said in *Walden*: "living lives of quiet desperation."[9] They know something is missing, but if there hasn't been a spiritual barometer before, they may not know what is missing. This is when the call to awake from the slumber can come to us.

The last half of life then becomes the quest for something spiritual, something deep within the heart. Joseph Campbell writes, "it will become the forming and structuring energy of your life, without care for achievement, without care for prestige."[10]

There are several famous people who have hit that wall later in life and had to re-evacuate and rethink. Leo Tolstoy, the Russian novelist, wrote his slim volume *"Confessions;"* Saint Augustine, the famous theologian, wrote his own "Confessions" centuries earlier, to reference just a couple.

IN HIS BEST-SELLING book *How to Change Your Mind*, Michael Pollan talks about the feeling he had upon reaching his fifties and feeling that something was missing.

> Carl Jung once wrote that it is not young people, but people in middle age who need to have an "experience of the numinous" to help them negotiate the second half of their lives.[11]

The "experience of the numinous" is that deep interior sense of the divine, the transcendent, The Presence. American psychologist William James wrote about it in his seminal work, *The Varieties of Religious Experience: A Study of Human Nature*. Rudolf Otto, in his classic work, *The Idea of the Holy* developed the idea further. The word "numinous" is from the Latin *numen,* which means "spirit." It is an experience because it comes with an overwhelming sense that something is mysterious, fascinating, overwhelming, and comforting all at the same time.

When religion is just primarily doctrine and dogma, it can leave us dry and empty, yearning for some touch of the divine, the transcendent. Feeling that something is missing can be the start of that call to a second adventure of faith.

Thomas Moore, the best-selling author of *Care of the Soul, The Soul's Religion* and *The Re-Enchantment of Everyday Life* and numerous other books, trained as a Catholic monk for twelve years. But then, just before he was about to be ordained, he decided "it was time for a major change," and he left: "I left seminary with the thought that I would never again regard religion and the priesthood with such devotion."[12]

His books were a great help to me when I left ministry; he became another guide along a path that was not well marked. Moore writes, "I was told to be a saint, but later in life I discovered that the real saints are people who go against the current of culture and often against church rules and expectations."[13]

I return to Meister Eckhart's quote: "The ultimate leave-taking is leaving God for God." I was leaving behind "a church and belief system" that had served me well for a time. But I was ready for more; ready to move beyond. Somehow, I knew "God" had to be bigger and more encompassing than my "Yahweh-Jesus" God from that "brand" of Christianity. I was able to look at my spiritual life after 43 as a "Second Call to Adventure."

LIVING DELIBERATELY

I first read *Walden*, Thoreau's account of his retreat to the woods at Walden Pond, way back when I was in the Air Force. I was struck by his desire to make sure that he lived life rather than sleepwalking through it.

I got so tired of hearing Christians talk of how believers were just visitors in this world; "we're just passing through" they would say. They add "our citizenship is in Heaven" and we should live for the next life, not this one.

Nonsense, I thought. I liked Thoreau's desire to face and live life.

> I went to the woods because I wished to live deliberately, to front only the essential facts of life, and see if I could not learn what it had to teach, and not, when I came to die, discover that I had not lived. I did not wish to live what was not life, living is so dear; nor did I wish to practise resignation, unless it was quite necessary.[14]

It was about being present, conscious, deliberate, possessed of life. Thoreau continues:

> I wanted to live deep and suck out all the marrow of life, to live so sturdily and Spartan-like as to put to rout all that was not life, to

cut a broad swath and shave close, to drive life into a corner, and reduce it to its lowest terms, and, if it proved to be mean, why then to get the whole and genuine meanness of it, and publish its meanness to the world; or if it were sublime, to know it by experience, and be able to give a true account of it in my next excursion.[15]

It's about awakening and living life with a conscious sense of processing and experiencing it. It's coming out of that slumber and coming to consciousness. I didn't want to come to the end of life and realize that I had not lived it, that I had not experienced life itself.

RECONSTRUCTION

There wasn't a clear line between the "deconstructing" phase of my faith and the "reconstruction" phase. I was reconstructing as I was deconstructing. Paradigm shifts, eureka moments and transformational experiences would happen often during the first few years of my life beyond church and ministry.

But I was meeting new people, new friends, new guides, and writers. I was dating and having a good time out beyond the tribe and its tent, in the actual world. My three children continued to be a positive support system, along with my mother and brothers, all who lived nearby in Central Florida. I finally landed a professional, career job in instructional design systems, writing computer-based training programs.

The mission video I directed, wrote, and helped edit from my Amazon Jungle trip had awakened my interest in video and film. The new digital video systems of the later 1990's opened up new possibilities. During my day job, I helped start a video department at two different training companies. Following some personal passions, I was having fun writing and submitting screenplays to Hollywood and getting good responses.

I confess it took me a good seven years after leaving ministry before I started feeling confident again about my newly emerging faith and freedom. After so many years in the safety of my familiar church shire, it took some getting used to navigate the wide-open terrain beyond my theological confines.

I had built up an impressive library of books in two decades of Christian ministry. I carted the dozens of boxes of books around through three or four moves in the first few years of leaving ministry. Finally, I went through all the boxes of concordances, Bible reference books, commentaries, church history, biographies, sermons, Christian classics, etc. I selected only the keepers (the books I knew I wanted to have around). I sold the rest to a young, seminary-bound student. I was building a new library.

CHAPTER 26
ALL THE SEAS OF GOD

Truth is one,
sages call it by various names.
—The Rig Veda [1]

LEAVING BEHIND....

The writer of the New Testament *Book of Hebrews* invokes Christians to "move beyond the elementary teachings" (Heb. 6:1-2) and go beyond toward maturity.

"Therefore let us move beyond the elementary teachings about Christ and be taken forward to maturity, not laying again the foundation of repentance from acts that lead to death, and of faith in God, instruction about cleansing rites, the laying on of hands, the resurrection of the dead, and eternal judgment."[2]

It's a two-fold call to the church to (1) "move beyond the elementary teachings about Christ" and (2) "be taken forward to maturity." Notice what the writer includes in his list of what we should move beyond. These are some of the most basic and routine things the church provides. The thing is, I never really felt that we, and the church in general, ever moved "beyond the elementary things" in Evangelicalism.

Most of the institutional churches, denominations and branches, seldom let us move beyond the fundamentals or elementary things. It's been designed that way since the earliest centuries when it was becoming an institution designed to be kept going by its own followers. We are the sheep, the branches of the vine, clay pots and cracked vessels, the sinners in need of forgiveness, the supplicants, the ones who bring sacrifices to atone and pay tribute.

And when the church does decide to "move beyond the elementary teachings," what does it usually resort to? Usually it means more Bible Study, more theology, more doctrine, more dogma. *Let's study end-times prophecy!*

I know why we do it. I did it. We like the holy huddle, the bubble. We don't want to have to rethink which religion or church we are a part of, we have that box checked, our dog tags make it clear.

We don't trust those other religions. We don't trust those other "secularists" or anybody not on our approved list. It's a slippery slope out there. If you leave our tribe, you're kind of on your own. We'll be here if you want to come back. But remember: Satan is just waiting to pounce outside these doors.

MOVING BEYOND THE ELEMENTARY THINGS

During these years beyond the church, I was being helped by Roman Catholic priests, from my good friend Father Walsh to Father Andrew Greeley and the authors I had discovered. I was reading about Jewish Kabbalism, the mystic branch of Judaism. I was learning new meditation techniques from Taoism. I was reading more from writers of other faiths, particularly Judaism, Hinduism, and Wisdom literature.

I was reading regularly from Walt Whitman and Rainer Maria Rilke as well as going back to classic literature. Thinkers and analysts like Carl Jung, Joseph Campbell, James Hillman and some others helped provide a wider context and a greater understanding of humanity and diverse spiritualities.

In reconstructing my faith, my goal was:

- a robust, flexible faith and spiritual path
- an intuitive and organic faith
- a faith that respected and embraced the Self, humanity, imagination, and soul
- an expansive view of God and the Goddess
- a spirituality that allowed for genuine spiritual breakthroughs and experiences
- a spirituality that was less doctrinal, not dogmatic

Writing in the second half of the 1800's, when to most American the country of India was a distant, exotic land, Whitman envisions traveling and embracing a far away, unfamiliar land in his poem *"Passage to India."* As his poem proceeds, India comes to represent more than just India; it represents the idea of exploring and venturing out to other unfamiliar lands. Reading again the passage that I have used as inspiration for thirty years, Whitman calls on his Soul, his traveling companion: "Reckless O Soul, I with thee and thou with me... For we are bound where no mariner has yet dared go...

Are they not all the Seas of God."[3]

Why fear? Whitman rhetorically asks in his line: "Are they not all the Seas of God." Yes, they are all the Seas of God. The eternal, omnipresent Supreme God. The Divine Presence is everywhere.

THE PRESENCE AND THE HIM-SHE

I grew weary of the common "God" term that had been so easily used; it was so common and nondescript it was almost like saying, "Hey You" or "Sir" or, for that matter, "dude." So I looked into other terms.

"HaShem" is a Hebrew term that means simply "the Name." The Hebrew (השם) term is often used by Jewish Mystics and in casual conversation. You may have heard the phrase "Baruch HaShem," which literally translates into "Blessed be the Name" or colloquially means "Thank God."

It's commonly said that God's name is "Yahweh" (or YHWH as it appears in Hebrew, without any vowel pointing). The great Tetragrammaton (literally "four letters"), as it is referred to, is the four-letter Hebrew word (יהוה – the four letters, read from right to left, are *yodh, he, waw,* and *he*) that God gave to Moses in the Old Testament when he asked, "Who shall I say sent me?"

God said to Moses, "I AM WHO I AM. This is what you are to say to the Israelites: 'I AM has sent me to you.'"[4]

The thing is, it's not really a name. The best translation we have come up with is, "I am that I am." The truth is, God never really gave us his name. "I am who I am" is not a name. My guess is that "God" never gave us his name because he didn't want just "one tribe" to have it. Or perhaps because it's unspeakable. So God wanted to keep his name private. There is a lot to unpack in that. Primarily, I wanted to use something other than "God" and "Lord." I didn't want to use Yahweh or Jehovah.

I noticed that Father Andrew Greeley at times used the "S/Him" or "S/He" moniker instead of the male pronoun for God in his book, *Confessions of a Parish Priest.*

I have used the term The Presence as a way to help me rethink my image of "God." Sometimes I use my own mixed male-female pronoun mash-up, the term "Him/She" to address the androgynous God/Goddess.

ORIGINAL GOODNESS

If you only read one of the Hindu scriptures, read the short volume *The Bhagavad Gita (Song of the Lord)*, which is a sub-section of the larger scripture *The Mahabharata*. I found that Hinduism has a better concept of the human self, the individual human being. I wish I had come upon it sooner.

In his recent translation of *The Bhagavad Gita,* Eknath Easwaran says:

> I grasped one of the most refreshing ideas in Hinduism: original goodness. Since the Self is the core of every personality, no one needs to acquire goodness and compassion; they are already there" (p. xliv).

The Bhagavad Gita is a 700-verse poem in which the Hindu God (Sri Krishna) instructs a young disciple, Arjuna. Dated to the second half of the first millennium BCE, it is considered one of Hinduism most sacred texts.

The Hindu God says this about his relationship with man:

> "I am the true Self in the heart of every creature.... The beginning, middle and end of their existence."[5]
> "I am the Lord who dwells in every creature."[6]

Here we read that God doesn't need to be invited into our heart or soul; he is already there; the spark of the Divine is within; which is just like Jesus' line, "the Kingdom of Heaven is within."[7] Jesus said this not to just his followers, but to people in general. God is already within us.

It is fascinating to me that the Hindu God uses the term the "Self" to indicate his Presence at the center of each of us. He equates the innermost "self" of the individual within the "body" with his own true Self.

"This supreme Lord who pervades all existence, the true Self of all creatures, may be realized through divine love."[8]

"The Self of all beings, living within the body, is eternal and cannot be harmed."[9]

This is the essence of original goodness. The self, the inner soul and essence of the individual, is itself divine; it's that spark of God within all people. I don't know what the Hindus say, but I say "Hallelujah!"

All the "self"-bashing of Christianity is seriously misplaced. And this God makes it clear that we have a "divine self" that is the essence of who we are; the body is not the essence of who we are.

"He who knows me as his own divine Self breaks through the belief that he is the body..."[10]

This is not something I ever heard in church.

"My eternal seed... is to be found in every creature."[11]

"I am the seed that can be found in every creature...."[12]

The closest thing to this in the New Testament is I John 3:9, where the writer says that his seed remains in him and he cannot sin. Unfortunately, too many Christians take this to mean they are therefore "perfectly holy" and cannot sin, which only confuses things.

The Bhagavad Gita also makes it clear that we need to rid ourselves of selfishness and self-centeredness. The text does not condemn the entire self as sinful. There is sin and turning from God. But it is refreshing to read that there is a divine self within each of us that is the essence, the spark of the divine God. God is the inner self, and "the inner witness"... "I am the only refuge, the one true friend."[13] As for those bodily punishments and penances made up by the Christians to punish the self, the Hindu God says: "Some invent harsh penances. Motivated by hypocrisy and egotism, they torture their bodies and me who dwells in them."[14]

Sounds like Jesus' warning that what we do to the least of these we also do to Him. Why hasn't the church ever applied that verse from Jesus to what we do to punish sin? This verse from the Hindu scriptures warns us that punishing our bodies is punishing God.

A BIGGER, HIGHER GOD

In Hinduism there is also the understanding that "God" is One, but has many manifestations. When Arjuna asks to see Sri Krishna, God appears in "A million divine forms with an infinite variety of color and shape... He appeared with an infinite number of faces, ornamented by heavenly jewels."[15]

In the Hindu image of God, there is more than a Trinity of three, there are millions of manifestations of God. "Neither gods nor sages know my origin, for I am the source from which the gods and sages come."[16]

This God does not have a problem with "other paths" or other religions: "Those who worship other Gods with faith and devotion also worship me."[17] "All paths, Arjuna, lead to me."[18]

This is a refreshingly unthreatened God, apparently with his own healthy self-image. Imagine that: a God with a healthy self-image, a God who is not a narcissistic megalomaniac. This is quite a contrast to the jealous and xenophobic Yahweh of the Old Testament scriptures.

MAN IS GOD'S FAIR FORM

I went back and began reading the Gnostic Gospels and the lost books of the Bible. Many of these were from the Dead Sea Scrolls and other hidden books that the early church branded as heretical. I remember getting a cursory introduction to these books in seminary. It is a shame some of them didn't make it into the canon of scripture.

What were they trying to keep from us? I see some of the problems because some of these books present quite different ideas.

I found some noteworthy comments about man in a particularly interesting Gnostic book titled, *"Poimandres or The Power and Wisdom of God,"* by the well-known mystic Hermes Trismegistus.

We are taught in Genesis that man was made in the image and likeness of God. The verse actually says: "Let us make man in our image and likeness." (We'll skip the whole issue of the pronouns *us* and *our.* But clearly there were more than one of them.)

In Hermes' vision, Poimandres appears to him as a "Being of Limitless Size" and reveals the secrets of creation. When God created man he says:

> *Man was fair, created*
> *in the image of God.*
> *Enamoured by his own form*
> *God granted him all His craft skills.* [19]

God was enamored of his own form in the human being he created. Let that sink in. God liked what he saw in the physical human form of man. It was good. It goes on to describe man as "God's fair form."

Here also, God uses the term "Self" (capital "S") to describe himself.

> *I my Self, I Am*
> *ever present to the blessed,*
> *good, pure, aware,*
> *compassionate, holy.*
> *The Presence of the Self*
> *becomes an aid.* [20]

God speaks as this androgynous Self, as The Presence. He continues:

I AM, as their Self,
will not permit these
defects to harm them.[21]

The Gnostic Gospels and numerous other books that were left out of the Bible are a great complement to the canon of the Bible. It is important to remember that the current Bible that we have was curated by a collection of influential men who were positioning Christianity to be a major part of the culture of the Roman Empire. The books of the Bible were not officially set until over three hundred years after Jesus' death. The Council of Rome officially set the Catholic canon of scripture in 382 A.D. and the Synod of Hippo in North Africa set the New Testament canon in 393 A.D.

Numerous other popular texts were excluded. But they weren't just excluded—they were banned and labeled heretical. Thankfully, many fragments and parts of these books have been discovered over the centuries.

On the theme of original goodness, Hermes Trismegistus wrote what the Divine being said to him about the regenerated man:

The body's senses rise up
and return to the Source
separating and remingling
with His original energy.[22]

Here we are being told that the body, along with our soul, can be reclaimed and return to the "original energy" from "the Source." That's a lot more positive and hopeful than being stuck with some ancient stain of total depravity and the "old man" of our sin nature.

The great library in Alexandria in the ancient world was a place where wise men from the East (the Oriental World), and the West (the Occidental World) may have met and intermingled. The Magi who visited the birth of Christ in the Gospel of Luke were from the Oriental World.

Writers like Hermes Trismegistus and writers from India most likely compared texts, prophecies, and theological thought. It is no coincidence that we find in ancient texts this similar use of the word "Self" by two different deities, one from the Hindu God in *The Bhagavad Gita* and one from this Christian God in the Gnostic text, *"Poimandres."*

"The First Book of Enoch" was written hundreds of years before Christ. It too was among the banned books of the Dead Sea Scrolls. It is clear that Jesus and the writers of the New Testament were familiar with that text because many of the terms used to describe Jesus were terms from *"The First Book of Enoch."*

It is not in the scope of this book to go into a whole study of comparative religions, but that is what I was doing during my journey. Without going into great depths in each, the point is that there is much to learn from other faiths and disciplines. If we are so dogmatic about our own faith that we cannot learn from those of other faiths, then it simply reveals a spirituality that is not adaptable or flexible enough to accommodate a broader concept of truth.

Up until the twenty-first century I had not met or been friends with any people who were Hindu in their beliefs. That was my loss. Over the last decade, it has been my privilege to become friends with a number of people of the Hindu faith from India, some of whom are now U.S. citizens. I am eternally grateful to them for filling in what was lacking in my religious diversity of friends and understanding.

World religions are all part of our story, the story of mankind on this ever-shrinking planet. We have more in common with other religions than we know or care to admit.

MOVING BEYOND

Before going to the Cross, Jesus said to his disciples that he had many more things to tell them.

"I have much more to say to you, more than you can now bear. But when he, the Spirit of truth, comes, he will guide you into all the truth. He will not speak on his own; he will speak only what he hears, and he will tell you what is yet to come." [23]

Apparently, the Disciples weren't quite ready to hear or to "bear" or to process the "much more" that Jesus had to say. But he promised that "the Spirit of truth," or his Holy Spirit, would lead them.

I don't think we have a term for the new emerging faith that many of us are trying to describe. A big part of me doesn't want to label it. When you label it, it tends to get categorized, systematized, and institutionalized. I have avoided writing this book as a step-by-step "how to" process specifically to avoid creating a "a program." Each person needs to personalize their faith and their steps on the journey. There are guidelines and mentors and particular journeys each has to make.

Thomas Moore's books helped me set a goal, a goal of blending the variety of religious traditions and beliefs into something more eclectic and diverse. I know that having grown up in America, my most basic religious cosmology was colored by my Christianity. I cannot escape its stories, texts, mythology. It's been ingrained in me for decades. I am at peace with that; I can appreciate the rich heritage of my faith and scriptures and the part they played in the first half of my life.

It was my "starter religion," my "first faith," and became the professional faith in which I was trained and educated. Thomas Moore wrote about the color of his Christianity and how blended it became for him:

It feels as though my Christianity has come to infuse every cell of my being and yet at the same time has grown less visible and tangible. The color of Christianity to me has blended with the different hues of Buddhism, Greek Paganism, Renaissance syncretism, Sufism, Taoist emptiness, and Judaism. This is not watered-down or diffused Christianity but a richer, more complex spiritual vision, one that acquires strength by not being defined in context with other visions.[24]

I couldn't say it any better. That was where I was heading. The color of my faith was blending. Someday we'll have better terminology to describe those of us who could not abide the singular tribal tent; those who needed to find our own new library of Alexandria where we could mingle with those of other faiths freely and thrive on the truths we can share as we seek to assemble this gigantic puzzle of spiritual pieces.

Looking back now on the last thirty years since I left the Christian church, I see that at every turn in my self-described "independent study" without a clear spiritual "path" for me to follow, I see that this bigger God, The Presence, my Him-She was directing my path even when I wasn't sure. It didn't matter that I was avoiding "Yahweh-Jesus" or ditching my "Jesus Doppelgänger" or letting my Bible gather dust on the shelf.

I admit: I went rogue. I wasn't looking for a "better" church or a "better" Christianity. I was looking for a blended spirituality, a richer cosmology.

Time and time again I was led to the right person, the right book, the right author, the right music when I needed them.

"The spirit will lead you into all truth."

CHAPTER 27
MY WHITMAN LITURGY

From this hour I ordain myself
loos'd of limits and imaginary lines.
—Walt Whitman,*"Song of the Open Road"*[1]

During seminary, when my twin boys were toddlers and just starting to stand up and take a step or two, I'd put on some of my favorite rock music and they would move in circles to the beat smiling and waving their arms. It was cute and completely innocent. I casually mentioned it to a couple at our church one morning and they said in all seriousness, "That's their sin nature."

Nonsense, I thought. Not wanting to get into a heated debate on the whole doctrine of man's sinful nature, I politely dismissed their comment and changed the subject. I grew tired of changing the subject.

The roots of Christianity's doctrine of man's sinful nature and total depravity are so woven into the theology of conservative Christianity that its tentacles have strangled out the truth of man's dignity and the wonder of our humanity.

THINGS I DIDN'T HEAR IN THE EVANGELICAL CHURCH

I was adopting beliefs from other faiths and wisdom. Hinduism's concept of the divine within each of us was much more representative of a good, kind, loving and truly Supreme Deity. Thomas Moore says in *The Soul's Religion*:

> In fifty years of church-going I don't recall ever hearing from any church pulpit about creating and discovering your own individual spirituality.... (I was) never encouraged to follow my intuitions and passions... I was told to be a saint...[2]

Looking back, it's sad to admit, but there are phrases I didn't hear in Evangelical circles and churches:

- Believe in your Self
- Trust your Self
- Know your Self
- Be Self-possessed
- Celebrate your Self

I certainly didn't hear anyone say, "Celebrate yourself." That was practically heresy. It was all "To God be the Glory." And when they turned to us, it was "Have you confessed your sins?" "What have you done for the Lord today or lately?" Before you know it, a kind of sacred, consecrated, and learned holy helplessness parades as spiritual devotion.

Other things I didn't hear in Evangelical churches:

- Follow your dreams
- Follow your heart
- Follow your instincts and intuition

Make no mistake, this is by design and in keeping with the mindset of the Onward Christian Soldiers on Christ's Great Mission. Make no mistake, there is a cold war, a war of words and ecclesiastical spin that is being waged against the individual, the very human beingness of you and me, lest any of us get out from under the guilt, manipulation, and control.

It's a denigration of the Self, a debasing of the self. It's a campaign against our humanity, a willful ignorance of human psychology, and a "theological" abhorrence of the human individual. My Christianity was dismissive of my humanity.

It's not in all these churches, but its tentacles run deep in their "anti" stance on nearly everything. You must ask yourself, as I did: Why are they so afraid? Will the house of cards topple if certain doctrinal cards are removed?

I realized enough to know that this "Yahweh-Jesus" I had constructed and my Jesus Doppelgänger were not the whole picture of the real God. They were the dystopian creations of my theological and dogmatic training and the conjuring of my Evangelical mind.

REPLACING OLD TAPES

I was sitting having lunch with a friend in a diner who had come to Christ through Campus Crusade. Campus Crusade had a higher profile than The Navigators, and Bill Bright, its founder, was a well-known Christian leader. Both parachurch organizations preached the mission of saving the world for Jesus and had a big impact on our lives as twenty-something disciples of Jesus. My friend was now in his forties, a businessman, a husband, and father of two children.

He said to me, "I'd like to find Bill Bright and kick his ass."

We both laughed, understanding our mutual change of heart on some of these things. But his comment was serious as well; it summed up his accumulated anger at how our youthful zeal had carried us away.

Another friend, who had been on the Campus Crusade staff, now in his sixties and on a similar path of healing and healthier spirituality, said to me: "I don't talk to Jesus anymore."

He put it using this analogy. He said in those early discipleship days as a new believer, "It's like we were wearing a football helmet with a narrow field of vision. One day you take the helmet off and discover there is a whole 360-degree vision out there."

Both men are still spiritual people. They just don't practice their faith the same way and their belief systems have changed and expanded.

The Christian church doesn't count the numbers of those who left or who they left wounded along the trail. Rarely do you get a church exit interview with a "Tell us how we're doing" survey. (They don't really want to know.)

I needed to replace "My Evangelical Discipleship Liturgy." I replaced it with "My Whitman Liturgy." It was part of deprogramming and reprogramming my internal operating system with inner dialogue that was more positive and healthy.

My personal Christian experience led to a fractured self, an alienated self, a lost self. I wanted wholeness, an integrated self, a free and celebrating self. All the lines in "My Whitman Liturgy" are straight from his poems (as indicated by abbreviations).

MY WHITMAN LITURGY

> *We understand each other then, do we not?*
> *What the study couldn't teach,*
> *what the preaching couldn't accomplish*
> *is accomplish'd, is it not?[3]*

You have not known what you are
you have slumbered upon yourself all your life.
I should have made my way straight to you long ago.
None has understood you, but I understand you.
There is no endowment in man or woman that is not
tallied in you.
I will leave all and come and make hymns of you. [4]

The sum of all known reverence
I add up in you whoever you are. [5]

I celebrate myself and sing myself
I lean and loaf and invite my soul.
Clean and sweet is my soul and
clean and sweet is all that is not my soul. [6]

I sing the body electric.
I too am not a bit tamed, I too am untranslatable.
I sound my barbaric yawp over the roofs of the world.
I am large, I contain multitudes.
I am larger, better than I thought
I did not know I held so much goodness.
From this hour I ordain myself
loosed of limits and imaginary lines. [7]

Allons! With power, liberty, the earth, the elements,
Health, defiance, gayety, self-esteem, curiosity. [8]

It's not that I actually read this liturgy regularly or memorized it exactly like this. But those were the new lines that were seared into my soul to help change the voice in my head.

EMBRACING MY HUMANITY

God didn't ditch his whole commitment to humanity and human beings because sin entered the world. God wasn't like Dr. Frankenstein turning in horror from his creation.

I have discovered time and again that my whole self (mind, body, soul, senses, etc., etc.) is part of my spiritual journey of awakening. I am a whole unit, and wanted to be a unified, integrated self.

To me, that whole self-abnegation path misses the difference between the true essence of the individual self, and the habits of self-absorption and self-centeredness.

Being swept up into the anonymity of the Giant Borg of God Energy doesn't appeal to me. Does God want a relationship, a connection with us? Or does God just want to absorb our human energy? Are we back to just being empty husks, hollow hosts for some nameless, amorphous divine energy to flow through? I think not.

Why did God bother making us "in the image and likeness" of the Gods only to have us reject that image and rid ourselves of it? I believe we are exactly as the Divine Presence wants us to be: human beings with bodies, minds and souls that are in the image and likeness of the Divine God and Goddess. We are still "God's fair form."

Why did the Creator create us with all this humanity, this capacity for intelligence and creativity, and this amazing range of senses, memory, and imagination, if we are to rid ourselves of it? It makes no sense.

I believe our humanity, our senses, our capacity for deep emotion, our ability to create and imagine are all the very things we were given because God wants us to use them.

I remember my surprise upon reading Whitman's lines in his poem "To You":

O I have been dilatory and dumb,

I should have made my way straight to you long ago,
I should have blabb'd nothing but you,
I should have chanted nothing but you.
I will leave all and come and make the hymns of you[9]

We sing hymns in churches to God. It's all about God's glory. Does God really need to hear us singing all these hymns to him? Our response to that in church was to say: "God doesn't need the songs, but we need them, to get our eyes back on God."

Did you catch the trick in their comeback? Did you see how they do that? They put the onus back on the sinners.

Is God in that much need of our praise? Is he a complete narcissist, a megalomaniac? Is he so insecure that he needs all our pep talks in songs and hymns? That God sounds too needy.

I remember hearing believers joyously say that "when we get to heaven we'll get to sing his praises for a thousand years." That never sounded like fun to me. I like to sing, but not that much.

I've heard singing so bad in some churches, I don't see how any of it glorifies God. I can imagine God motioning with his hand to stop hurting his ears. God does have perfect pitch, you know.

Whitman wrote in the voice of a divine messenger, announcing a fresh beginning. It was uplifting to hear Whitman say he will make "hymns of you." I don't need a song about me. I don't need God to sing me a hymn. I don't need to be praised. What I needed was God to say: I celebrate you; I like you. You're neither cursed nor a constant disappointment.

DURING THESE YEARS of reconstructing my faith, I started picking back up things I loved that I had set aside or left behind. I went back and listened to rock music, classical music, and musicals I had loved or missed; some were artists I never had time to listen to or I didn't think were important to my spiritual life. I read books I had passed up because of my faith. I went to art exhibits I wouldn't have gone to in the past.

At an international food festival at the nearby University of Central Florida, I wasn't prepared for how it would affect me. I walked around and was overcome by emotions. It seems silly now looking back, but this was part of the new sense of celebrating life that hit me. It was not just the samples of food that I tasted; it was also the great realization of the wonder and diversity of mankind.

I approached it like Whitman taught me: to embrace and celebrate the wonders of God's diversity of humanity.

On a trip to Paris, I was stunned by the art at The Louvre. I was moved by the massive size of some of the paintings and the attention to the details of people, faces, and expressions. More than anything, it was the sculpture that really amazed me that day. The size, bulk and beauty of these stone men and women transfixed me. The smooth marble beauty of the two lovers Eros and Psyche in Antonio Canova's classic sculpture "Psyche revived by Cupid's Kiss" is a stunning tribute to the human form.

I took my daughter to New York City for her high school graduation. We were sitting in the theater waiting for the musical *"Les Miserables"* to begin. Kim and I had listened to the CD and memorizing songs at home. I'll never forget the look on her face when the first two notes from the orchestra began the production. We knew this was going to blow us away. The Broadway's adaptation of Victor Hugo's novel is an affirmation and celebration of love, forgiveness, and the hope of life after death "beyond the barricade."

I couldn't imagine Yahweh or Jesus celebrating their "creation" after Genesis Chapter 3 and the whole fall and judgment of man. Yet, I turn to *The Bhagavad Gita* and Krishna says, "Wherever you find strength or beauty or spiritual power, you may be sure these have sprung from a spark of my essence."[10]

I was listening to songs from the *Les Miserable* production while driving the Blue Ridge Parkway on my way to Mount Mitchell during my week-long sabbatical months before resigning from the church.

One song in particular helped me when I was at my lowest point. It's the prayer Jean Valjean sings asking God to let the young Marius survive the coming battle in the streets. It's called *"Bring Him Home."* It is one of the most beautiful songs of the musical. Winding along the narrow switchbacks through the mountains, I was praying and hoping to bring myself home.

CHAPTER 28

BEFRIENDING DREAMS

Befriending the dream begins
with a plain attempt
to listen to the dream.
—James Hillman[1]

I was a Samurai Warrior in gold-colored battle armor locked in a ferocious sword fight with another Samurai Warrior. It was intense. Somehow, I knew this was not a drill, this was a death duel. The other Samurai Warrior had a mask covering his face. One of us would die. The two of us were alone on a ridge as we clashed swords and traded blows. We fought for what seemed like a long time, then he struck a blow that knocked the sword from my hand. It was over. He won. I dropped to my knees, bowed before him. Then in one swift swing he decapitated me. My head rolled on the ground like a cantaloupe and I fell dead.

I woke terrified from the dream. I wrote the dream down in my notebook. I had no idea what it meant—but I knew who would.

It was a small circle of friends who helped me get through my most difficult times of transition from church world to real world, from unemployed pastor to instructional designer at a computer-based training company. It was an unlikely circle that included my gay best friend and a couple of his gay friends, unchurched folks, a couple of old Christian friends, a few divorcees, new people I was meeting at work, and two counselors. My children, grown now, have always been a source of strength for me, along with my mother and brothers.

Father Walsh helped me through a second divorce. I met someone and rushed into things after dating for a couple of years. I probably shouldn't have married, but five years after my leaving and separating, I remarried. The relationship helped at the time; we had some wonderful times together. But it was short-lived. Eventually it became clear that she was on a different trajectory than I was. The last couple of years were awkward and strained. Although we parted amicably, that didn't mean it was without pain.

SURRENDER

The biggest lesson I learned during my outbound journey from the church was surrender. I had learned a lot about surrender in my Evangelical years. But I was learning it at a deeper level—or, to use the metaphor of the spiral circle, I was going through it at a higher level.

Spiritual surrender is not resignation, not passivity, not giving up, but a spiritual frame of mind that does not seek to grab, cling to, or bend things to my will. Most spiritual paths teach the way of surrender. It is an essential mindset of peacefulness and acceptance. I was about to have one of the most vivid examples of the results of surrender.

I dreaded returning to my house one night after work; I did not want to face the awkwardness of being divorced while my ex-wife was still living there but getting ready to move out. My son, Scott, fresh out of two years in the U.S. Marines, was living with me at the time, as was my daughter, Kim, who was a recent high school graduate.

Scott called me up at work that night. "Dad, she moved out, all her stuff is gone. Just like that, she moved out." I knew it was going to happen, I just didn't know when. After I hung up, I didn't want to face walking into that house.

Driving home I prepared myself for the big letdown upon entering the front door. I had been practicing surrender for months, so I was already on a spiritual path. But it was bound to be shaky.

Then something supernatural happened. I use that term sparingly. But that day, I knew something happened that was not of me. I walked into my house and instead of being overcome with the sadness, I felt lifted up by something other than myself. I knew I didn't have it in me because I was drained, empty, down, and depressed.

The minute I opened the door and walked in there was a new lightness and a feeling of clarity. It was as if the Spirit had swept through the house, clearing the air, exorcising any latent, lingering darkness, leaving it new and fresh.

I walked around the rooms of the house and the new positive energy was unmistakable. It was one of those times when you just can't quite find words adequate to convey the moment and experience. That day I felt The Presence lift me in a way I will never forget.

I didn't know it at the time, but a whole new learning phase was beginning.

DREAMS AND INTERPRETATION

After the first couple of years of counseling with Father Walsh, we moved into an informal period where he saw me as a friend, confidante, and fellow Christian professional. During these times, we delved more deeply into dreams and dream interpretation. I called Father Walsh my dream whisperer.

I remember early on when he said, referring to the spiritual life, "I love the mystery of it." I was confused. As a young Evangelical disciple and as a pastor we were trained to have an answer to almost every question. We were trained in apologetics in order to defend the Gospel and Scripture. I was trained to have a verse for almost everything that could be thrown at me.

"I thought we were supposed to have the answers," I said dumbfounded to Father Walsh. "We're supposed to clear up the mysteries, right?"

He smiled, knowingly.

We still had a lot of work to do.

There was a point in my counseling when Father Walsh said to me, "Write down your dreams and bring those each time to our sessions."

"Dreams?" I asked.

"Dreams. The kind you have when you're sleeping."

He told me to keep a pen and paper by my bed and when I woke in the night from a dream that I should jot down as much as possible (with the lights out) before going back to sleep. He said that we always think we'll remember that vivid dream in the night, but then by morning it's all gone or vague. So I started writing down my dreams. I was having some pretty scary dreams at times. The kind where a Samurai warrior lops your head off and you wake up in the dark and can't get back to sleep.

I brought the Samurai Warrior dream to Father Walsh. He always broke into a wide smile after I recounted a troubling dream. For him dreams were like a coded message or a puzzle, a riddle to solve from the unconscious, and he liked the challenge. And He always smiled at however terrifying my dream was. He was never deterred by the horror or violence, which was part of the lesson; the dream is figurative, imaginative and metaphorical.

. . .

ROBERT A. JOHNSON's book *Inner Work* is one of the most helpful primers on dreams and interpretations that I have found:

> Dreams show us in symbolic form, all the different personalities that interact within us and make up our total self. The multiplicity of dream figures reflects the plurality and multidimensional structure of the inner self.[2]

James Hillman writes:

> The classical Jungian attitude toward the dream is expressed very well by a term I would borrow from existential analysis... This term is to befriend the dream. To participate in it, to enter into its imagery and mood, to want to know more about it, to understand, play with, carry and become familiar with—as one would do with a friend. As I grow familiar with my dreams I grow familiar with my inner world.[3]

Befriending dreams? It was a new approach to me.

Most of us don't take dreams very seriously. Maybe we have a scary dream after we watch a horror movie and the dream is just a reaction to the movie. Occasionally we may have a dream that seems significant or meaningful, but it may seem confusing, so we wind up dismissing it or forgetting it, never imagining that it may be trying to tell us something.

In the alchemy of the Self the unconscious and subconscious are active within us, even when we choose to dismiss their activity and occasional messages.

> The purpose of learning to work with the unconscious is not just to resolve our conflicts and deal with our neuroses. We find there a deep source of renewal, growth, strength and wisdom.... We learn to tap that rich lode of energy and intelligence that waits within.[4]

From my Christian training, I was taught that dreams were basically of no use; they were of this world, maybe demonic. The typical first verse used to put down dreams is: "In the past God spoke to our ancestors through the prophets at many times and in various ways, but in these last days he has spoken to us by his Son, whom he appointed heir of all things."[5] The "various ways" was usually meant to be dreams and visions. In my old Evangelical world, dreams were one of the old ways God used to employ, but now he only needs Jesus. Thus dreams are inconsequential. The goal is to get people back to the Bible, because Jesus is Word, and the Bible is the Word of God.

However, in the Old Testament, Yahweh is ready to reveal through visions and dreams: "Listen to my words: 'When there is a prophet among you, I, the LORD, reveal myself to them in visions, I speak to them in dreams'"[6] Daniel, one of the great Old Testament characters, was known for his gift of dream interpretation.

The New Testament *Book of Acts* says clearly: "In the last days, God says, I will pour out my Spirit on all people. Your sons and daughters will prophesy, your young men will see visions, your old men will dream dreams."[7]

This is another authority issue for the church. They don't want people to run off seeking visions and dreams, or delving into the unconscious; it opens up a can of worms, a Pandora's Box that the church can't control. We operate within our theological boundaries. Discounting dreams and visions was another way of keeping us "Christian Biblicists" and making sure that we didn't come up with any crazy ideas, or that we were delving into any "Liberal Christian" territory. It was also another way to be dismissive of the complexity of the inner self.

DURING MY DARKEST TIMES, and there were many of them, my dreams began to show me how closely connected I was at an unconscious level with the Holy Spirit within. I associated my dreams with a verse in *The Book of Romans*. The verse uses a strange phrase: "groanings which cannot be uttered," as the King James Version puts it. In a new translation it states: "In the same way, the Spirit helps us in our weakness. We do not know what we ought to pray for, but the Spirit himself intercedes for us through wordless groans."[8]

I began to see through Father Walsh's wisdom that The Presence was prodding me and communicating personally through my dreams. These were not prophetic dreams, nor were they weird "messages" for others. They were deeply personal messages from within my unconscious and subconscious, "wordless groans" that came through in dream images like my Samurai Warrior dream.

It was as if the Holy Ghost, the Presence, was teaming up with Father Walsh to specifically show me that the Presence can reach me through my dreams. It was like a three-way messaging system: (1) Me having a dream; (2) My dream, like some groaning from the Presence down in my unconscious; and (3) the Dream Interpreter, Father Walsh, interpreting the dream picture.

Our human senses have limitations. A dog can hear frequencies humans can't; a hawk can spot prey from the sky hundreds of feet away; whales can communicate with other whales from miles away. We could go on and on with examples of how nature's senses are more heightened than human senses.

We also have limitations in our abilities to connect with our unconscious and subconscious. We certainly can't see through this earthly dimension into the celestial plane.

"Each dream communicates information that isn't known consciously by the dreamer."[9]

Fr. Walsh always found the positive and spiritually uplifting interpretation of my dreams, no matter how crazy, weird or horrific they were. My Samurai Warrior dream was an easy one for him, especially since he knew me so well by this time.

In Walsh's interpretation, I was *both* Samurai Warriors in my dream. I had seen myself in the dream as the Warrior who was killed. But I was also the one who won and cut off the head of my opponent.

One of the key principles of interpreting these kinds of dreams is that every person in your dream can be a representation of the dreamer.

Walsh pointed out how I had lived most of my Christianity from my head, all that scholasticism and knowledge, all the doctrine and having the answers. My masked opponent Samurai was my emerging self, the self who wanted to be whole—my heart, soul and integrated self. He said the dream is me putting an end to my "head and mind" oriented spirituality and moving toward an integrated, heart, soul, and mind approach. I had won the samurai match.

It seemed so simple once he said it. He was right. After we discussed it, I saw that it was a way in which The Presence was affirming via my dreams the path I was on. It was my unconscious giving me a picture in a dream, affirming that in the deepest part of my inner self I was putting to death the head-oriented, scholastic, theologically based faith, and instead seeking a holistic spirituality, something that integrated the whole of me.

The mystery of dreams is something that I would never have delved into in my Evangelical days. If they were scary that's because they were from Satan. That is what I was taught. I discovered nothing could be further from the truth. If David, Jacob, Mary and other Biblical characters were given dreams and visions, why can't we receive them also? God's "figurative hands" cannot be tied by any religion's taboos or cultic limitations.

Why is it that as an Evangelical I limited how the Presence can break through?

Clearly there are dreams that carry no spiritual import, that are just nightmarish responses to some recent movie we watched or some such thing. But I discovered that during some of my most trying times, times of change and upheaval, dreams can be one of the most intimate ways in which The Presence can reveal truth and encourage us.

PERSONALIZED DREAMS

It's not my intent to enumerate all the steps and principles of dream interpretation, but there are some basics that help. Robert Johnson's book *Inner Work* is a good place to begin for those interested in understanding dreams.

Some dreams provide valuable insights, like my Samurai dream. But you have to work with the dream to get something out it. Then there are many dreams that are compensatory. Compensatory dreams are those that bring us some compensation we are missing, need or desire. There are also dreams that are not of any particular significance; the silly or scary dreams you have after watching a horror movie or some such thing. But don't dismiss that "horrific" dream too readily. Jung broadly categorized dreams as little dreams and big dreams. I was having a lot of big dreams and Father Walsh was enjoying being the dream whisperer.

I remember having a couple of dreams in which I met people from my past and our encounter resolved something for me or gave me something I needed at the time. One such dream was as simple as me running into one of the guys from the military ministry whom I had not seen in 25 years. He was always a gregarious, warm, welcoming friend who would give me big bear hug. In my dream one night during a difficult stretch, I ran into him in a dream and received that warm, loving greeting and hug. I woke up right after than dream and literally felt as if I had been hugged by my friend. It was compensatory; it helped compensate for the cold time I was going through.

I was discovering that my dreams were ministering to me and making me aware of things in a revealing way. Over these last three decades, my important dreams have always become more frequent and fascinating when I was going through times of transition, change and hardship.

Another key principle I learned from Fr. Walsh is that most often in "message" dreams the key people in your dream represents an aspect of the dreamer. So what are these other selves telling you through other people in your dream? In my Samurai Warrior dream, I was both warriors.

Another short example is a recent dream I had about my father. As I said, my dad died when I was 25, and I have missed him often over these decades. But oddly enough I have only ever had two dreams where my dad showed up and those were late life dreams. I've often prayed to have a dream about Dad to bring to Father Walsh, but Dad never showed up. It was strange to me. Then one night, I had a dream in which Dad appeared.

It was a very short dream. I was approaching a house for an outdoor party in the yard. It was Dad's house (not our real home but I knew it was his house in the dream) and he was throwing the party. I walked into the backyard and there was my dad coming toward me with a tray of food. I lit up and was so glad to see him, but it was as if he didn't see me at all.

As we passed each other, he never acknowledged me; it was as if I was invisible. He walked by me as I stood there downcast and disappointed and he continued carrying his tray of food to a table. There were several people milling about in the white picket fence yard and he smiled and chatted with them, but never with me.

My dad didn't recognize me at all in the dream. I woke from the dream nearly in tears. I finally saw my dad in a dream, and he walked right by me and we never got to talk. Do I get mad at my dad? No, I knew there was a message here for me.

I wrote down the dream and figured I would think about it the next day. By this time, much to my loss, Fr. Walsh had passed away. So I did what I've been doing since he has been gone: I ask myself. "What would Fr. Walsh say? How would he tackle this?"

I went back through the dream the way Father Walsh taught me. Then it hit me. "Your father is you in the dream," Fr. Walsh would say. "You know how you don't recognize your own gifts and talents? How you tend to put yourself down or belittle your own accomplishments. The dream is not about your dad at all. It's about you not recognizing yourself for all you are."

The dream was a metaphor, "meeting" my father was not literal; it was a backhanded message from my unconscious to remind me of some positive circumstances. Instead of a sweet reunion in the dream with my Dad; the Spirit used the one person who could hurt me, my Dad, make me realize how I had been hurting myself. It's an example of the Genius of the Holy Spirit working within my own unconscious to tell a story, a parable, if you will, to play a scene from a movie. Scenes and stories stick with us more than the lecture from the professor.

If I had ignored these kinds of dreams and the Samurai Warrior type dreams, I would have missed out on a special "mysterious" aspect of how The Presence was reaching out and through the deepest groanings of my innermost self. There's a holiness to that, a sacred personal communion. This Divine Presence is at the very center and core of my Self. It affirmed my belief in a personal, transcendent Presence.

The key is to work with the dream. Don't dismiss it too readily. Think of it as a riddle or a puzzle to work through and solve. You may find some treasures.

CARL JUNG'S writings on dreams and visions were monumental and have inspired many other writers and researchers. In his autobiography *Memories, Dreams, Reflections*, Jung writes, "The dream is a little hidden door into the innermost and most secret recesses of the psyche," the inner self.[10]

Dream activity varies in intensity for me. I pay attention and write down my dreams before I forget them. There are other times, like when life seems peaceful and under control, that I have had fewer significant dreams.

I am so grateful for all the hours Father Walsh spent with me and all he taught me. Walsh was a Jungian counselor, a priest, and a deeply spiritual man, which is also a hard breed to find. But if you are having interesting dreams or are open to looking into them and discussing them, you may find that interpreter you need.

Another quick note: I don't look to dreams for prophecy or to reveal the future.

Most books on dream interpretation are not that helpful. Dreams are highly personal. So for any book to list "how to interpret dream symbols" is presumptuous. A meaningful image in your dream may mean something completely different in my dream.

Dream principles are more important than a catalogue of what animals and symbols mean in your dreams. Each dreamer may have a different set of dream symbols. Meaningful dreams come at specific times, relate to specific happenings in our lives and cannot be forced into some "typical" pattern of interpretation.

When my son, Scott, was stationed in Croatia serving with the Marines, he called me one day and said, "Dad, I had a dream about grandpa last night." Now my children never met my dad in this life; he passed away three years before Scott was born. He had only seen photographs of my father.

I was so thrilled for Scott to have a dream encounter with my dad. He said it was a simple dream. Scott was playing his guitar and singing a song while my dad sat and listened encouragingly. I have to admit that I was jealous of his dream. My dad never sat and listened to me play and sing.

I now have four notebooks of my dreams and interpretations covering thirty years of my life. I am always amazed when I have a dream that I know is worth meditating on, deciphering the code in the postcard, solving the riddle, and discerning the message. I miss Father Walsh, my dream whisperer, and his delightful smile as he dissipated the horror of my dreams by showing me the positive messages I was being sent.

Befriending my dreams would also become a factor in the unusual connection I had with the next woman I met and who became a true companion on our shared journeys.

CHAPTER 29

THE PARK BENCH
DIALOGUES

*Dreams are the first of the two great channels of
communication from the unconscious;
the second is the imagination.*
—Robert A. Johnson[1]

I came in through the front door of the ministry home where I was living after I was discharged from the Air Force, except in my dream, it looked different. There was a party going on as I put some gadget I was carrying on the small table by the door and figured I would get it as I left. It didn't matter what the gadget was; I'll call it a watch. Just like it didn't matter that the house looked different in my dream. I knew it was the house where I was being further trained for ministry. Dreams don't have to be literal or historically accurate.

As I was leaving the house after the party, I went to pick up my watch, but it had been knocked to the floor and was in pieces: springs, gears, tiny screws and too many pieces to put it back together right there. I knelt down and began picking up the pieces, and my mentor (the owner of the house) knelt down to help me collect them.

I had all the pieces in my hand as I said good-bye and told him I would put it back together later.

I had that dream many years after my two years of living in the ministry home. It was a picture of how I felt when I left ministry: I had all these pieces of myself that I needed to put back together. The gadget or the watch was a metaphor of me moving on from one stage of ministry and life. More than once, I found myself picking up pieces of myself after being figuratively knocked off the table. Deconstruction and reconstruction go hand-in-hand.

It was never my premeditated plan to get divorced, let alone to get divorced a second time. But there I was after a second marriage finding that my wife and I were going separate ways.

I took some solace in Ulysses tale of women giving him passage home in Homer's *The Odyssey*. After fighting in the Trojan War for ten years in Homer's *The Iliad*, Ulysses is on his way home in *The Odyssey,* which took another ten years. Joseph Campbell's insight on Ulysses' journey home is that the story shows us how Ulysses was being prepared to go home back into his more female-inflected world, leaving his warrior ways behind and being aided by women along the way.

The Odyssey is full of adventure and challenges, it's a lot like a dream with fantastical creatures, monsters, witches, gods, and goddesses. At every turn, it is women who give Ulysses passage toward home. As the story goes on, Ulysses loses more and more of his ships, men and armor, until at last he is the lone survivor washed up on Calypso's island in tattered clothes needing to be nursed back to life.

From Circe, the witch, to Calypso, who takes him in when he is shipwrecked—and a series of other female characters in between— Ulysses is getting reacquainted with the feminine world, which is different from his ten-year-long battlefield world he left behind in Troy.

The Odyssey" is the debriefing of a warrior. He has got to get back home, to leave his warrior ways behind him and return to the female-inflected world of home and bed.[2]

It reminded me of Father Andrew Greeley and his concept of viewing his pilgrimage as a journey to the tender heart of God. In his novels, many times it is the passionate love of a woman in the story that reveals the passionate love of God to the main character.

I, too, was on a journey to the tender, female nature of the Divine. Women became an important part of my journey. My second wife had helped me in a number of ways on my journey. She gave me the freedom and permission to boldly pursue a new life beyond the church. But after nearly seven years together, she was going in a different direction.

I was about to sit down at a table in a bookstore café when I heard a female voice call my name. I looked up and saw the familiar face of a lady I'd worked with on some transportation projects in my new career since leaving ministry. She was at the next table and invited me to join her.

I always liked Helen (I'll call her Helen); she was a couple of years older than me and was always professional, personable, and cool all at the same time. I sat down with my iced tea and some book I was checking out. She quickly asked how I was doing and commented that I looked a little down.

I tend to wear my heart on my sleeve and my face. I felt comfortable telling her: "I just got divorced a second time."

I'll never forget her response and how it helped me that day. She tapped me on my arm and said with a calm smile, "I've got you beat. I've been divorced three times."

I was kind of stunned and we both immediately laughed. I remember how positive and encouraging she was. It wasn't that she or I were cavalier about any of our relationships or divorces. She was able to put it all in context, to see how all the relationships had their place. Maybe we were both just "the marrying kind."

About this same time, I also discovered an old high school girlfriend via social media. She had been living in Florida for almost as long as I had. I called her on the phone; her voice still sounded the same after being out of touch since high school (it had been over thirty years since we talked). She too had been divorced and had been happily remarried for many years. When I told her I had just had a second divorce, her reply touched me. She said knowingly, "Sometimes it takes a couple of times to get these things right."

In the Evangelical church, there is no greater "sin" than divorce. In fact, some have facetiously joked that you'd be better off bumping off your wife than divorcing her, because the church will forgive you for murder, but not divorce.

It was a third woman at this time that really helped me with the stigma of my second divorce; someone I least expected.

ACTIVE IMAGINATION

In addition to my dream work, Father Walsh and I explored the practice of "active imagination" as another tool for meditation and self-help.

Robert A. Johnson's book *Inner Work* provided some practical information about Jung's psychological approach using dreams and active imagination.

> Active imagination is a special way of using the power of the imagination to develop a working relationship between the conscious mind and the unconscious. It is an age-old process that Jung reformulated into a technique that modern people could use.[3]

Johnson's book, along with June Singer's *Boundaries of the Soul*, were the best distillations of Jung's writings on the inner workings of the self that I have found. Jung's extensive writings can be very dense, and I have found that it's best to get an introduction to his works by others like Singer and Johnson before diving into Jung's books themselves.

Active imagination is a way of having a conversation with people in your life who may no longer be alive or who you may have a hard time communicating with in real life. It is like practicing a conversation or a debate and imagining what the other person might say. It is another technique or discipline, another form of meditation that can help unlock information or insights not yet evident to us. However, it is not the same as simply talking to yourself.

June Singer writes:

> Imagination, employed this way, is not the same as fantasy. Jung called this use of the imagination by the term *active imagination*, to distinguish it from the ordinary passive imagination which is nothing else than self-propelling fantasy. Active imagination is entered into consciously...[4]

Prayer is a form of active imagination: the believer talks to God, imagines or believes God is listening, and hopes to receive a word, an assurance, a verse of scripture or an insight from the engagement. Believers will say things like "I talked with the Lord this morning," when they mean that they prayed and the scripture they read spoke to them.

Active imagination actually employs the imagination, and it is called "Inner Work" because it takes work to develop the technique. It is just like any "discipline" you learn, like playing an instrument, a piano or guitar—the beginner practices and develops techniques to acquire the skill. There is a skill and discipline to active imagination. It's not just telling ourselves what we want to hear.

Robert A. Johnson writes: "Active imagination is not like some current 'visualization' techniques in which one imagines something with a goal in mind. There is no script..."[5]

Because there is no script and because the goal is not to "tell yourself what you want to hear" or already know, active imagination, when approached as intended, can reveal things to us, can help us work out what we're feeling and can unlock inner connections we can't quite see yet.

THE PARK BENCH

Active imagination is a form of meditation in which you play out a conversation with someone in your head or on paper. Say for instance, you need to work something out with an estranged or deceased relative, so you imagine a conversation you might have with that person.

This practice has become important to me over the years, but it was especially important during the time when I was single again. I used the exercise of active imagination during my nightly walks around a lake near my house. The walk around the lake is almost exactly a mile, and a boardwalk crosses the lake at either end. At one end of the lake there is a single park bench sitting on a large patch of grass under a giant oak tree about fifteen feet from the lake. I would start my walk at the oak tree and park bench and end my walk there as well.

My exercise went like this. I would walk around the lake twice. I used markers on the lake to divide up the walk, so that I gave each of my different emotions and thoughts center stage for a portion of the walk. So, for example, if I was truly angry or down or both, I would give my anger center stage on one side of the lake, then I'd allow my next emotion to have center stage from one boardwalk to the next.

Then during the last quarter of the walk, I would clear the stage and clear my mind. I would clear my mind of emotions, thoughts, and any premeditated ideas. Then in the last thirty yards before the oak tree, I'd ask myself: "Who is waiting for me on the park bench tonight?"

Then as I stepped off the sidewalk onto the patch of grass and headed to the park bench, I imagined a friend or relative waiting for me. Those sessions became so real and helpful that I called them "The Park Bench Dialogues." Usually I met a relative who was no longer alive: my dad, grandfathers, grandmothers, etc.

The secret to making this refreshing was two-fold: surrendering and not having a preconceived notion of who would be there. It was the surprise of who popped into my head that made it meaningful, spontaneous, and not pre-meditated.

ONE PARTICULAR NIGHT, as I approached the end of my walk and asked, "Who is waiting for me on the park bench tonight?" To my surprise, it was my paternal grandmother, Nana Shields.

My father's mother, Mabel Shields, had been my favorite grandparent growing up. She had been deceased for nearly twenty years when that night, to my surprise, I imagined her waiting on the park bench for me.

Nana Shields was always good with children; she was playful and fun. I remember Christmases and Easters at her home in Richmond Hill, Queens, New York. I remember spending weekends at her house when I was a kid. She was always kind, friendly and generous. She worked at a small Presbyterian Church just a couple of doors from her house. She was a good Christian lady.

That night I sat down on the park bench and was a bit teary-eyed when I confessed to Nana that I had just been divorced a second time. I was able to imagine her there and we both stood up and walked to the water's edge.

Then, as clearly as if she were standing there in person, I heard her say in my head, "You remember that I had three husbands, don't you?"

I was astounded. I had not remembered that; it must have been somewhere in my unconscious memory, but I had completely forgotten.

She recounted: "Remember, your dad's father, Guy Davis, my

first husband, died when your dad was thirteen. Then, I married Charles Lysagdt. He turned out to be a gigolo and ran off with some of my money."

I never knew my dad's father or her second husband. It all happened before I was born. As she spoke, I vaguely remembered that Dad said one time that he never liked "that man" (her second husband) and he ran off with a bunch of Nana's money. Dad called him a gigolo.

Nana continued, "Then I met James Shields, my third husband, the one you knew as Pop. He was good to me and we stayed married until our passing."

I was floored. I remember that I cried, right there by the lake. My kindly old, good-Christian, church-going grandmother reminded me of family things I had completely forgotten. My Nana ministered to me that night in a way no one else had, and it was all through the practice of active imagination.

THE UNCONSCIOUS IS AN AMAZING FACILITY. There are things down in there that come out in dreams and in unexpected moments. On that park bench over the span of two intense years, I had conversations and comforting times with deceased relatives.

The key to making active imagination fresh and not just "talking with myself" is to practice surrender in such a way that the mind is open to hear what that person you imagine might actually say. It's truly amazing when you hear them say something that you never would think to say to yourself. So in imagining the other person, the key is to allow them and their personality, their voice and their individuality, to come through.

I "saw and heard" my long-deceased grandmother so clearly that night. I felt that I was touched from the other side; it was a brushup against eternity, a thinning of the veil, a peek from behind the curtain.

That night I thought about my grandmother's whole fascinating and difficult life. How hard it must have been for her losing her first husband (the love of her life), when her son (my father) was only thirteen. It was during the depression years of the 1930's.

And yet, she and my dad never talked about it. I find it all so hard to understand why my dad never talked about his father. His dad was a decent and loving father. I could tell from the photos I have of my dad when he was a kid with his mom and dad.

My dad never talked about this gigolo who married his mom and ran off with her money. By the time I came along, Nana had already been with Pop, her third husband, for some time. Somehow you never really think much about what your grandparents were like when they were young.

By this time in my life, my mother had recently passed away. Now both parents and grandparents were gone. So I was the elder in my family, fatherless and motherless at 51.

Yet these few years before meeting another woman and marrying a third time proved to be vital years in my spiritual soul journey.

CHAPTER 30

THE WOODEN SHARD

Transcendence is the goal of all religions.
—Russell Shorto[1]

I was kneeling on a king-size bed feeling a sharp pain in my right side, toward the back just above my hip. I was in shorts and a T-shirt at a friend's condo in Saint Petersburg, Florida, loaned to me for the weekend. I yanked off my shirt to see what was happening. I looked around at the spot and saw a large wooden shard sticking out of my side. The rough-hewn piece of wood was huge and thick—a foot-long chunk, four by six inches thick, of dark weathered driftwood, like something from an ancient shipwreck. It was buried about four inches into my side.

I didn't panic. There was no blood and though the pain seemed real, I knew I didn't need to go to the emergency room. I called to my friend in the next room. I knew what this was and that I had to pull the wooden shard out myself.

I was about an hour into my first LSD trip.

THE MARSH CHAPEL EXPERIMENT

Leading up to Easter, during high holy week, twenty seminary students gathered at the Marsh Chapel on the Boston University campus to participate in a voluntary experiment. The doctors administering the test explained that the experiment was designed to explore "the psychobiology of religious experience."[2]

It was Good Friday, 1962, and the experiment was designed to test the effects of psilocybin (the psychoactive agent in LSD and "magic mushrooms") on the religious experience. Half of the students received the drug and the other half were given placebos; none of the students knew which they had been given.

The seminary students then participated in a two-and-a-half-hour Christian worship service. After the experience the students were given questionnaires and interviewed: once immediately after the service and once six months later. Twenty-five years later there was another follow-up with a number of the students. The experiment is also referred to as "the Miracle at Marsh Chapel" and "the Good Friday Experiment."[3]

Eight of the ten participants who had received the psilocybin reported both right afterwards and twenty-five years later that the experience was one of the most impactful religious/spiritual experiences of their lives. It was reported by those who followed up with the students: "Each of the psilocybin subjects felt that the experience had significantly affected his life in a positive way and expressed appreciation for having participated in the experiment."[4]

Several of these students went on to careers in social and political activism. One particular student, who became a pastor, in a follow-up interview years later, confessed to his congregation that he had taken part in the LSD experiment and said he wished his congregants could experience legally what he had experienced in that 1962 experiment.

I first read about the Marsh Chapel experiment in Russell Shorto's book *Saints and Madmen* years before my own LSD trip. I wished that my seminary course curriculum had offered me such an experience.

Through my own research, I was hoping to create my own experiment somehow. In the course of my independent study, as it often happened during these years, I would be in the right place (at a Bohemian Artists friendly bar downtown), at the right time (a Happy Hour afterwork gathering with co-workers), to overhear just the right conversation that led me to the right person to help me open the next door.

That was how I wound up in my friend's condo in Saint Petersburg, Florida, kneeling on the bed with the very real hallucination of a wooden shard in my side.

My eight-hour guided LSD experience was one of the most impactful spiritual experiences of my life. I did not go about this experiment lightly. I was fortunate to meet someone who had been a guide to others taking LSD and who had positive experiences.

TESTIMONIES

A similar experiment to the Marsh Chapel one was performed on prison inmates in 1961. This was during the time in which psilocybin and other hallucinogens were just being developed and explored; before they were labeled illegal in the U.S. in the 1970's; before all the excesses and misuses gave them a bad name.

Researchers from Harvard University in 1961 gave psilocybin to thirty-five prisoner volunteers. The test was to see if the drug had any effect of the recidivism rate. The results were impressive. At the time the recidivism rate averaged 64 percent for the prison population as a whole, but only 25 percent of the "hallucinogenic prisoners had been re-arrested six months after their release."[5]

"What surprised the researchers was that during and after the drug experiences the prisoners... talked of the experience in terms reminiscent of the great mystics of world religions."[6]

Many people don't know that Bill Wilson, the founder of AA (Alcoholics Anonymous), attributes kicking his addiction to alcohol to his hallucinogenic experience.

> "He credited his own sobriety to a mystical experience he had on belladonna, a plant-derived alkaloid with hallucinogenic properties that was administered to him at Towns Hospital in Manhattan in 1934.
>
> "Few members of AA realize that the whole idea of a spiritual awakening leading one to surrender to a "higher power"—a cornerstone of Alcoholics Anonymous—can be traced to a psychedelic drug trip."[7]

In Michael Pollan's *How to Change Your Mind*, the author extensively researched the many clinical trials that have been performed since the 1990's on a variety of patients in controlled situations. After the negative reactions and excesses of LSD use in the late 1960's, most of the research on the drug's benefits was shut down by the government in the U.S. Things began to change in the 1990's, when research began again. I highly recommend Pollan's book for those interested in this topic. There is also an excellent four-part documentary series (with the same title as the book) featuring Michael Pollan and people participating in the various experiments.

The testimonies in Pollan's book of those helped by their LSD trip are impressive.

Aldus Huxley recounted his "trip" in his now famous book *The Doors of Perception* (published in 1954). In a letter Huxley wrote after his trip, he said: "It was without question the most extraordinary and significant experience this side of the Beatific Vision."[8]

The drug gave him "unmediated access to realms of existence usually known only to mystics and a handful of history's great visionary artists."[9]

In the 50's and early 60's, numerous Hollywood celebrities were undergoing LSD therapy.[10] Movie star Cary Grant underwent sixty sessions and extolled "the benefits of LSD therapy" in a 1959 interview.[11] Grant said that the therapy helped him overcome his narcissism and improved his acting and relationships with women. He continued: "All the sadness and vanities were torn away." (He was 55 at the time.) "I had my ego stripped away... I am no longer lonely and I am a happy man."[12]

Bill Richards, the noted psychologist who led many guided psychedelic journeys in the 1960's and 1970's, said, "In the big picture... these drugs have been around at least five thousand years."[13] Richards, who has graduate degrees in psychology and divinity, said he "never doubted the validity of these experiences."[14] He writes:

> This is the realm of mystical consciousness that Shankara was talking about, that Plotinus was writing about, that Saint John of the Cross and Meister Eckhart were writing about. It's also what Abraham Maslow was talking about with his "peak experiences,' though Abe could get there without the drugs.
>
> ...the experience of the sacred reported by both the great mystics and by people on high-dose psychedelic journeys is the same experience and is "real"—that is, not just a figment of imagination.
>
> You go deep enough or far out enough in consciousness and you will bump into the sacred. It's not something we generate; it's something out there waiting to be discovered.[15]

Some of the most fascinating results recounted in Pollan's book are the clinical trials on terminal cancer patients. These were patients who were months away from death. One of the doctors running the trials was surprised by what the patients were saying in their post-LSD interviews with the patients:

> I thought the first ten or twenty people were plants—that they must be faking it. They were saying things like "I understand love

is the most powerful force on the planet.[16]

Patients who had previously expressed fear of their cancer and fear of death and what lies beyond were coming away with a new sense of their future: their fear was removed.

In 2016, articles in the *New York Times* reporting on the clinical trials conducted at NYU and Johns Hopkins said that "some 80 percent of the cancer patients showed clinically significant reductions in standard measures of anxiety and depression, an effect that endured for at least six months after their psilocybin session."[17]

Patients experienced similar feelings of extreme connectedness to loved ones, a sense of sacredness, surrender and acceptance. Many of these people were not particularly religious, and yet they felt they had encountered something out there and beyond themselves, a positive spiritual experience.

In general, people who have these mystical mushroom or psilocybin experiences have remarkably similar transformational experiences: "Even the most secular among them come away from their journeys convinced there exists something that transcends a material understanding of reality; some sort of 'Beyond.'"[18]

I managed to get through the 1960's as a teenager and never did any drugs. I remember going to parties at three different houses in three different states—New York, Florida, and North Carolina in 1969 and 1970—at which a potpourri of hallucinogens and sex partners were available in different rooms. I remember the dark music, the dark rooms, the smoke, the clouds, the gaggle of bodies strewn about on floors and couches. I remember that I didn't stay long at any of the parties; I didn't feel comfortable and decided not to participate in the activities.

It's not that I didn't want to. It was all tempting. I wanted the magical mystery tour, but I usually didn't trust the situations and sources of the drugs. The excesses ruined it for others.

During those years in the sixties and seventies there was a lot of experimentation and excess that left a lot of people damaged and some destroyed. We lost rock stars, movie stars and others to the excesses of the times. I didn't trust the substances and wasn't interested in just tripping and seeing pretty colors, or worse, having a really bad trip. So I abstained back then; looking back I was glad I did at that time.

MY OWN MARSH CHAPEL EXPERIENCE

I read about how to prepare for an LSD trip,[19] how I should have a responsible, experienced guide to lead me through the experience. I met my guide through friends. My guide had me prepare for three weeks prior to the event. I went on a special diet, I had a medical checkup to make sure I was in a good shape physically, and I prayed and meditated as I usually did during the time leading up to the evening. I approached it like a sacred rite.

I want to make it clear that I am not recommending an LSD trip to the readers of this book. However, I will say that it was another once-in-a-lifetime transformational experience in my spiritual journey for which I am thankful. I did not go looking for an LSD experience, the opportunity opened when a friend made a chance comment. That person turned out to be my guide.

A friend loaned me his vacation condo in St. Pete, and my guide told me to bring some of my favorite music and literature. My guide brought the LSD tab, which had been prepared by a credible, local elderly hippie, known for producing the purest substance. The trip typically lasts eight hours.

When I first took the little LSD tab, my guide and I were sitting on the beach in St. Petersburg on the edge of the Gulf of Mexico watching the sunset and the slowly darkening night sky. We were reclining on big wooden cabana loungers by the water outside some hotel. It was a magical start to an unforgettable evening.

When I saw that most of the night stars had colorful astral trails, I knew the LSD had kicked in. The sky lit up for me as it never had before.

It was my first and only LSD trip. It was so meaningful that I never felt the need to take another one since, and that was over twenty years ago. As with many spiritual experiences, descriptions can never quite convey the full impact of the experience.

MYSTICAL EXPERIENCES often have what has been called a noetic quality. America's great psychologist, William James, observed in *The Varieties of Religious Experience* that the mystical experience is ineffable and noetic.[20] Both point to the fact that the experience leaves such an impression that the individual knows something at a level they didn't know before and that it is so deeply felt that the words used to describe it are inadequate.

A noetic experience means that the mystical experience impacts the individual not only as a feeling, but as a state of knowing. The person comes out of it with a profound sense that important truths have been revealed. For example, in the case of the terminal cancer patients in the clinical trials, their fear of death is lifted.

RATHER THAN DETAIL my psilocybin trip, which was eight hours of magic that I wrote down in detail after the trip, I will mention a few points. After we left the beach and returned to the condo, the wooden shard experience hit me. Kneeling on the bed in some angst, I looked at this large rough-hewn wooden shard sticking out of my back. My guide assured me that only I saw the wooden shard.

I knew instantly what the wooden shard was. It was my old Evangelical Christianity. It had been nearly ten years since I had resigned as a pastor and left the church. I had worked through a lot with my counselors and on my own, so I was on a positive path by this time.

I looked down at the giant splinter sticking out of my side and knew only I could take it out. Once I acknowledged it was my old Evangelical Christianity, the pain subsided, and I realized it was part of the learning experience of the trip. I reached around and pulled the shard out and it instantly dissolved. The pain was gone.

During my eight-hour-long trip, my heightened sense of awareness was so clear that after the trip I was able to recall everything that happened during it. At one point my guide played some of my favorite music on a small portable CD player. I never heard those songs so clearly or so beautifully before. At one point, while I was lounging on the bed listening to the music from the other room, I saw the group of singers as they leaned into the microphones and sang.

During another part of the trip, I read out loud from Whitman's three-page poem "To You." The words were seared into my soul with tremendous poignancy.

The best way to describe the effect of the eight-hour trip for me was that afterwards I felt I had made peace with myself at a level deeper than I could even put into words. I had never quite used the term "peace with myself" before. I had been focused for many years on peace with God. The trip had revealed that, deep within, I had been at war with my conflicting selves. I felt as if the LSD itself was the unseen guide leading me.

As I said, I am not recommending this experiment to the readers. I am recounting my journey and my personal need to experiment for deeply spiritual reasons.

I did not enter into this without research, prayer, and preparation. If not for discovering a friend who had taken LSD a couple of times and knowing that the results were positive, I would not have had the opportunity. But circumstances, opportunity and timing converged.

My LSD trip was one of the most significant transformational experiences of my life. I related to the Hawaiian minster who, when interviewed twenty-five years after his Good Friday Marsh Chapel experience, still spoke about how impactful it was for him.

I had pursued the experience from a spiritual desire. I wasn't going into it to see all the pretty colors or wild hallucinations. Many people have bad trips or experience very little that is transformational.

"GOING TO THE GODS"

Robert Johnson in *Inner Work* writes:

> When ancient and primitive cultures spoke of "going to the gods" in their rituals, it meant in their archaic language that they approached the great and terrible archetypes of the collective unconscious.
>
> In our time it is still the fashion to think of all this as naïve and superstitious. But other cultures had a great advantage over us: They at least recognize the *existence* of the psychic realm.[21]

Russell Shorto's book *Saints and Madmen* explores how pioneering psychiatrists are discovering that what once were regarded as "spiritual afflictions" were often medical disorders that could be treated by unconventional disciplines.

Many cultures and religions around the world have used hallucinogens socially, spiritually, and ritually. "The earliest evidence for the ritual use of psychoactive drugs dates back to 800 B.C. Soma, the elixir of the gods used in Vedic sacrifices in ancient India."[22]

I must admit, the words Jesus used to describe what the church now calls "Holy Communion" and "the Lord's Supper" can sound downright primitive and cannibalistic: "Truly, truly, I say to you, unless you eat the flesh of the Son of Man and drink his blood, you have no life in you. Whoever feeds on my flesh and drinks my blood has eternal life, and I will raise him up on the last day. For my flesh is true food, and my blood is true drink." [23]

"Whoever feeds on my flesh and drinks my blood has eternal life" could be lines from a horror movie or a demonic cult ritual. How repulsive and strange Jesus' words must have sounded to his Jewish disciples, who wouldn't even eat pork.

"Eating flesh and drinking blood? What—are we cannibals now?"
"Where is Jesus going with all this?"
"I'm getting a little queasy."

So why were the Spanish priests and missionaries who reached Central America suddenly surprised when they heard the local indigenous people talking about their tribal sacrament of eating the "flesh of the gods"—which is how they translated "mushrooms"—the ones that are psychoactive and produce visions?[24]

The "flesh of the gods" sounded an awful lot like the Jesus' words about eating his flesh. Now in the Christian church, Holy Communion has been sanctified, homogenized, pasteurized and institutionalized and the "body of Jesus" is just a silly paper-thin wafer, and the wine is cheap grape juice in most churches.

The Native Americans of the New World had been using "magic mushrooms" (the flesh of the Gods), peyote, San Pedro, and ayahuasca for centuries before the Westerns came. Shamans in the South Americas use substances from different plants than those in North America. Ayahuasca and San Pedro come from the cacti that grow in their regions.

The Inquisition and the subsequent outlawing of the use of these natural stimulants by the Church didn't do away with their sacramental use by the Native Americans, it just drove it underground.

A big difference between the Church's sacramental elements (the wafer and the wine) and the Native Americans' natural stimulants was that one required an act of faith to believe something sacred had transpired, while the other delivered a direct effect, an undeniable experience. So who had the better sacrament?

MAKING PEACE WITH MYSELF

Right after, months after, and years after my one LSD trip, the overwhelming feeling I came away with was that somehow and someway in that eight-hour trip in that little St. Pete condo, I made peace with my Self at a deep level. All from a tiny quarter of an inch square paper-thin tab of LSD.

My Evangelical Christianity had put me at odds with myself. My Self had been essentially my enemy—the old man and the new man dualism. I was taught to lose, crucify, and distrust myself. My deepest self was not at peace with itself. How could it be, according to all my old theology?

My LSD trip had opened the door; that caged self was freed. Somehow, in an inexplicable, noetic, efficacious way I made peace with my divided self. It was something that happened beyond words, beyond detailed explanations.

The wooden shard that was protruding from my side was removed. A bond and a treaty were established in a way that all my religion and training had not provided me. Go figure. I knew that deep within myself was the kingdom of heaven and at the heart of it was a Divine Presence.

A few years after my LSD experience, I was working with the Navajos on the Navajo Nation in New Mexico and Arizona. I was with a company doing GIS work and making a video to promote their scenic byways. I worked with them over the span of six years. During my travels, I met and became friends with a few Navajos. I talked with some of them about their Native American church services and a couple of their elders explained how they use peyote to help heighten the worship experience. The congregants get just a pinch of the substance. The Navajos are slow to invite Anglos like myself to their ceremonies. I never asked or imposed, I just prayed that one day I would be invited.

Finally, after six years, I was invited to two peyote ceremonies. Unfortunately, I was not able to go back and take them up on the offer at the time.

My prayers would be answered in a different way a few years later.

CHAPTER 31
"THE WIND BLOWS WHEREVER IT PLEASES"

In my own personal religious life
I began to appreciate that my faith
was one of mystery, wonder,
and above all surprise."
—Father Andrew M. Greeley[1]

One thing had become clear to me during my reconstruction years: the Divine Presence was surprisingly creative. My journey outside the bounds of any one religion didn't matter to this Presence, this Him-She, this God beyond images, this Androgynous Rogue Spirit. I was discovering the mystery and unpredictable ways in which the Great Spirit moves and guides, which I was reminded of by Jesus words:

"The wind blows wherever it pleases. You hear its sound, but you cannot tell where it comes from or where it is going. So it is with everyone born of the Spirit."[2]

Think about what Jesus said: "you cannot tell where it comes from or where it is going." That's not how the church talks about what God can do. What I discovered time and again was that the categories and boundaries that had previously concretized in my Evangelicalism were being removed, erased, challenged, and jack-hammered and the Spirit was not handcuffed in my life.

I turn again to Maria Popova's book *Figuring,* with its insights on transformational experiences and the paradox they present us:

> Because our imagination is bounded by our existing templates of how the world as we know it works, we fail to anticipate the greatest transformations—the events and encounters so unmoored from the familiar that they transfigure our map of reality and propel us into a wholly novel mode of being.[3]

Popova uses the term "existing templates" in the same sense as I use "paradigms" and "paradigm shifts." She notes that these templates (which constitute our mindsets, doctrines, belief systems, etc.) limit our imagination of how our reality works.

Meanwhile our religions try to formulize, systematize and program how the Divine is expected to work. Our religions want to define and label the "orthodox" and the heretical. The church has been wrong many times about whose ideas and discoveries were heretical.

Sometimes our religious constructs can box God out; religion can be one of the greatest obstacles to spirituality. *"The Spirit blows where it wills."*

What happens when things happen around us that are "unmoored from the familiar" or are out of the ordinary? What happens if we are unable to process these within the scope of our expectations, beliefs, and existing mental constructs?

Modern man is hesitant to acknowledge the supernatural and the mystical and instead looks first for scientific explanations and empirical proof. That makes sense. I'm all for that. I've heard Christians all too often attribute something to God, when clearly they didn't look closer. We trivialize God and make him some kind of genie in a bottle with unlimited wishes. (I'm sorry, but praying for a parking space close to your favorite store and then finding one is neither an epiphany nor cause for a big "Thank-You, Jesus.")

What if the "unmoored" event challenges our paradigm of how the unexplained interacts with our personal "map of reality?"

MY MOTHER'S PASSING

When my mother passed away, something happened that didn't quite fit into my "existing templates." My mother, June Lillian Davis, had been treated for breast cancer for a year. Then suddenly one day she fell at home and was taken to the hospital. She contracted pneumonia and over the next week she went into a coma. She was only 73, but she didn't pull out of it.

After a few days in intensive care, it was clear she was barely breathing on her own and was close to the end. We met with her doctors.

My brothers and I were standing around her in the hospital bed just before they took her off the breathing device. She was unconscious and we had no way of knowing if she heard us. I prayed and held her hand. It was January 2000, the turn of the century. I counted the years and I realized that she had been a widow and single now without my Dad (her only husband) for 25 years. She never wanted to remarry after Dad died, even though we all encouraged her to meet someone.

I think she didn't want to face a new century without him. She was a true romantic, I probably got that from her. I talked to her more than prayed to God. I told her we didn't want her to leave, but if she felt she wanted to, we understood.

Moments later the machines were turned off and she breathed her last. I couldn't take it. I was a wreck. She had been such a beautiful, loving, strong soul, a wonderful person, human being, and mother. She had moved to Florida in the mid-1980's to be close to my family and her first grandchildren. All my brothers had moved down here also, so she finally left New York to come and live near all of us.

I walked out of the hospital room. I needed to walk so I wouldn't collapse in tears. Something unusual and, for lack of a better word, mystical happened. I was distraught and overcome with emotion.

As I stepped into the hospital hallway outside mom's room and turned the corner to another hallway, a powerful gust of wind blew through me with such force that I stopped for an instant to make sure there wasn't a huge hole in my abdomen; it was that real. It was clearly not an actual gust of wind, but it was as unmistakable as if someone opened a window and a strong storm wind hit me. I steadied myself by placing my hand on the wall. Was this mom's spirit blowing through me and off somewhere that these spirits go?

Then, as I continued walking the hallway, my eyes blurry, something else out of the ordinary happened. I hesitate to tell this story, because I don't want it to seem like this is weird or these things happen often to me. They don't. But at the same time, that's exactly what transcendent moments are: they are out of the ordinary and timely.

I had a lucid dream as I was walking and awake. Clearly, I had entered into an altered state in my grief and devastation. I didn't want to go to the hospital crying room, I needed to walk and be alone. I needed to hold myself together at the hospital; I could break down later at home. To this day, I don't know how to explain this, so I'll just tell it like it happened.

As I got to the end of the hallway where it turned in two directions, I noticed to my right two locked double doors, each with a round porthole-like window. I turned and looked through the porthole windows, which were blackened. There was nothing to see in the dark windows. I tried to open the doors; they were locked.

When I peered again through the blackened window, I saw a panoramic scene: a big, lush garden of greenery, and way down below in the garden were my mom and dad standing together, as vivid as a Technicolor movie.

My vantage point then changed, like it does sometimes in a dream. Now my point of view in the dream was as if the camera were behind my mom and dad, without them knowing I was there. From that viewpoint, far off in the distance high above the forest of green, I could see what mom and dad were looking at in the sky.

They were looking at a porthole far in the distance with me peering through into this garden. That was when my mom said, "He's not coming now, is he?" My dad said, "No, not yet."

The lucid dream ended right there, and I was standing at the dead end of a hospital corridor looking at darkness through a porthole. I turned around and kept walking the hallways to collect myself before going back to talk to the doctor and the rest of my family.

HOW DO YOU DESCRIBE THE MYSTICAL?

I don't know what that was empirically—the wind and the dream. But I know the gust of wind and the lucid dream were as real as my mother passing away that day. I counted it another gift from The Presence; another reminder of both transcendence and immediacy; both deeply personal and unexplainable.

We read in the Bible of people having visions and dreams that seem otherworldly. The prophets especially had some strikingly visual visions. But usually, the church tells us, these special moments are reserved for the prophets and saints.

Maria Popova's explanation helps clarify these moments for me:

There is a singular strangeness to those moments when we find ourselves unmoored from our own being, when something seems to pull us beyond ourselves and shock us into recognition, however momentary, that the self is not a static monolith we take it to be but something dynamic and situationally sculpted into various possibilities of being.[4]

The dynamic self and the dynamics of spirituality can operate beyond the bounds of the existing templates we each construct by our individual belief systems, religions, doctrines, experiences, and sciences. I was pulled beyond and outside of myself. The wind and the dream that day helped me from falling apart and being admitted to the hospital. More than any theological construct of the afterlife, those two happenings that day gave me hope and comfort when I had nothing left.

ALTERED CONSCIOUSNESS

Call it a transformational experience, or a paradigm shift, or a remapping of how I thought the world should be. Call it a mystical experience with a noetic and ineffable quality. My consciousness was altered in my last moments with my mother; I was speaking to someone it a coma, I believe she heard me, as did The Presence with us in the room and in each of our souls. In my grief, I went into another level of consciousness as I walked the hospital corridors blocking out all other people for those few moments.

I remember other times of altered or heightened spiritual consciousness. I remember the altered state of consciousness I had singing with 700 other men at a Christian conference in the Blue Ridge Mountains in the 1970's. I remembered altered states of consciousness I had in a handful of other memorable worship services. I've had the occasional altered state after having a few glasses of alcohol.

We are all used to the jolt from caffeine in that first cup of coffee in the morning. There are a variety of altered states of consciousness we experience.

I know my mother left this earth with a flair that I will never forget; the gust of wind and the vision of the garden. I knew she was at peace and so was I.

Michal Pollan writes that "the human brain is an inconceivably complex system—perhaps the most complex system ever to exist."[5]

EVOLVING STAGES OF THE JOURNEY

Whenever I get too settled in my image of who "God" is and what "God" can do, it is as if the real Cosmic Presence (both within and without) swoops in and challenges my assumptions and images. This Deity, the Him/She, the Androgynous Other defies my images. I remind myself:

It's a journey. Don't get too comfortable in the Shire just yet. This is a nice spot to linger for a while and refresh, but the trail leads on. There are more surprises just around the next bend, over the next ridge.

Herman Hesse's famous novel *Siddhartha* has spoken to seekers for decades as it has for me. Hesse's father, mother and grandfather were strict Christian Pietist missionaries. He spent his early childhood in a dormitory for missionaries in Switzerland. He escaped at 15 from a Protestant boarding school housed in an old monastery. His battle with these early religious influences is the subject of many of his novels. He wrestled with this education that was designed to subdue and break the individual personality.

Set in India with a quasi-Hindu spiritualism, Hesse's *Siddhartha* tells the story of a young man on a spiritual journey, a quest, and the stages or passages he goes through in his continual awakening. Siddhartha leaves his home and goes in stages from ascetic withdrawn from the world, to his rejection and dissolutions of the self, to a stage of immersion in the world and the senses. He experiences love and beauty from the beautiful courtesan, Kamala, and success in business. But still not finding the peace he is looking for, he leaves all that behind and ultimately finds peace with himself when he learns to live in harmony with all of life and what it has to teach us..

On his journey he must reconcile the conflicts of the opposite worlds; but neither strict asceticism nor the complete immersion in the life of the senses is the answer. It's in the balance.

Hesse's book sought to break down the dualisms of Eastern and Western religions and spirituality and to help imagine a bridge between the Western and Eastern paths of spirituality. Siddhartha's first stage is essentially the "unselfing"[6] and freeing himself of everything. We are told that "he killed his senses, his memory." [7] "I do not desire to walk on water," said Siddhartha. "Let old samanas content themselves with such tricks."[8]

After exhausting himself on the ascetic path, which is similar to Christian asceticism and denials of self, he awakens and realizes: "I was afraid of myself, I was fleeing myself!.... I will no longer let Siddhartha slip away.... I will no longer murder and dismember myself... I will be my own pupil."[9]

Debasing the self is not the answer in any spirituality that hopes to heal the soul. The journey varies for each seeker; but many aspects and stages of the journey are archetypal for all seekers, regardless of church membership or religion.

DEFYING CONVENTION

Losing my mom was another personal blow. At the age of 51, I was now the "elder" of the family: both my parents were gone, all my grandparents were gone. During these few years of being single again I met a friend who challenged my presuppositions in new areas and ways.

She was not a "born again" Christian, she was not raised in the church (even though she was from the south and Bible Belt country) and yet she was more "Christ-like" in so many ways than most church or "Christian" woman I had known. We recognized each other as seekers on a spiritual quest outside the typical religious paths.

We first struck up a friendship while working together; she was the first person I met other than Father Walsh who had not only read

Carl Jung, but could teach a course on him. I was impressed. It seemed she was one of the few people who could talk about "the spiritual journey" in terms other than the predictable Christian terms. She was farther along on the path than I was in many ways.

Maybe my mom was sending me an angel of sorts, the right woman at the right time.

CHAPTER 32

THE GODDESS I NEVER KNEW

The eternal feminine draws us on.
—Goethe[1]

I t was coming up on Easter. It had been 24 years since I left ministry, tore my study Bible in half and began a second journey of faith. It had been 48 years from the time I accepted Christ at age 19 and spent the first 24 years of my life as a "disciple," lay minister, seminary student and local church pastor. The symmetry of the 24 years "in" and 24 years "out" struck me.

How had leaving my first faith gone? How had this second journey of faith gone in these most recent 24 years? How had the "reconstruction" of my faith gone? Was I in a better place spiritually and otherwise?

As I've been highlighting in my story, I had left a number of things behind. I had changed the voice of God in my head. I had completely reimagined "God," the Transcendent Divine, The Presence, the Great Spirit. Gone for the most part were the old "Yahweh-Jesus" Doppelgängers.

I had avoided joining any one local church, denomination, or institutional religion. I had a string of new mentors and writers who helped provide new insights and expanded views. I had close friends and mentors who helped me along. I was now a grandfather with more grandchildren on the way. Life was good and getting better. There were still more spiritual highs and spiral circle inclines and vistas to come.

UNUSUAL GRACE

I spent four years being "single" after my second divorce. I dated and traveled. I met a woman through work and we were friends and co-workers for six years before ever striking up a dating relationship.

She challenged more of my old Evangelical Christian assumptions and categories of thought. She was from the Bible belt south but had not grown up in the church, yet she was deeply spiritual. She had a goodness and clarity about her that drew me. She was brilliant, a great artist. What struck me was that she was so open and interested in the spiritual journey, yet she was on that path without being in any church or organized group.

I remember being confused and intrigued by her clear-eyed ability to see the value in various spiritual disciplines and the best of people. She had a BA degree in Art and Film and was knowledgeable in a wide variety of disciplines like literature, psychology, Gnosticism, Hermeticism, music, the tarot and astrology, as well as being one of the best read people I knew. She was brilliant.

My old "evangelical" categories of thought popped up: I had never looked into the tarot and astrology much. These types of things were always viewed as "satanic" or black magic by Evangelicals.

As she explained them and demystified them for me, I could see that they were not Satanic at all. Maybe some people misused them,

292

but they were not Satanic. Here again were my old categories of thought being corrected. I was both impressed and intrigued by this gracious, intelligent woman who exuded goodness and kindness. I was drawn to her goodness and her ability to not be corrupted by these things.

It reminded me of the passage where Jesus corrects his listeners and says that it's not what goes into us that defiles us, but what comes out of the heart. Is there a purity of heart and an incorruptible spirit in some of us?

This was also a time of intense dream activity for me. Father Walsh was working with me on these in my counseling sessions. I was reading and learning about the Kabbalah and Taoism and meditating using the Tree of Life from these traditions.

I would eventually date Stephanie after we had known each other as friends and co-workers for eight years. We discovered that we both had seminal dreams about each other long before we were dating. Our spiritual paths wove together. This was someone who "got" me. We eventually married and she has been a godsend for me. We are also business partners and owners of a multimedia company.

Stephanie and I soon found others like myself who had also left their first faiths and were on the path to a more embracing spirituality. To my surprise, I was not alone in my unorthodox spiritual journey. I found to be true what I had read about in one of my favorite author's works. Thomas Wolfe, the American novelist, wrote:

> *To lose the earth we know for greater knowing,*
> *losing the life we have for greater life,*
> *and leaving friends we loved for greater loving,*
> *to find a land more kind than home, more large than*
> *earth.[2]*

THE GODDESS

One of the aspects of my Evangelicalism that I sought to change when I left ministry was the "Trinity Boys Club" patriarchal-heavy Christianity. One of the things that helped me change the voice of God in my head was relating to The Presence as the Goddess, the Feminine Divine Presence. Music and poetry had played a big part in this. When I prayed and "dialoged" with "God" it was mainly with the Female Goddess, not the "Father" or male God.

MUCH OF CHRISTIANITY is an extremely patriarchal religion. It wasn't always that way. Reading the early Gnostic Christian writings there was more emphasis on the female. Unfortunately, in the first couple of centuries of Christianity, there was a battle between the different factions of this nascent religion. One faction wanted the Church to become a respected institution in the empire and won out over the Gnostics (and others), who were not as concerned about "institutionalizing" the faith.

I was listening to more female singers after I left the church. I was seeking a more tender female voice, image, and presence of the Divine.

The Divine Presence is many things, can appear in many forms; it contains male, female and androgynous characteristics. I realize not everyone sees the Divine as a person, or a type of being as such. In my spiritual constructs, I have always imagined "God" as a person, a being in whose "image and likeness" we were formed. I grew up in Protestant churches, where God was Father, Son, and Holy Ghost; they were distinctly male, a patriarchy. It was not something you could escape when I grew up. It's strange to me that none of us asked: "Where's the mom?" It was too big a theological leap for Protestants to see Mary as the Mother of God like our Roman Catholic friends did.

For some reason, when I approach the Divine Presence as female,

I find I open up differently and feel less guarded. Perhaps relating to the female Goddess-Mother frees me from so many of those associations of the militaristic, mission-oriented, commander-in-chief Yahweh images that took root for so long. Perhaps it's because in the family I grew up in the men tended to be silent, the women talked more.

I remember first noticing this after returning home after my four years in the Air Force. I remember there was a big party for me with family and friends. I paused for an instant between the family room and the kitchen and took in the sight: the men were gathered around the TV watching football, not talking; the women were gathered in the kitchen cleaning up and talking. I went into the kitchen to be with the women. That's where the family energy was, the laughter, the casual warm conversation. You got to know their personalities and their kindness. When I hung out in the TV room with the men, the conversation was about the game; you didn't talk about feelings and personal stuff. The men tended to be guarded and self-sufficient. The women tended to be open and honest.

From then on at family events and church gatherings, I made sure I gravitated over to where the women were gathered, because the conversation was usually more engaging, personal and fun. I knew what the men were talking about: usually sports, cars, work.

I liked Father Andrew Greeley's concept of viewing his pilgrimage as a journey to the tender heart of God and the Goddess.

My mother and her gentle, consistent acceptance and love had been an example of the Goddess mother. My grandmother, who had married three times, was an ever-pleasant joy and a light. It was Stephanie, who seemed truly to be one of those "angels" from a higher plane, who came down to engage with me.

A PERSONAL JOURNEY

My journey has been rather unorthodox; my own independent study course. In one of Joseph Campbell's analogies about the personal nature of the spiritual journey, he likens it to each of us facing a great dark forest:

> "Each entered the forest at a point that he himself had chosen where it was darkest and there was no path. Where there's a way or path it is someone else's path; each human being is a unique phenomenon."[3]

An analogy from the American West has helped me understand that different types of people have different motivations and identities in the great adventure. There are explorers, pioneers, and settlers. The Explorers and Discoverers are the ones launching out into the frontier and finding what's out there beyond the ocean, beyond the Mississippi River, beyond the Rocky Mountains; they find the routes, the water and the destinations, mark the trails and make maps. The Pioneers come after them; the ones who follow the new maps and trails and carve out a place on the frontier. Then come the Settlers with their families; they help build, fill out and establish the towns.

I found out I am more an Explorer and Discoverer type. I enlisted in the Air Force and took my chances; I was the first in my family to leave my home state and move far away; I planted a church as a pastor. I worked with two start-up companies in industry and started my own company with my wife. Some people are the pioneers, some are the settlers. I would be fine out on the spiritual frontier; I had sufficient tools and training to know how to make my way.

Not everyone needs their own independent study course, like I did. Many need the steady security of a good local church. But don't be lulled to sleep.

FROM GOTCHA'S TO AHA'S

As I mentioned previously, my Evangelicalism had become a continuous program of rooting out every possible shade of sin. This determination to "be ye holy as I am holy," this calling from Yahweh wound up morphing into a "Gotcha" kind of Father Superior inner accuser. It was a sin-oriented system with a minefield (and mindfield) of "Gotcha's."

> *"Oh, you feel good about your Christian progress?"*
> *"Gotcha! Now you're guilty of pride and lack of humility."*

It took the better half of my first ten years away from the church to root out the many tentacles of that mindset. Father Walsh would remind me again and again, "Phil, you're not a fundamentalist. And it's okay." Reprogramming our mind is a process.

I read a few of Father Andrew Greeley's books. He was a Catholic priest and novelist. In his novels there were always depictions of what I describe as the Aha's of grace. I replaced the "Gotcha's" of my strident, perfectionist Evangelicalism with "Aha's" of grace. These are moments of realization, sometimes epiphanies, of a great good divinely unfolding for me.

In his novel *An Occasion of Sin*, a young Catholic priest is assigned to investigate a recently deceased priest who is being considered for sainthood. The investigating priest had some negative impressions of this possible "new" Saint from previous encounters; and his investigations reveal some reasons he thought the priest should be disqualified from sainthood. However, the investigating priest also discovers that this priest he is learning more about had clearly been used by God in some astounding ways. He discovers both the "Gotcha's" and the "Aha's of Grace" in this flawed but saintly priest. Greeley uses these masterful "comedies of grace," as he calls them, to show us the surprising Aha's of God's grace that come upon us when we least expect them.

Father Walsh giving me the permission to move on from my first faith meant a lot. I was not an Evangelical and it was okay. My new "blended faith" was being enriched by the wisdom of other religions.

I also took permission from Walt Whitman's poetry. The debate about Whitman's sexuality goes on. Was he gay? Was he bisexual? Did he have any children? Whitman never said. However, he did love women and men. It was irrelevant to me. I believe it is precisely Whitman's ability to relate to men and women, his celebration of the beauty of both sexes, that make him such a great celebratory herald of the Divine and the Human.

Whitman challenged me to continue my journey and experience life and spirituality firsthand, not second or third. Here are some of his lines that really hit me from *"Song of the Open Road"*:

> *From this hour I ordain myself loos'd of limits and imagi-*
> > *nary lines...*
> *Listening to others, considering well what they say,*
> *Pausing, searching, receiving, contemplating,*
> *Gently, but with undeniable will...*
> *I am larger, better than I thought,*
> *I did not know I held so much goodness.* [4]

This was a time for me to accept and experience the mystery. Thomas Aquinas, the great theologian, put his finger on the great paradox, the great irony of knowing the Divine. In *Summa contra gentiles*, he writes: "One can know God only when one knows that God far surpasses anything that can be said or thought about God." [5]

Michael Pollan talks about being the doorkeeper of our thoughts and what goes on in our head. He says we should address the voices in our heads, the thoughts that sometimes gain the soapbox, the megaphone inside. We should ask, "What are you doing in my mind? What do you have to teach me?" [6]

This central locus of control within each of us (the Self) is what I was asked to crucify and hand over to Jesus (aka Yahweh-Jesus) as a young Christian convert. But now, I had finally taken personal adult responsibility for reconstructing my connection to the Divine Presence.

After 24 years outside the Evangelical church, I was able to see the beauty and wisdom in many of the world religions and mythologies. I was able to move beyond a faith that was based largely on scholastic dogma and belief in certain rigid doctrinal and theological constructs, to one that was more experiential and open to all wisdom and truth.

After 24 years on the outside of institutional religion, I found that The Presence was on the outside with me the whole time.

CHAPTER 33

INVITATION TO MY SILENCE

To you my prayers are no blasphemy.
—Rainer Maria Rilke[1]

A fter doing a minor spiritual inventory of my progress, I was on my way to my favorite beach that April morning. I had just realized it had been 24 years since leaving the church. It was a weekday. I had managed to take the better part of the day off to spend a couple of hours at my favorite sanctuary: an hour away on the soft sand, gentle surf beach of the Atlantic Ocean at Canaveral National Seashore in Florida.

It had been one of my spiritual health practices to regularly spend a half day at the beach; when I hit my sixties it was usually weekly. I had spent many hours on these beaches over the 48 years since moving to Florida. From my days as an Airman at Patrick Air Force Base in Cocoa Beach, from long walks and meditations along the beaches from Indialantic Beach and New Smyrna Beach to these beaches and dunes at Canaveral just north of the Cape and NASA's facilities.

I distinctly remember what I said under my breath as I approached the boardwalk through the dunes, with my backpack on, carrying my beach chair, umbrella and iced tea. I decided quite spontaneously to talk to "Jesus" for the first time in many, many years. I was still in the habit of praying and meditating and seeking the Spirit all during these years, but I had stopped specifically addressing "Jesus" and his Father (Yahweh).

But this morning, as I set foot on the boardwalk passage through the dunes, I said in prayer quite bluntly: "I won't give you any crap about your stuff, if you don't give me any crap about mine.... I invite you, Jesus (just Jesus, not Yahweh) into my silence." It was that straightforward, and somehow, I knew I was understood.

And with that I proceeded onto the beach and enjoyed two hours reimagining Jesus. At one point, I opened my well-worn copy of Rainer Maria Rilke's *The Book of Images* randomly, as I used to do at times with my Bible, to see what I would read at that moment.

A brief note about Rainer Maria Rilke, the poet, who along with Walt Whitman, were the poets who helped me regain some sanity.

Rilke's mother had hoped she would have a girl. When she delivered a baby boy, she was so disconsolate that she gave him two girl's names—Rene Maria—and raised him for the first few years as a girl. When Rene Maria Rilke left home, it was one of his early lovers (Lou Andreas-Salomé) who suggested he change his first name. She gave him the more masculine name "Rainer" (pronounced "Riner" like diner in German), which meant "Pure" in German. He wrote his *Book of Hours* poems in Russia, adopting the persona of a cloistered monk to compose his poems to God.

I find that Whitman and Rilke are excellent complements. Walt Whitman is the herald, the prophet. Rainer Maria Rilke is the monk, the mystic. Whitman is the orator out among the people. Rilke is the quiet one, alone in nature. Whitman is the magnanimous, free-spirited God who loves and celebrates his creations. Rilke is the quiet contemplative writing poems, trying to paint God to get inside the head of this Dreaming God. Whitman expounds and waxes on without apologies. Rilke compresses and chooses words carefully, packing a lot into a few words. Whitman preaches and sings the glory of humanity and all the world. Rilke prays and liberates God, humanizes and personalizes the Divine. Both voices are in me, and I find expression through both these poets especially. Walt is my Gospels and Psalms; Rainer is my "Book of Common Prayer."

Whitman's poems are contained in one volume: *Leaves of Grass*. Rilke's poems were released in several volumes; however, the two that I use most frequently contain primarily his spiritual poems: *Book of Hours* and *The Book of Images*.

A BRIEF NOTE of personal context: At this time I had been writing and producing music with a band that I formed, Peyote Moon, for about seven years. We had released several CD's of our original music on iTunes, Spotify and the usual online outlets. I had built a music and recording studio in one of our bedrooms. We had been performing out around town for six years at the time.

I had rediscovered the creative outlet that music was for me. Songs came pouring out and music became a part of my working through my inner processes. I wasn't doing it to make money; I discovered it was part of who I was as an artist.

The first poem I read that day on the beach, upon randomly opening my Rilke volume, while imagining a fresher "Jesus" there on the beach, was titled *"Music."* Using active imagination, I imagined Jesus picking up and reading the poem:

> *What play you, Boy?... Lo! Your gypsying soul....*
> *Your young life is strong, but how much more strong*
> *is the longing that through your music sighs.*[2]

It all seemed personal and surprising. Rilke's poems always hit me personally, but I was surprised at the direct connection with me and my music. I had written and recorded nearly a hundred songs by this time.

The poem even went on to say be still, be silent. I imagined Jesus reading as if he had selected the poem. Rilke's words were like an uncanny nod to my "invitation to silence" and the bad tapes and old dialogues from my Jesus-Doppelgänger Evangelicalism.

I thought, *"Hmm, Jesus knows his Rilke better than I do. He went right to that poem."*

The nod and encouragement to my music seemed remarkably personal. I always felt a large part of my music reflected my spirituality. One of my more personal "prayer" songs was inspired by a Rilke poem.

I often sit out by a campfire on cool nights on my back porch by the pool. I wrote a very personal song, "Circling." It was inspired one night when I imagined myself sitting with Jesus at the campfire. It began: "Not really sure where we stand these days; been so long since I've been down on my knees." I used Rilke's lines from his poem *"I Live my Life in Circles"* for the chorus with slight variations: *"I circle about God"...through millenniums...am I a bird...or am I a wild storm or a great song."*[3]

I put Rilke's book aside and pull out from my backpack Whitman's *Leaves of Grass*. Whitman titled many of his poems as songs: "Song of Myself," "Song of the Open Road," "A Song for Occupations," "Song of the Answerer," "Song of Joys," etc."

It was almost Easter and it was the 15th week of the year (according to my iphone). Whitman didn't number his stanzas, but the publisher did. There are 52 stanzas in "Song of Myself," one for each week of the year. So I imagined Jesus turning to Stanza 15 of Leaves of Grass where he read: *"The pure contralto sings in the organ loft.... "*[4]

Whitman starts off his long montage of people with a singer of a song. What follows is like the script of a music video. Whitman gives us a rapid fire series of vignettes of people, humanity, in homage to mankind: children, wives, shore men, prostitutes, peddlers, trappers, brides, presidents, carpenters, opium eaters, and on.

There was no MTV or YouTube then; so Walt paints word pictures. Along the way he mentions Thanksgiving and when he mentions the 4th of July it hits me: it's "Jesus" reading Walt Whitman and it is Easter week: Independence Day and resurrection to new life all in one. There is no great story in Stanza 15; the story is the people, individuals, the great colorful diversity of humanity. Whitman, the great "everyman," identifies with all:

> I am of old and of young, of the foolish as much the wise,...
> Maternal as well as paternal, a child as well as a man,
> Stuff'd with the stuff that is coarse
> and stuff'd with the stuff that is fine...
> A learner with the simplest, a teacher of the
> thoughtfullest...
> Of every hue and caste am I, of every rank and religion[5]

This is Whitman, a modern Jesus, "the caresser of life" (Stanza 13), the great Androgynous Him/She who embraces one and all. Like a God incarnate, he relates and inhabits the breadth of humanity. He picks up the song/music theme:

> With music strong I come, with my coronets and my
> drums,
> I play not marches for accepted victors only,
> I play marches for conquer'd and slain persons.[6]

Whitman has been called our "American" Jesus because he embodied the greatest of Jesus' ideals: love, grace, peace, mercy, goodness, and acceptance. Harold Bloom in the introduction to this anniversary edition of *Leave of Grass* writes: "We are accustomed to Whitman as Asian (Hindu, Buddhist): he is our *Vedas*, our *Bhagavad-Gita*, our *Sutras*. But he is also our *Zohar*, an esotericist or extraordinary originality."[7] Whitman embraces all people, all spiritualities and wisdom without ever being "religious," so to speak.

That morning, an Easter week morning (or the 4th of July spiritually), there on the soft sand beach, I imagined a long-haired Jesus in t-shirt and board shorts reading Walt Whitman to me in a beach chair under a beach umbrella. The Great Presence, the ever-present Holy Spirit, is well-versed in Whitman and Rilke.

I had not been to an Easter Sunday service in over twenty years. I did not go to an Easter Sunday church service that week either; I had other plans.

Instead, I started a new ritual that morning. For the next four years I would meet the Presence on the beach on Easter Sunday alone and have my own Easter Sunday early morning sanctuary time. Each of those next four years on Easter Sunday I would discover a Rilke or Whitman passage that would be one of my themes for the coming year.

So did this time on the beach mean that Jesus was "back" for me? Did it mean I somehow saw the light again in Christianity and had my second "coming to Jesus" moment?

That's not what happened. This particular encounter that day on the beach did not mean that I was back with "Jesus," that we were close again. It just meant that maybe—just maybe—I was able to deal with that particular mask or image of the Divine again from time to time. Maybe.

CHAPTER 34

SETTING BOUNDARIES WITH "GOD"

I had to wrench myself free of God,
so to speak, in order to find that unity
in myself which God seeks through man.
—Carl Jung[1]

When Yahweh appears in the Bible, you can never quite be sure how he'll appear. He appeared as a Burning Bush to Moses, as a Pillar of Fire to lead the Israelites through the desert, as an Angel of the Lord, as a man wrestling Jacob, and as a baby in a manger to the Wise Men, to list a few.

Whenever the Angel of the Lord appears in the Old Testament, he was terrifying, because the first thing he had to say was, "Fear thou not," to the prostrate humans. To the prophet Ezekiel, God appeared and "looked like a human," but he was blazing like fire and was surrounded by strange creatures with various animal features.[2]

When Moses asked to see God, he was told that he couldn't

handle it and it would kill him. So Moses hid in a cleft in a rock because God needed to pass. As God passes, Moses sneaks a peek.

There is more between the lines here. What does Moses see when he peeks? God's back. Notice how God describes himself in human terms from the passage in Exodus.

"But," he (God) said, "you cannot see my face, for man shall not see me and live." And the Lord said, "Behold, there is a place by me where you shall stand on the rock, and while my glory passes by I will put you in a cleft of the rock, and I will cover you with my hand until I have passed by. Then I will take away my hand, and you shall see my back, but my face shall not be seen."[3]

God speaks of his face, his glory, his hand, and his back. Moses was allowed a glimpse of God's back, but not his face. Whether this is a literal event or mythic moment, one message from this incident is that mankind is not able to see the full countenance and glory of Yahweh without it doing damage to our physical being.

When Jesus appeared in his resurrected form and body to the two disciples on the road to Emmaus, he was clearly viewed by them as just another human on the road. It was only after he left that they realized it was Jesus. In a way Jesus was kind of messing with them. Jesus could have appeared to them in a way they would have immediately recognized—as he looked when He was among them. But he chose to appear incognito, undercover.

In Greek Mythology, the Gods and Goddesses often appear to men and women in some disguise: as an animal or a mythical creature or some such earthly manifestation that they could perceive. Christians seem to think it strange, even primitive, when we read of Gods doing this in other world religions. Yet, there is an underlying truth in all these instances, Christian or otherwise. These celestial beings, Yahweh and whoever, need to alter their appearance because humans cannot see the Divine Presence without being disintegrated or imploding or however our death would ensue.

It makes sense, then, that they would have to appear to us in some less terrifying form to avoid annihilating us. So they cloak themselves in some fanciful form. When Moses peeks, God is already ahead of him and in his "cloaked" form. Seems God chose a Titan appearance, a towering human barely clad, which was kind of a sign of how close God felt toward Moses. God could have appeared in armor or royal robes, but there is a clear picture of God willingly granting Moses a peek at his human-like personage.

We read in *The First Book of Enoch* that when Enoch is raised into the heavens and given his vision, Enoch says that the divine luminaries were shining bright and could morph into human form at will. "Those who were there were like flaming fire and when they wished they appeared as men."[4]

OVER THE YEARS of deconstructing and reconstructing my faith, I came to understand that my Christianity, training, and indoctrination came with pre-packaged "images" of Yahweh and Jesus. It's telling that in the Old Testament Yahweh tells his people not to make any "graven images" of Him. And yet, we do make images, even if it's not a literal "golden calf" that we construct. From all the many paintings of Jesus with fair skin and an Anglo look, to the scores of medieval paintings of judgment, and the gaggle of bodies suffering in Hell, Christianity has depicted our faith for us in countless images, usually suited to our race or ethnic preferences.

As a Christian it is difficult to escape the "images" that come to mind when describing Yahweh in the Old Testament: He is vengeful, angry, jealous, capricious, short-tempered, xenophobic, patriarchal, dangerous, and shows extreme favoritism. It's clear Yahweh was male, a definite "He," who is portrayed in anthropomorphic terms. Anthropomorphic simply means having human characteristics.

I knew I needed to change these predominantly Evangelical Christian "images," or as Joseph Campbell calls them, "masks of God." They are the faces, the looks that God chooses to show himself through, manifestations of something and someone so otherworldly and celestial that the only way we can relate is through "earthly" imagery we understand.

It took some time, but I was able to move on beyond those primary Yahweh-Jesus masks and realize that this Divine Presence, this Supreme Spirit, is far more diverse and complex than the Yahweh-Jesus images that I had limited the Presence to. The Presence manifests itself in multiple masks, faces, or images.

When Walt Whitman wrote that he "contains multitudes," I was reminded that so does The Divine Presence.

Hinduism recognizes that the Divine Presence manifests itself in thousands of Gods. Our Christianity has limited God to a Trinity of Father, Son and Holy Ghost. Roman Catholicism allows for Mary, the Mother of God. But it all begs the question, "Where is mom? Where are the Female Goddesses?"

I believe that the Divine Presence is One, but contains many. I believe the Divine Presence is energy, but also is being and person. I believe we are "in the image and the likeness" of the Divine Presence regardless of how we got here. I believe that we are "God's fair form" and that our physical being reflects that Divine Presence which is within and without.

I would still get tripped up from time to time by Yahweh taking the soap box and inner spotlight. It was usually triggered by something. Going to an Evangelical or similarly conservative Christian church became difficult. After Father Walsh recommended that I should "not go to church for a long time because it made you sick," I stayed away a long while and have not returned.

I would on occasion attend a service conducted by Father Walsh at his Catholic parish; or my friend Father Bob's Episcopal Church, or the big European-style Episcopal Church in downtown Orlando because I could connect with the awe through their remarkable choir and glorious architectural surroundings.

The three or four times I visited a church, usually at a friend's request, I came away knowing I couldn't go back, not yet. It was not that the service was unpleasant. It's not that it was objectionable or offended me. It's just that some things now trigger a whole slew of connections that I have long since severed or changed.

I know I could go back to some churches, and I'd probably be fine. Someday, perhaps, I'll feel compelled to attend regularly again. But for now, I have my own spiritual rituals and sanctuaries.

SETTING BOUNDARIES WITH THE OLD "GODS"

I remember one particular neighbor who would always pop up whenever I was outside. He would want to talk and talk and command my time and attention. I had to kindly set boundaries with him to let him know that I have a life and things to do. We set boundaries in relationships and move them as we need to. It's the adult, mature thing to do.

I realized that I have the freedom to set boundaries with these old images of "God." It was my episode at the beach and the invitation to silence, as the previous chapter recounted, that helped me see that.

A week later I went back to the same beach, that sanctuary stretch by the Atlantic Ocean that I go to regularly. I went back and thought, "Let me see if I can read some passages from the New Testament." So I brought one of my old Bibles. I still have a collection of my old study Bibles. I still have the Bible I tore in half that day in 1993 when I left. I have several different translations of the Bible. I also have a large Davis Family Bible from the 1800's and I have an old German Bible handed down from my grandmother. But that day I brought with me my first leather Scofield Study Bible purchased a week after accepting Christ as a young Airman in Cocoa Beach in 1969.

I started reading some passage in one of Paul's epistles. It was a bad idea.

It's difficult to explain how some old passage that used to contain a wealth of theological information for me could now have the effect of a really bad trip or hangover. It brought up a lot of old pain, consternation, and disagreement. For one, I believe that Christianity today is more Paul's religion than Jesus'. I can appreciate some parts of scripture, but Paul's epistles can be problematic.

I knew I couldn't read some of this stuff anymore with the same constructs I had when I was in my twenties. Not yet anyway. It carried too much old baggage that I had painfully discarded. Now it was like some old family wound brought up and ripped open at a reunion.

I thought, "This is why it was an invitation to my silence." I don't need Yahweh-Jesus to start their usual "We need you on our Mission for God" guilt trip routine.

I had said to Jesus, "I won't give you any crap about your stuff if you don't give me any crap about mine." I can't do this again. They always want to get their teeth into me, always the guilt trip, always something they want me to do for them. It's tiresome. It's their way or the highway, just like so many of their Christian churches.

For me, the tentacles of the old mindsets of the tribe, the cult, can easily reappear in full force. They were and they can be relentless: all the guilt, sin, possessiveness, purity, Lordship demands, plus all that "We're on a mission for God," Trinity Boys Club, Warriors with a Battle-Cry Zeal that winds up rearing its Taskmaster Head.

I HAD another scuffle with Yahweh-Jesus right there with the waves of the Atlantic slapping my chest with a crash. It hit me that I don't trust this "Yahweh-Jesus" mask of God. It always ends up with the "Gotcha's" and the guilt.

For me it is a different kind of trust now.

Technically the words belief, trust and faith can be used interchangeably and are supposedly synonymous. But "trust" in someone's character is different from belief in doctrines or statements of faith.

I don't trust the old Yahweh-Jesus I used to trust; I no longer trust being in relationship with them. They are too demanding, and for all the talk of faith and peace, it's way too transactional with them. All the talk of God's love and peace and comfort doesn't work any longer for me. I spent too many years under their thumb.

The God and Goddess beyond the single particular Evangelical mask is who I want to glimpse, to get a peek of the back of the Divine if nothing else.

I felt used after a while, fodder for their mission. I don't want a God who is a Warrior on a Mission, even if He says that now he's a Prince of Peace. It's the same mission! Like Father, like son, like Holy Spirit. I don't trust a "God" who needs to be appeased with blood sacrifice.

I don't want to have to defend Yahweh's Old Testament record or the church's theology and authoritative stance. I don't want to have to defend Jesus as some one and only savior. I believe that I can relate to a Divine Being beyond all that, a more loving, caring Divine Presence without the theological pillars of Evangelicalism, Christianity or any one religion. It's a blended faith for me. These days, I have more in common with mysticism and Hinduism than Evangelical Christians. Today, I'm more comfortable with an honest atheist or agnostic than with most Evangelicals.

In healthy, adult relationships, people have to set reasonable boundaries and negotiate the terms and expectations of the relationship. When people marry they have to do this, whether it's conscious or unconscious. People need their space, privacy and times of social engagement and intimacy.

We need to relate to the Divine Presence as adults, not as children or sheep. In setting boundaries with "God" I wasn't choosing to limit what the Presence could do, I was limiting how we related and how I thought of and imagined "God."

That day, I decided that I needed to negotiate the terms of my relationship with "God," the old Gods, and any of the Gods seeking to take over and dominate me again. I had managed to unconsciously set boundaries with Yahweh-Jesus when I left the church and when I asked God to let me have my house back.

MY OWN HOME AND PRIVACY

So I deliberately set boundaries with those Gods. That's how adult relationships work. It may seem strange or contradictory to, on the one-hand be open to anything the Presence may bring my way, but on the other hand to set boundaries with "Gods." But it's more like not allowing yourself to go backward. It is about knowing yourself and being your adult self. It is like knowing your body's dietary needs and precautions.

Out beyond the boundaries of my old religion, I found a magnanimous, celebratory, outlandish, and beautiful Divine Presence. I wasn't going to go backward to the old gods and their masks.

I broke up with my Yahweh-Jesus roommates years ago and had them move out. Recovering my own house, my own self, my own locus of control and healthy adult freedom were what I needed in order to heal. I wasn't going to have them move back in and take over my house again. The terms were different now. I had moved along and I felt bad that they seemed stuck in who they were. But I realize now, they are just the particular tribal masks of God that had concretized in my culture and religion, and I had grown up with them as the old acceptable masks. The bigger Deity, the Presence was always within; an inner flame, a light and quiet goodness, a spirit that can lead me into truth. I no longer want a faith chained to one "God" image, one religion, or one book.

WRESTLING TO EARN RESPECT

I never thought my Evangelical Yahweh-Jesus "God" conveyed any real respect for the individual.... No respect for privacy, our humanity. The whole "lose yourself and deny yourself" strangulation of the individual, and the debasing and dehumanizing of man killed that faith for me.

Yes, you can find verses that say God loves, "chooses," and forgives individuals.... But my Evangelicalism left me feeling "that God" and "his people" don't really respect the humanity of man, my human-beingness; it shows in the dogma, practices and overall veneration of "doctrine" and the institution over the "person" and the believer.

I have felt more spiritual connections, at deeper levels and more experientially, since leaving the church than my first faith provided a foundation for. The journey does require some work, some effort, putting in the time on the trail. Today people want the quick experience, the formulaic instant karmic experience, as if it was a pill that imparts the mystery and meaning of life.

In my seventieth decade now, I feel more at peace now. And I see how this was probably the only way I could have gotten here. I see now that the path was there even when I thought I had lost it.

There is so much to learn, embrace, celebrate, and experience in life and in the spirituality and wisdom of many other religious and world traditions. I choose to not be limited by the Evangelical Yahweh-Jesus doctrinal tribe. Nor do I believe any one religion has the corner on the truth or the One and Only God. There is one truth, there are many paths, some marked, some not so much, some still to be discovered.

It's complicated for me to communicate why I choose to avoid the institutional churches now. Perhaps the analogy of work and retirement suits it best. Going to church for me is like going to work, back to the workplace, after I have retired from there. I don't experience church quite the same way as I used to. It served me then; but now I've moved on.

As I've said all along, this is one man's story. Others have found their place and their peace with their Christianity. For some of us, the deconstruction and reconstruction of our faith were necessary for our souls and well-being.

PENANCE OR FORGIVENESS

Set in South America in the Eighteenth Century, the movie *"The Mission"* (1986) has Jeremy Irons playing a Spanish Jesuit priest as he establishes a mission among the tribal people deep in the jungle beyond the waterfalls. Robert De Niro plays a slave trader who preys upon tribal people. He kills his brother in a fit of jealousy and is imprisoned.

There is a wonderful scene of penance and the surprise of forgiveness that reminds us of why stories can be so powerful, and how true grace is beyond our expectations. The imprisoned De Niro prays with the Jesuit priest and decides to enter the Jesuit order to atone for his crimes. As they journey to the mission deep in the jungles, they come to a waterfall that they must scale and go beyond. De Niro feels compelled as an act of penance to carry all his warrior armor in a heavy bag as he climbs the waterfall to meet the tribal people in the mission.

We watch as he climbs barefoot up the slippery rocks alongside the Falls with this impossible weight of his past sins. At one point, the priest mercifully cuts the chords of the weight of his armor and lets it fall into the water below.

Then at the summit of the waterfall De Niro kneels facing these angry tribal people. These are the very people who he used to hunt and sell as slaves. He kneels before his enemy. They have every right to kill him and he knows it. He kneels in surrender, awaiting their knives...when much to his surprise and relief, the tribal people start to laugh and instead of killing him, they welcome him in all forgiveness and grace.

That is what it is to realize Divine grace and forgiveness. The weight of all those sins and the torturous penance we feel compelled to endure to "pay for our sins" and to appease our own inner tormentor are not necessary. For me the weight I carried was a jumble of Evangelical dogma, a patriarchal "God" who rarely if ever was satisfied, and images of that Deity that were old and limiting.

The cord is cut. The weight falls.

I finally had the weight cut and watched it drop into the water, I finally realized I didn't need to climb the waterfall carrying all that to punish myself for my past—and for just being human. I finally was beyond the angry greeting and knew it was a friendly celebratory greeting that embraced me.

It was after reaching this point of peace and nearing my seventieth birthday that I would be surprised again by another transformational experience.

CHAPTER 35

SAN PEDRO CEREMONY

Judaism and Christianity are popular religions...
They ought to be a little more available than they are
to the opening of the door to transcendence."
—*Joseph Campbell*[1]

On my last trip to the Navajo Nation, I finally received two unsolicited invitations to one of their Native American church peyote ceremonies. Though I had prayed that I would be invited, I had not mentioned the subject to either of the men who extended the invitation. Unfortunately, I was unable to take up either offer because at the time I was due back in Florida. Both men gave me their cards and said I should call them the next time I came back. Several years passed and I had not been able to make the journey back to the Navajo Nation. But something else came along instead.

SAN PEDRO

A friend of mine invited me to a Pan Pedro Ceremony close to home in Florida. The San Pedro Ceremony was conducted by a Shaman. It was an all-day event with 14 others at the home of a friend. San Pedro is the South American "sacred cactus" similar to North America's Peyote cactus.

San Pedro (*Trichocereus pachanoi*) is the sacred cactus (Huachuma) that has been used for 5,000 years by South American Shamans, specifically in the Andes Mountains of Ecuador and Peru. South American shamans and healers (curanderos) consider the San Pedro cactus a visionary teacher plant used for healing, spiritual guidance and traveling in other dimensions.

San Pedro is a hallucinogen. Though not as strong as Peyote or Ayahuasca, it does have some mescaline in it. The San Pedro Ceremony is essentially a heart opening ceremony that can bring a healing effect on partakers.

The timing could not have been better for me. I had been making good progress writing this book about my spiritual journey. But for the previous two months I had found myself drawn back into some of my old anger about my Fundamentalist/Evangelical roots. Going back, reflecting, and writing about some of those earlier passages of my life sucked me back down into old dark spiritual thinking.

I did some research on San Pedro, which I had not heard of before. I will admit that I was a little suspicious. They say that during these ceremonies participants often "meet" San Pedro (Saint Peter from the New Testament).

I doubted that, but thought I'd give it a try and go with an open mind. San Pedro Ceremonies are healing ceremonies. I felt I could use some inner healing and I was grateful to have been invited.

MY SAN PEDRO CEREMONY

The Ceremony Day would be a 10-to-12-hour time of reflection, meditation, healing and hanging out with the other people who were attending. It was much like the format of many church retreats, conferences, and workshops I had attended over the years, but the similarity ended there. I was not prepared for how profound and life changing my San Pedro experience would be.

The Shaman was unassuming in appearance. He looked like one of the attendees; he was a middle-aged man in shorts, sandals, and a white Oxford shirt. He was handsome, smiling and warm.

We were all on the tile floor in a house somewhere outside of Miami on sleeping bags or mats with our pillows as the shaman began. He explained that the purpose was for each of us to go deep inside ourselves, to surrender and let San Pedro work. There would be three sessions in which we would be guided by his chants and music. Each ceremony session would last an hour to 90 minutes. In between the sessions we would take breaks to sit outside in nature, have a small group session with the Shaman and have a meal as the day went along.

We each drank our small cup of San Pedro. It tasted horrible, so I just chugged it down and washed away the dreadful taste with some water. The Shaman also made it clear that we may meet San Pedro, who has come to be called the gentle grandfather. I was a doubter, but okay, let's see what happens.

The Shaman then began chanting and singing in Spanish, blowing smoke with his ancient tribal pipe and alternately playing recorded music. I felt myself slipping into a meditative state.

Whole scenes played out in my mind's eye, as if I was watching a movie with my eyes closed. For me, it was like a Technicolor lucid dream. I came home that night and wrote down everything that happened to make sure I remembered every detail.

This is an account of what I experienced, heard, and saw in my

San Pedro Ceremony. This all took place with my eyes closed, lying on my back on my sleeping bag on the tile floor at a home somewhere west of Miami.

SESSION ONE

At first there was a long period of darkness as I waited to get to my place of surrender. The Shaman led us through a series of breathing exercises. During this time, I was acknowledging some of my anger. "Where are they?" Where are those Old Testament and Medieval Gods, the wrathful punisher, those cold, harsh judgmental Gods of antiquity that took root in me from a young age? I need to clear up some things with them.

To be precise and honest, what I really said was, "I want to talk to the S.O.B.'s!" That's how ornery I felt that day.

The first words that came to me from another voice in my head were: "Forget the Book, the Bible. It's about Spirit," the gentle voice said. That wasn't my voice. I have been meditating and going deep within for years; I know my voice from other voices.

Then in my vision, it was as if I stepped out from behind a black curtain. I was now walking down a white stone staircase in a bright white, enormous, outdoor amphitheater down toward a ceremony at the center of the open-air festival. I was wearing a robe with a boy walking right in front of me, my hand on his shoulder. He was about chest high, and I didn't ask who he was, though later I would realize who he was.

I was aware that I was a Priest and that my calling, ordination, and path as a pastor years ago still counted. Then suddenly there appeared behind and around me my five grandchildren (I now have two more grandchildren) and we were heading to the ceremony below.

And at that moment, in the room where we were physically lying on the floor on sleeping bags, the Shaman blew some powerful smoke from his pipe on my chest. It was as if he knew the right moment to do it, like he was in my vision, as if his smoke were a kind of ceremonial acknowledgement of my being a pastor/priest.

I spoke my intentions in the vision as we continued down the white stairs: "I have come seeking a new voice, to make a new peace with these Old Gods. I want to return to the peace I had a few months ago."

It was a beautiful scene as my grandchildren were now leading me forward. Lucas, age 9, was on my left. He held my hand and arm as he led me forward. Faith, age 14, had my right hand and arm leading on the other side. Leon (8), Kajus (6) and Leja (4) were on either side next to me. And there was a young boy about 12 years old walking with us, right in front to me. I didn't wonder who he was; somehow, I knew.

I was aware there were a couple of figures far off at the bottom of the stairs where we were heading, but I couldn't really see their faces. I was aware that in this amphitheater there were other people way off in other directions, but I didn't look to see what they were doing. Lucas was leading us toward the figures waiting down on the center stage. "Come on, Pepa, we're almost there," Lucas said.

It was clear that Lucas was leading the way, as if he had been here before or felt very comfortable here. (I believe now it's because his mother is from Mexico, so he was connected with the part of the Mexican, South American world of the Shamans and San Pedro. He knows Spanish, so he understood the chants, although I didn't.)

Then as we approached the two figures in white, Lucas said to them as our spokesman: "This is my Pepa, he has come for help. Can you help him?" ("Pepa" is how "Papa" came out when he was little, so it has kind of stuck. I've always liked it.)

The scene then seemed to fast-forward, and I was lying on my back on a straw mat in the same enormous white amphitheater center stage and the five grandkids were around me like nurses, making sure I was comfortable. They were covering me with flowers and sage. Leja was drawing her little designs on small pieces of paper and putting them on me, while Kajus was running toy cars on my legs, and Leon had his hands on either side of my head. He leaned in and said, "There's no danger here, Pepa."

Faith was next to my head and said, "I think they will come soon, there's nothing to fear here." Lucas was on the other side of my head, saying, "You'll be okay, Pepa. These are the good guys." I realized I was the offering, and they were presenting me, preparing me for what was next.

Then I was standing up and they were all behind me and I was moving forward, not knowing where.

"Show yourself," I asked nervously, still feeling uncertain and a little ornery.

I heard a clamor of voices.... But saw only two nebulous figures asking what I seek.

"I come seeking a new voice. My voice has become garbled these last months and I have been sucked down into the old darkness of my struggles with these Old gods. I've been drawn back into the void and want to be restored as I was months ago when we were at peace." I said none of this out loud, but it was clear in my dream vision.

Then the Shaman called us out of the session. He took a couple of groups of four into private prayer sessions while the rest of us went outside to enjoy nature and reflect. I recounted in my mind my meditation session out under a beautiful giant Camphor tree. I was hoping somehow there was a way back to that scene that was interrupted.

SESSION TWO

Before the second session, the Shaman offered another cup of San Pedro to those who wanted it. I took another cup, chugged it down in two gulps, washed it down with water and tried not to hurl. Then the Shaman began his chants, pipe smoking and blowing of smoke to the four directions. I was on my back, eyes closed, wondering what's next.

The challenge of these sessions is getting to that place of meditation where your mind is open and surrendered. It is like a waking dream state, in which your mind is free and things come to mind that you would never dream up yourself, the way we have wild and imaginative dreams that come upon us in our sleep.

Remarkably, when I went into my meditative state, I was back in the white ceremony amphitheater where I left off the last time. There we were again: me on the offering matt, the five grandkids kneeling around me. (I really was surprised to find myself back in the vision. Typically, as in a dream in the night, once you wake out of it, it is hard to get back into the same dream.)

Lucas was calming me down, "Don't worry, Pepa, this won't be scary."

I was feeling fearful now, because I was expecting to be in trouble with "God" (Yahweh, with whom I had the biggest beef). I was expecting a "talking to" with recriminations and some rebuke. I had broadened my spirituality way beyond my Evangelical roots and believed things differently than I did, so I was expecting to be called out for not being an "orthodox" Christian.

My fourteen-year-old granddaughter, Faith, was describing what was happening. She said, "I think they are going to take you to another place alone, but it will be okay."

Suddenly, I was standing before a big white altar, knowing I am going to speak to "God" or some celestial representative.

Then I was walking up a different white narrow stairway. It seemed everything was white and blue, like the colors in those photos of the Greek Island Santorini.

Glancing back and way down below I saw my three grown children, each with their children: Steve was with Lucas and Leon, Scott was with Kajus and Leja, Kim was with Faith and she's holding Hope (my four-month-old sixth grandchild). But they are so far down below they appear barely two inches tall. Yet I had only walked a couple of steps.

I heard someone say, "Papa is a Priest, he is going now where the priests go. We have to wait for him here until he comes back."

Then I was sitting on a simple, blue corner couch with room for several people and I was looking through a blue tinted glass and way down below I could see my children and grandkids standing and waiting.

Then I was aware of His Presence next to me. This Person was suddenly there on the couch next to me and the Boy who had been with me was sitting on his opposite knee. The Person was large and exuded calmness and clarity. I didn't see his face, his head was within inches of me, close to my right ear, and his arm, nearly weightless, was around my shoulders.

He was so close to my ear, he practically whispered as he said in a soothing, calm voice of genuine apology: "Forgive me, forgive us…. If we have somehow failed to come through to you as we really are. You know there are no Dark Gods here. Forgive me, us… if we were misrepresented to you."

He said "you know" in a way that implied that he knew I knew. His voice and words were so clear. He just asked me to forgive Him.

The nearest I can get to describing this person is that he was oversized, like a seven-foot-tall NBA basketball player. I was aware this was San Pedro. We each knew who the other was; there was no need for introductions.

I am not embellishing or exaggerating. This was as clear to me as a movie on a giant color HD screen. What struck me was an over-whelming sense that he knew me and had been with me all my life. I had an unmistakable feeling that he was truly glad to see me. Few words were spoken; much more was communicated without words. I had an overpowering feeling that this being was pleased to see me. I had a sense that he trusted me.

I couldn't draw his face, but his eyes and mouth communicated the warmth and joy he exuded. There was not a hint of accusation or disapproval, no recriminations, only an overwhelming sense that I was family, we had a bond.

Looking down on my family below through the blue tinted glass, he said, "They can't see us now. But it will seem like you were gone for just a second."

Then San Pedro said with a tone that communicated we were somehow on the same level and frequency, "You know what is right and good about us... don't let the dark moments steal the knowledge that we are good."

There it was again: he trusted me, my inner soul self.

He turned to the Boy sitting on his knee and he said to me as a Grandfather might say casually with a smile to his son, "Take care of this Boy." It was said not as an order but in love. I could tell he adored the Boy.

But who was this boy? I wasn't sure at the moment.

And he said, "Again, forgive me and us for however we may have failed you... and him in the past." I was utterly humbled, my anger gone, replaced by more tears.

All during this time, the Shaman was moving around the room chanting, but I was on the floor, my eyes closed and fully immersed in this experience. I was in tears on the tile floor of a house in Miami. I felt my body shaking as I tried to contain my tears.

I asked San Pedro with a bit of an edge, "Where's Jesus? I want to see Jesus."

San Pedro said, "You don't need to see Jesus now... it gets kind of crazy when he shows up. People fall on their knees and start asking all these questions he's been asked a million times."

Then we were walking. San Pedro hoisted the Boy on his shoulders. "I want to show you something."

Within seconds the three of us were engulfed in what I could only refer to as the Hall of the Gods. A chorus of "OM's" (as in Hindu meditations) in deep mysterious voices overtook the room. Remarkably, the Shaman's music seemed timed to this moment.

325

How did he do that?

I was enthralled and awestruck. The Halls of this room extended up to the dazzling darkness of the heavens. It was like a cylindrical cathedral of stone columns extending high up until they dissolved into the darkness of the night sky, a dazzling darkness accompanied by the celestial sounds of a chorus of baritone OM's.

For what seemed like a long time, I stood with San Pedro and this Boy listening and caught up in the mystery and otherworldly and beautiful sound of the chorus of OM's. I was never so moved in all my life by a sense of the Divine. I never felt the need to fall to my knees. I felt lifted up, humbled to be there and have this experience.

There were no words, just Spirit, oneness, yet a personal separateness, a distinct me and this Boy. I now understood that this Boy who had been with me through the whole vision of San Pedro, that the Boy was my Soul Self, my eternally youthful soul self.

Then at that moment on my sleeping bag on the tile floor, the Shaman asked me to sit up.

I sat up but kept my eyes closed, as the Shaman blew smoke from his pipe on the top of my head, and then down the back of my shirt, and on either side of my head. Then he took both my hands and sprinkled water over me.

It again seemed like remarkable timing by the Shaman, as if he knew what was going on and as if he was in my San Pedro vision. How could this be? I was trembling with tears, awe, and wonder.

Then San Pedro took me and this Boy back out of the Hall. He said, "You are not able in your human form to fully comprehend or see the Gods. It is part of the earthly limitations."

Then we were back behind the blue tinted glass on the blue couch, and I saw my family way down below, still standing and waiting.

San Pedro's final words were: "You know what's good and right about us. We know you know. So hold tighter to that than to the grip of lies and dark ruminations that can suck you down into despair and untruth."

San Pedro then looked at the Boy Me and his final words were, "Take care of this Boy." He said it with a smile as he jostled the Boy's hair.

As if right on cue, the Shaman called us out of the session.

How did he do that?

CHAPTER 36

TAKE CARE OF THIS BOY

Who are you that wanted only to be told
what you knew before?
—Walt Whitman[1]

T he San Pedro Ceremony was finished, but there was more to the day. The Shaman took groups of five into private sessions with him. He took my prayer group of four to an outside porch where it was quiet. The Shaman never asked any of us about our sessions or what we went through or saw during the ceremony. But then, using a stack of Illustrated Cards (with paintings of gods, goddesses and mythological characters from various cultures and religions), the Shaman asked me to break the deck and restack it. Then he drew four cards for my "reading." He did this with each of us in the group one by one.

THE ARCHETYPAL CARDS

Here is the part that further amazed me. The four cards he drew from the top of the deck that I shuffled were so representative of my San Pedro vision that I was astonished. I will explain them below. I had never seen any of these cards or this type of card deck. But here are the four cards he drew for me. The Shaman went counterclockwise starting with the upper right card laid out on the floor: Pluto, Daimon, Phanes, and Arete.

The Pluto–Hades Card represents not negative dark things, but the deep mysteries of God and the underworld. Pluto guards the mysteries of the Deep, the underworld. I had just been to what, for lack of another term, I called the Hall of the Gods and the dazzling darkness.

The "Daimon–Genius" Card was the one that particularly struck me. The card shows an Adult man with a smaller, golden, illuminated figure of a Boy in front of the adult. The card points to the higher self or the spirit double within each of us. This was a picture of what I had seen in my session vision. The Greek word "Daimon" refers to a lesser guide or guiding figure.

The Phanes Card is the card of "unconditional love." And the image again reinforces the young, innocent Child-like nature of the Soul. Phanes in Greek mythology was the generator of life; his name means to "bring to light."

The Arete–Virtue Goddess Card once again reinforced the words of San Pedro: you know what's good and true. The Greek Goddess Arete sits above the clouds in the mountains and calls us to virtue and excellence.

I never told the Shaman or anyone in my small group what happened in my ceremony experience. I was nearly speechless. I was so moved at how the cards lined up with my meditation vision.

REFLECTIONS

In all my years on the spiritual path, this San Pedro ceremony and vision was the most profound and overpowering transformational experience. I was in awe; I felt humbled and honored. My years-long anger and suspicion had evaporated, due to an unexplainable lucid dream on a sleeping bag on a tile floor in a small modest cement-block home in the suburbs of an old Florida neighborhood.

I was struck that there was no hint of recrimination or rebuke from this "San Pedro" figure. There was no sense of guilt or acrimony. And there was no list of things I was being given to do other than the main one: "Take care of this Boy." His use of "you know" when he spoke indicated that he knew that the truth was within me and he trusted me. Imagine a God who would trust us as adult human beings.

In fact, the presence of the Boy-Me was a sign to me that I have recovered that young eternal soul within me. He didn't need healing; rather, he was my healing. I had worked at recovering him since my early sessions with Father Walsh in the mid-1990's when his counseling showed me how that young boy me had been crushed under a dark Fundamentalism.

Though I could not describe San Pedro's face, the details of the face were not what was important; it was beyond an "image" or a face. It was more the look; what he conveyed in his eyes and smile. It's interesting to me that everything else in my vision was crystal clear, like a movie before me, but San Pedro's face was just beaming eyes and a smile. Even more memorable were the calm, soft voice, and the powerful, safe Presence.

I had an overwhelming sense that this Being, this "San Pedro" was encouraged to see me and this Boy and felt affectionate toward us both.

Our souls are the young Boy or young Girl within us. Our souls have that youthful, childlike goodness and innocence that children have. But sometimes our Soul Spirit Child is lost, damaged, abused, and hard to recover. Our souls get locked in a cage or are barely recognizable anymore.

Our souls can also be abused, just as children can be abused. It's not always about the harsh abuse; abuse can come in incidental ways, seemingly casual, innocuous ways; we can hurt our souls like children with words, sometimes in ways that neither of us understands in the moment.

I will never forget and never get over San Pedro asking, "Forgive me... us." I never in all my years of theological studies, reading and spiritual practices ever heard anyone suggest the idea that God or the Celestials would ever ask us to forgive them.

In my Evangelicalism, it was always me asking God for forgiveness. Those words from the San Pedro Ceremony were the most moving thing of the whole day.

Certainly, after centuries of all the ancient texts and religions that man has birthed, the Gods must feel a bit misrepresented.

I was also amused by San Pedro saying, "You don't need to see Jesus... things get a little crazy when he shows up." I could go into a lot about all that. I understood the wisdom of San Pedro on that point. Things do get a little crazy when Jesus comes around. I'm fine meeting with the Lesser Angels.

GOING INTO THE DAY, I never actually thought I'd meet San Pedro. My cynical, suspicious New York City boy thought, "Yeah, right."

The Shaman said people do meet him all the time. But I had set my expectations low for the ceremony, because I wasn't sure how it would go and didn't want to have the bar set too high and then be disappointed.

The other thing that struck me was that San Pedro used my grandchildren in the vision. What's interesting is that San Pedro is called the "Gentle Grandfather" shamanic experience.

To quote a *Huachumera*, a San Pedro Healer:

San Pedro teaches us to live in balance and harmony; it teaches us compassion and understanding; and it shows us how to love, respect, and honour all things. It shows us too that we are children of light—precious and special—and to see that light within us.[2]

How can a plant do that? What is it in a natural, magical substance, be it cactus or mushrooms, that can communicate so consistently something so spiritual? If you want to know more about these things, read Michael Pollan's 2021 book: *This is Your Brain on Plants.*[3] He covers how caffeine, opium, and mescaline work. He, too, has experimented.

How is it that a plant can produce such an altered consciousness in me? How is it that the shaman's cards lined up so succinctly with my lucid dream? And how is it that the shaman seemed to enter my dream as if on cue? Perhaps the greater consciousness that inhabits the natural world and our own consciousness is all connected in a way that allows the Divine Presence to move freely. The Spirit moves as it pleases.

WHENEVER I TALK about this experience, I will affirm that as supernatural as it may sound, "I met San Pedro," or whoever that celestial being or lesser angel was. Perhaps it was the True Self within, as Krishna said in *The Bhagavad Gita,* that God is the True Self within each of us. Just as Jesus said that the Kingdom of God is within. If you go deep enough within you will find the Divine Presence. I don't know the color his eyes or hair, but I heard his voice, saw the look and caught a glimpse of his smile. I will carry his words with me until I see him again. For me, it was similar to a lot of the near-death experiences people have reported.

I am not suggesting or encouraging you or anyone else to participate in a San Pedro Ceremony. I am merely reporting back my experience for what it's worth.

The Shaman and others I've read say that the San Pedro Ceremony is often transformative and healing. The Ancients have used the cactus and the ceremony for 5,000 years to help heal, get direction, and sort things out in people's lives. Though these Shamanistic practices were squelched by the Roman Catholic Church when they took over South and Central America, the Shamans never stopped their work.

In lieu of my peyote ceremony with the Navajo in Arizona, I was invited to a San Pedro ceremony in Miami. It came to me, I didn't even have to sign up or engineer it. Synchronicity had been working.

That day in that modest room, all the Shaman's prayers and chants were about God, his grace, goodness and how each generation must find God for itself. I didn't know that at the time, but a friend who was also there knew enough Spanish to tell me what the songs and chants were about.

The Ceremony was healing and life-changing for me. If I never participate in a San Pedro Ceremony again, that will be fine. I was transformed by my one San Pedro Ceremony.

PART FIVE
ENLARGING MY FAITH

CHAPTER 37

THE GARDEN OF THE WORLD

Man, like the rest of creation,
is simply God become concrete.
—Carl Jung[1]

EASTER SUNDAY

I make my way early on Easter Sunday to the beach, passing the launch pads, the block-like VAB (Vertical Assembly Building) at Cape Canaveral in the distance. Thick overcast clouds of varying shapes and layers cover the sky. Rain is forecast for about noon. I come prepared; I have layers of clothes.

Today, the ocean is a slate gray color, a limpid sea with single rows of waves rising lazily and then nonchalantly cresting with little intent but to creep along to the damp sand.

To the north there are a few people well over two football fields away; to the south, a fisherman or two. I have plenty of private space.

I come with songs today, my own hymns. With a little portable speaker, I play four new recordings I wrote with my band; these are the pre-mixed tracks: songs of a seeker; dialogues with The Presence.

. . .

I OPEN to Whitman's *Leaves of Grass* and select his *"Children of Adam"* collection of sixteen poems. The first poem is only twelve lines: "To the Garden of the World;" Whitman packs a lot into those few lines. The first line is: "To the garden of the world anew ascending."[2]

Whitman's new Adam is a resurrected man. No longer in the Garden of Eden, he is launching out into the Garden of the World. This new Adam is not exiled, fallen, or descending into darkness; rather, he and the world are "anew" and "ascending."

Content with what life was in the dreamy Garden, the new Adam awakens to his new world, as if from a slumbering dream.

Whitman's new Adam is not turning back and trying to reenter the idealized Garden. What's past is past. We're not meant to return to childhood. We will again when another cycle is repeated.

This Adam sees the Garden of the World not as a descent, not a demotion, not a letdown after the cozy comfort of the past, but an ascending. He is not dissolving into Satan's world, but this new Garden is every bit God's world, full of potential, meaning, being.

Whitman's Adam continues:

> *Potent mates, daughters, sons, precluding,*
> *The love, the life of their bodies, meaning and being,*
> *Curious here behold my resurrection after slumber.*

This new Adam, rather than fallen, has been resurrected "after slumber." He is looking forward to the sons and daughters he will bring forth. He stands curious. He has been reawakened. Whitman returns to his theme of slumbering to refer to a previous state of semi-consciousness. He is now on the verge of a new life, a new world.

I am wearing a white t-shirt under a white long-sleeved pullover today; Easter Sunday white. The sun suddenly bursts through the clouds. I look up and see that the wall of clouds is moving off. I remove my long-sleeved shirt. Maybe it's not going to rain after all.

Whitman's new Adam is awestruck:

> *The revolving cycles in their wide sweep having brought*
> *   me again,*
> *Amorous, mature, all beautiful to me, all wondrous.*

He is part of these revolving cycles of life in which we grow. Arrested development was never in the cards for this Adam; this is about ascension, a cycling up the spiral staircase.

Whitman, ever the Hopeful Herald, is turning our "concretized" image of the Garden of Eden and Adam and Eve on its head. We were not expelled; we chose to know what the Gods know, the knowledge of good and evil. It is the essence of life itself, growing from children, to mature adults, to fathers and mothers, to grandparents. Whitman's new Adam sees it is "all beautiful" and "all wondrous."

Whitman is aware he is speaking to a new era, to the Modern Man and Woman. He is challenging the religious conventions of his day. Whitman is presenting an alternative to the Victorian Era that had taken hold of his times with its repackaged Puritanical constraints based upon its high horse of Biblical judgments. Why are we still shackled and chained to these ancient stories of this harsh God? Whitman challenges. Why must we be subjected to a millennia-old story that man was doomed from the start because some "first couple" had the curiosity and desire to know what the Gods know?

Whitman sees the exit from the mythical micro-Garden of Eden as an awakening from slumber, a coming to consciousness.

> *My limbs and the quivering fire that ever plays through*
> *   them*
> *for reasons, most wondrous.*

As if just thrust from the micro-Garden, his limbs and body are still "quivering" and tingling from the fire of the two flaming swords at the garden's gate. This is his new consciousness, a new level of seeing and feeling. He is a new Resurrected Man. It's "most wondrous." He awakens to awe, not despair, not a tarnished, desultory existence. It is still good. He chooses to see and believe it is good.

He is not at odds with his Maker. Whitman's God has not turned his back on his creation, but released man and woman. There is no talk of a God who regrets his "creation." There is no talk of a God who is somehow surprised that his creations ate of the wrong tree and now he must punish them. This world, contrary to some religious beliefs, is not God's Plan B—it still is plan A.

> *Existing I peer and penetrate all,*
> *Content with the present, content with the past.*

Whitman's twelve-line poem is one long sentence with one period coming at the end of the last line. "Existing I" is his self-recognition, his awakening to himself, to consciousness. He takes it all in: "I peer and penetrate still." There is much to take in, much to explore, much to ponder, and much to experience first-hand.

The Resurrected Adam, the new man, is "content with the present" in his new Garden of the World. He is "content with the past." There is no blame, no pointing fingers, no remorse, no "woulda coulda shoulda."

This is not about the debasing of man and his humanity; none of the degrading and shaming of God's greatest creation.

What more could he ask for? He is resurrected, he is curious, he is at peace, self-aware, and feels the "quivering fire" pulsing through his being; that eternal spark of life and love. He is sentient and able to feel and sense.

The short poem ends with this:

> *By my side or back of me Eve following*

Or in front, and I following her just the same.

This new Adam is not blaming Eve for taking the fruit; he has not made her pay or made her subservient. Whitman's new world for the Modern Man has not become a Patriarchal world where women are lesser than man. The new Adam has the new Eve at his side, equal. In the new Garden of the World ascending, the new Adam can lead or follow Eve, it's not an issue; the woman is just as sacred and resurrected as he is.

IN WHITMAN'S following fifteen poems in the "Children of Adam" collection, he expands and elaborates on the wonders of being human; it is a poetic montage, a kaleidoscope of human beingness. These are some of his most graphic lines as he praises the female and male bodies and souls. Whitman, the magnanimous herald of God, now becomes the celebratory new resurrected Adam discovering the richness of life and being. I'll not go into these poems, but the titles themselves tell the story. Here are some:

- *"From pent up aching rivers"*
- *"I sing the Body Electric"*
- *"A Woman Waits for Me"*
- *"Spontaneous Me"*
- *"One Hour to Madness and Joy"*
- *"Out of the Rolling Ocean the Crowd"*
- *"We two, How Long we were Fool'd"*

Whitman's new Adam is openly inviting and engaging with life in this new garden of the world and his humanity. *"I swim in it as in a sea,"* he sings in *"I sing the Body Electric."* He is not a fractured, divided or alienated Self, but a unified, integrated Self. *"All things please the soul."* He sees his *"soul reflected in Nature."*

"The man's body is sacred and the woman's body is sacred" and *"If anything is sacred the human body is sacred."*

> *I say these are not the parts and poems of the body only,*
>   *but of the soul,*
>   *O I say now these are the soul.*

For Whitman's new Adam body and soul are not disconnected. The new Adam is at one with himself, not at war with himself.

Whitman knows exactly what he is addressing in the mid to late 1800's in America and the World for that matter. He has seen and lived with the thinly veiled Biblical and Victorian morality that made hypocrites of most upstanding people of his time. He is boldly going where no one had gone before. The world the "Creator" gave this new Adam is still pronounced good.

THE SUN IS BLAZING NOW on the beach. The Ocean is glorious and glistening. I strip down to my swimsuit and feel the warmth of the sun on my skin. I spray some sunscreen on my chest and back. A few more people dot the beach.

I brought some mini-chocolate donuts today for my "communion." (The convenience store I stopped at on the way was out of my usual mini-cinnamon donuts). I sit back down and have my own communion in prayer: my iced tea for the wine and the mini-donuts for the host: The body and blood of the Divine becoming one with me and my body and blood.

I think of the words in the opening chapter of *The Gospel of John*: "The Word became flesh and dwelt among us." Jesus, the divine, became flesh just like me and dwelt among us.

The ocean is a dazzling 180-degree display of blue water clear on to the horizon line. The water is a gentle procession of rumbling, rolling surf. I wade into the water.

The waves greet me: crashing, slapping, and splashing on my

chest, face and hair. I linger in the playful edge of another world. I know why the ancient people gave names to their waters.

Jesus' resurrection reminds us that we are resurrected men and women. Beyond the Cross is the empty tomb and new life. Jesus' life is also an example of our spiritual renewal. Resurrection does not need to wait for this life to end. I am not just "passing through" this life, I am participating in it.

Whitman's *"Children of Adam"* collection of poems ends as his new Adam stands on the beach *"Facing West from California's Shores."* It is the next to last poem in the collection. The journey of these poems was envisioned as crossing the globe and the continent; Whitman's own "Manifest Destiny" included acquiring more than one continent; it started when the new Adam went west into the "garden" of the world and moved west around the globe, the Earth— the "circle is almost circled."

> *Facing west from California's shores,*
> *Inquiring, tireless, seeking what is yet unfound,*
> *I, a child, very old, over waves, towards the house of*
> *   maternity,*
> *the land of migrations, look afar,*
> *Look off the shores of my Western sea, the circle almost*
> *   circled.*[3]

The new Adam recognizes the paradox of age and maturity, the man with the soul of the boy: "I, a child, very old... toward the house of maternity." He is moving toward motherhood, the female world, the cycle of rebirth.

We were always east of Eden, the birthplace as it were; and in Whitman's poem we were always traveling west to cross the whole span of the garden of the world, to take it all in. Who wouldn't want to know all that is in this garden? We are both owners and immigrants of these lands, "the lands of migration."

His line "seeking what is yet unfound" is not a note of discouragement or dissatisfaction; rather it is an expression of the hunger and longing for that unseen world beyond this one.

> *For starting westward from Hindustan, from the vales of*
> *Kashmere,*
> *From Asia, from the north, from the God, the sage, and the*
> *hero,*
> *From the south, from the flowery peninsulas and the spice*
> *islands,*
> *Long having wander'd since, round the earth having*
> *wander'd,*
> *Now I face home again, very pleas'd and joyous.*

He has circled the planet, circumnavigated the globe and taken it all in. Yet he knows there is still more, something unfound. There is that final temporal barrier that in this life keeps us earthbound, a dimension away from the unseen, the veiled.

The next and final poem of the series focuses on Whitman's resurrected traveling man. "As Adam early in the morning" walks "forth from the bower fresh'd with sleep" he pronounces his benediction. "Behold me where I pass, hear my voice, approach, touch me."[4]

Easter Sunday on the beach at the edge of a vast Ocean Presence, I wade into the waves a second time. The sun has burned off all the clouds and lights the whole sea, sky, and sand brilliantly. The ocean glistens in a million tiny mirrors of light on a water trail mosaic toward the sun.

The poets mediate for me. The natural elements mediate for me. Sacraments all. This ocean shoreline, a border land of sorts, is where we meet out on the edges. Brush up against eternity. I celebrate it all: resurrected, brought back to life, a new life, a new man. Grace abounds.

CHAPTER 38

A MOVEABLE
SANCTUARY

You, the great homesickness
we could never shake off.
—Rainer Maria Rilke[1]

Two of my older friends, mentors, and father figures passed away while I was in my sixties: Father Walsh and Marvin Chamberlain. Father Walsh was many things for me—mentor, priest, older brother, dream whisperer, companion on the journey. Marvin was the age my dad would have been had he lived; he was like my own father in his quiet dignity and gentle spirit.

I am fortunate to have several close friends, men who are more like brothers, men I have known for over forty years now. I value their friendship and brotherhood. I am fortunate to have wonderful children, who are in their forties now, and two actual brothers, Glenn and Chuck, who live nearby and whose loyalty, friendship and Davis goodness I value more each year. I have bandmates with whom I've written and produced music for over ten years now and whose fellowship through music has been one of the highlights of the last ten years plus.

Then there are the poets: Whitman and Rilke, mainly. I brought both poets today, as usual to the beach. When I go to my favorite nearby beach as I am today, I go for sanctuary. The quiet, stretches of vacant and less populated tropical beaches provide regular sanctuary for me. With my beach chair, umbrella, and backpack of Whitman and Rilke, I connect with the Presence.

I dig my toes into the soft sand of the Atlantic Ocean beach near the Cape. The ocean glistens in her full glory in the tropical sun only two hours over the water horizon and it's already hot. It's May in Florida.

This morning the surf is gentle, as if the morning waves were just falling out of bed and getting ready for the day, like a child still wiping the sleep out of her eyes on the way to the breakfast table. It's a freestyle collection of small, irregular breaking waves, "there to an ocean fullness his mercy doth expand" in a full 180-degree span of ocean and brilliant blue sky.

I have a big stretch of white sand beach to myself today. I sit down under my beach umbrella in the small patch of shade.

I imagine my good friend Father John Walsh is here; I imagine he is his 28-year-old self, but full of his wisest self. It was Father Walsh who said I was a "romantic mystic" with a poet's soul.

I imagine him reading Rilke as I open my slim volume of *Book of Hours;* the Anita Barrows and Joanna Macy translation captures the poetic, intimate, feminine sweetness of Rilke's humanity.

LIBERATING GOD

Rilke wants to liberate God from our old images and icons in his *Book of Hours* poems. He writes early in Book 1 about how our own images can disguise and hide God. He addresses God:

We must not portray you in king's robes,

346

you drifting mist that brought forth the morning.
Once again from the old paintboxes
we take the same gold for scepter and crown
that has disguised you through the ages.
Piously we produce images of you
till they stand around you like a thousand walls.
And when our hearts would simply open,
our fervent hands hide you.[2]

Often my images of God stood around me *"like a thousand walls"* disguising and obstructing the view of the whole God. Religion can be the biggest obstruction to spirituality and can obstruct a bigger view of the Divine; like the horse with blinders on or like seeing only a corner of the enormous painting mostly hidden behind the curtain. "Now we see through a glass darkly...now we know in part," the verse says in the New Testament,[3] reminding us that we have some earthly limitations. At best, we "know in part." It's a reminder.

So I needed to change both the voice and the images of God when I left the church. I removed a number of the pillars of my faith and discovered The Presence does not need my dogma and theology to reach me, doesn't need those orthodox images of Yahweh-Jesus to get to me and for me to reach through to the other side.

I continue in Rilke's poetry, still imagining Father Walsh reading:

I come home from the soaring
in which I lost myself.
I was song, and the refrain which is God
is still roaring in my ears.
Now I am still
and plain:
no more words.
.... I'd gone very far, as far as the angels,
and high, where light thins into nothing,...
But deep in the darkness is God.[4]

Stripped down to my swim trunks I wade into the ocean. I let the waves slap against me as I move out deeper. Dolphins, sharks, jelly fish, right whales and pools of fish live in these waters. I know they are there, occasionally I see them. Pelicans soar and dive for fish just beyond the shallow waves.

I find Rilke gives voice to my soul. We've given many names to the Gods and Goddesses across the globe, but they still remain the Nameless Ones. I understand that now and am at peace with it. The mystery fascinates.

Again from his *Book of Hours*:

> *If this is arrogant, God, forgive me,*
> *but this is what I need to say.*
> *May what I do flow from me like a river,*
> *no forcing and no holding back,*
> *the way it is with children.*
> *Then these swelling and ebbing currents,*
> *then deepening tides moving out, returning,*
> *I will sing you as no one ever has,*
> *streaming through widening channels*
> *into the open sea.*[5]

My Sea of reference is this tropical, soft sand and gentle surf Atlantic Ocean. This immense body of water clear on to the sky endlessly rushes its waves to the shore.

Both Walt Whitman and Rainer Maria Rilke helped liberate God for me from the singular imagery of my Christianity and confines of my Evangelical theology. I believe the Presence, the one we call God, is personal, not impersonal. I feel and experience the Presence now at a personal, intimate level.

Jesus was a heretic. They arrested, tortured and crucified him for it. He challenged and disagreed with the religious leaders of his day. He felt they missed the whole point. After thousands of years, they had added laws upon laws to ensure their followers would be holy;

they added dogma and theology to clarify and define who and how God works.

Jesus would be a called a heretic today as well. Today's "Christianity" has too much Paul and too little Jesus. Paul came along after Jesus and his books in the New Testament went a long way toward helping "institutionalize" the church, and in that process Jesus kind of got diminished.

NEW WINESKINS FOR THE NEW WINE

Walt Whitman was a socio-religious heretic in his time. Releasing *Leave of Grass* (1855) as England's Victorian Era moral constraints were wearing thin on both continents, Whitman was scandalized for pushing the boundaries, crossing borders or what was deemed acceptable. He said it right up front that he was calling for a new religion for the modern man. He proposed a spirituality of the body and soul. He would have none of this harsh religion that de-humanized or devalued man or women.

I pick up my thin 1st Edition of *Leaves of Grass*; I imagine my good friend Father John Walsh reading (I imagine Whitman's voice sounded like John's):

> *I am the poet of the body...*
> *and I am the poet of the soul*
> *I am the poet of the woman the same as the man...*
> *I chant a new chant...*
> *I am he who walks with the tender and growing night*
> *I call to the earth and sea...*[6]

I catch sight of a dolphin's fins about 300 yards out in the water. I watch as another twenty pass heading north.

In the Gospel of Mark, Jesus and his disciples are seen eating and drinking with the "publicans and sinners" (2:15) and having a good time hanging out. The Pharisees didn't like it. They come to Jesus and ask: "How is it that John's (the Baptist's) disciples and the disciples of the Pharisees are fasting, but yours are not?" (2:18; NIV)

This is quintessential Jesus; he answers with the now famous words:

> No one pours new wine into old wineskins. Otherwise, the wine will burst the skins, and both the wine and the wineskins will be ruined. No, they pour new wine into new wineskins.[7]

These wineskins are more than just the "new covenant," or new worship services; the interpretation at its basic level is that this new "Jesus Spirit Wine" was not designed for nor will it fit into the old religious cracked and brittle wineskins, buildings, temples, church services, liturgy, dogma and doctrines. We are the wineskins. Each of us individually are the new wineskins: body, mind, spirit and soul.

What I love about Whitman is he is not identifying himself with any one religion; he's embracing the best of them all, minus the dogmas, for contemporary man. He's championing humanity; he's championing the new wine of Jesus in human bodies and souls; a non-religious spirituality; a blended faith. He doesn't have to name it:

> *There is that in me—I do not know what it is—but I know*
> *it is in me...*
> *... it is without name... it is a word unsaid,*
> *it is not in any dictionary or utterance or symbol.*[8]

Whitman became a guide to me when I left the church for a more organic, intuitive spirituality. Whitman's single volume *Leave of Grass* stands as perhaps the greatest declaration of spiritual and personal independence.

The ocean waves come in rows, four deep now; rows neatly spaced so that every other wave is breaking; two at a time; while the other two wait their turn. I swim out to the "in between"—in between the second and third rows of waves—where I can bob with the undulations of the water; float in the calm rise and then slide down the backside of a soon to crest wave. I watch a line of seven pelicans glide by without moving their wings; they skim just inches above the crest of the waves, gracefully and effortlessly.

I had a dream recently. In the dream, I was sitting on this same vacant stretch of beach where I usually visit. It was a beautiful sunny day, a brilliant blue sky with a big friendly white cloud just out over the water. I looked up to my left and in the cloud was a small square hatch opened and people were climbing through the hatch up behind the clouds. Then I looked to my right and saw a huge metallic cylinder extending from the sand up through the clouds. There too, in the clouds, next to what I realized was a giant rocket ship, was a square open hatch in the clouds with spacemen climbing up behind the clouds.

A Jacob's ladder type dream; the mysteries of inner and outer space. The ladder and the hatch are always there. I come to this beach for exactly that; there is always a palpable sense of the Great Presence here at the edge of this Ocean on these pristine, soft sand shores. On a sandbar of a beach, a barrier island within view of the Kennedy Space Center, I can see the top half of the Vertical Assembly Building at the Cape peaking just above the dunes between the sea oats and sea grapes. I've been here five times recently when a Space-X or some such rocket was launched. The ground does rumble.

Back under my umbrella in the shade, for my beachcomber communion, today I have watermelon and grapes. Even as I go through my casual ritual of the "wine and the host," I am reminded that all of life can be a sacrament.

I return to Whitman:

> *Do you see O my brothers and sisters*
> *It is not chaos or death... it is form and union and plan*
> *...it is eternal life...it is happiness.*[9]

Whitman knows that this *"that is in me"* shares the connection with the divine; the order and connectedness of it all. There is an innate spark within: the Presence, the Self, in the deepest part of one's own self.

My 14-year old grandson calls me often on his own cell phone these days. He thinks he might want to be a pastor (his maternal grandfather in Mexico is a pastor; and I was one for a time). I must admit, down deep I feel torn. I hear all my own idealism from my monkish boy years in him. I remember those good feelings. I won't discourage him. He is such a great kid and will probably be a better pastor than I was.

He is ready to learn and asks me what he should be reading. So, first I tell him to slow down and enjoy his teenage years and we can talk about books as he's ready. He says he doesn't really want to read about other religions. Again, I remember that feeling. I ask him, "How can you expect someone to respect your religion and what you have to say, if you don't have any respect for or interest in theirs?" "Oh, yeah," he says. He gets it.

REIMAGINING MY FAITH

Like the explorer in Kipling's poem hearing the call—"something lost and hidden behind the ranges, go and find it"—I figuratively grabbed my backpack and took to the road less travelled and barely marked. Clearly, for me, my first faith took me to a peak along the way, a stopover, a village, but there was a trail that led to higher mountains and other oceans to cross. Whitman is on the road. There are open hatches in the clouds waiting.

It's the treasure in a field that a man sells all he has to buy the field. It's the pearl of great price. A man awakens to his soul... his "whisper woke to hound" him and he can't stay home. He can't be the maintainer; he's the explorer priest.

It's a reimagined place, masks and faces of the Divine. Sometimes it's a "still small voice;" sometimes it's being knocked off your horse and seeing a light. Sometimes it's a verse read in a dark closet by a thread of light streaming in. Sometimes it's a knock on the door by friendly strangers who invite you along. Sometimes it's the day you know you are supposed to go. Sometimes it's a hunch, an intuition, a knowing deep inside that you have to trust. You know you could stay home and not rock any boats; but this time you know you can't.

Sometimes you know they won't understand; you were called to be a priest, an explorer. Some stay and are fine. But you can't be satisfied with the liturgies, limited sacraments, and this sole scripture.

While Jesus was talking with the Samaritan woman, she asked a contemporary question, basically asking, "Where should we worship?" Jesus responded: "Believe me, a time is coming when you will worship the Father neither on this mountain nor in Jerusalem.... a time is coming and has now come when the true worshipers will worship the Father in the Spirit and in truth."[10] It's not where you worship; it's not a particular church or place. You don't have to be in the Holy City of Jerusalem.

I imagine a God, a Presence, who is not bound by any one religion or dogma.

I imagine a Divine Being who delights and celebrates his creation, his human beings, "God's fair form."

I imagine a Divine Being who trusts individuals, who wants to meet us on mature terms, adult to adult, soul to soul. It's time to move beyond the elementary things, time to put away childish things.

I imagine a magnanimous God cheering us on as a proud effusive parent, not one who needs to rule and dominate us.

I imagine a Divine Presence who honors, respects, and welcomes our individuality, personality and human beingness—we who bear the divine "image and likeness."

I imagine a Divine Presence who does not debase human beings and their humanity, but values and celebrates our humanity; we are ever "in the image and likeness."

I imagine a Divine Presence who is both within and also totally other; one with us yet separate. A God/Goddess who is personal and immanent yet who is beyond complete comprehension to our human limitations; a Divine Presence that is one but contains multitudes and manifests itself in many faces, forms and objects in this visceral world dreamed into existence by its imagination.

Like this vast, immeasurable Ocean before me, I imagine a Divine Presence that cannot be bound or contained by any one religion or sacred scripture.

WHAT THE GODS DREAM

The 2017 remake of the sci-fi movie *"Westworld"* in miniseries format featured Anthony Hopkins as the mastermind or creator of this world that people pay to enter to essentially live out their controlled fantasy. We find that Hopkins the creator programmed everything—to a point. It's an interesting meditation on God and his "created" world here on earth.

We eventually discover why things are going "off-script" in Westworld's programmed immersive adult fantasy. At one point, Hopkins, the mastermind of this fantasy world, admits that as the bored genius he programmed into the system "the Reveries." The Reveries were the glitches wherein pre-programmed androids, that resemble humans in every detail, could choose to do something not programmed. They could decide to go off-script; they could exercise free-will. Some were becoming sentient beings. While Hopkin's engineer is trying to fix the glitch, the Mastermind tells him not to, he says: "Permit me my mistakes." It's really a striking point.

I like that he named them "the Reveries." The word reverie is synonymous with the word dream. We wake from one dreaming state into a daydream. The creator, mastermind programmer of this

"Westworld" wanted to see what they would do in their own dream state.

The ones waking out of their slumber begin to feel their emotions and their connectedness to life in and around them. The Reveries are the ones becoming human.

I believe we are the Reveries. I believe the Presence, the Great Divines, are delighted to see the Reveries becoming human. We are what the Gods dreamed. Not merely what they dreamed once upon a time, but we are what the Gods and Goddesses still dream. We are part of a greater consciousness.

What are we to make of a Divine Superior Being who only wants robotic creatures without a free will to serve him or her? Apparently, that's what the Angels were designed to be. Did he need men and women to be a lower form of angels? The Angels were envious of man, the Bible says.

Perhaps the whole idea was to see how it would work out if the Divine Presence gave these creatures the freedom to choose.

Could this supposedly "Great" Being chance it? Could this allegedly Divine Being allow the Reveries to become human?

Would this becoming human thing completely ruin God's nice neat fantasy? How many would seek, ask, knock, and choose a higher path? How many would find their way to the wizard behind the curtain?

CHAPTER 39
TO THE YOUNGER BROTHER

Perhaps it is time to abandon Christianity
in favor of the Christ.
—Thomas Moore[1]

MATANZAS INLET

We were spending a week in Saint Augustine, renting a house while we did some work and some vacationing. It was an overcast morning, but I was going to spend a few quiet moments on a beach I had not been to before. I walked out on Matanzas Beach on the Barrier Island, near the bridge on A1A over the Inlet.

I knew rain showers were threatening and I spotted a gnarled old tree by the dunes. It was a rare sight, a rather large tree with most of its branches growing up over the dunes. It formed a shelter of sorts. So I was able to sit comfortably on dry sand, lean back against some branches, and stay out of any rain. There were a few solitary people walking on the wide sandy beach off in the distances. The tide was out, so the ocean was far from the dunes.

Fort Matanzas National Monument, just on the other side of the Inlet, is a coquina shell-stone fort that was named for the Matanzas River and the slaughter or *"matanzas"* (Spanish for slaughter) of a band of French Huguenots along its shores in the mid 1700's. The Roman Catholic Spanish and the Protestant British and Huguenot French took turns battling each other in Florida back then while praying to the same God for victory against each other, no doubt. All "in Jesus' name" I'm sure.

I acknowledge my gratitude for living in the time and place that I have—America in the twentieth and twenty-first centuries. I am grateful to be living in a country that has offered me so much education, freedom, and opportunity. I know I have lived in a time of great progress and relative peace.

I settled into a nice curve in a thick branch of the tree that rested partly on the sand. Its branches formed an impressive little alcove. I positioned my iced tea and backpack and reached for my books. I had a Rilke, a Whitman, and a Joseph Campbell. I had been sifting through each of them while on vacation. I chose Rilke. I knew the rain could chase me back to my car if it came hard. Rilke usually says the most in the fewest words.

I opened at random after a short prayer anticipating something good. It's my newer edition of Rilke's *Book of Hours*, the Barrows and Macy translation; I needed a fresh copy because my old copy had too many notes and underlines.

I opened to one of the few "titled" or "addressed" poems in this volume. Rilke addresses this poem *"To the younger brother."* It is Book I—The Book of the Monastic Life, poem 38.

> *You, yesterday's boy,*
> *to whom confusion came*
> *Listen, lest you forget who you are.*[2]

"Yesterday's boy" is to remain true to himself; Rilke is not referencing some outdated boy. Yesterday's boy is that innocent young
monk who will be preserved as today's boy, the ever-youthful soul
self.

Rilke is writing to a younger monk, imagining himself as the
older brother, addressing him as "yesterday's boy." I am reminded of
my words from the San Pedro Ceremony: "take care of this boy."
Rilke has some advice for the younger brother: that he not forget
who he is. He reminds him:

> *What chose you is the great desire*
> *Now all flesh bares itself to you.*[3]

Elsewhere in this Rilke volume, he says that God is "the great
homesickness we could not shake off."[4] "The great desire" is what
also seems to have chosen me; a longing, a hunger, a desire to know
more. Rilke as the older monk sees himself in this younger brother.

I find in this poem my own older self looking back at my younger
self. I am at a point in the journey where I can see the arc of my story
and life. I was fortunate to have a few good mentors.

I am reminded of another line from Rilke that has stuck with me.
Rilke's *Book of Hours*, poem II, 3 opens with a line that reminds me of
my early days as a Christian convert: *"I'm still the one who knelt before
you in monk's robes."*

I was one of the monkish boys those first four years as a new
believer and young airmen at Patrick Air Force Base, not far south of
this beach. Actual monk's robes or priestly garb are not necessary for
the metaphor of the monk to hit home.

I am known at the deepest levels as I always have been. The
Kingdom of Heaven has always been within. The Divine Presence has
always been at the heart and soul of my True Self.

I turn to that poem and read those lines again:

> *I'm still the one who knelt before you*

in monks' robes, wanting to be of use.
You filled him as he called you into being...

And you are ever again the wave
sweeping through all things.[5]

Still the monkish boy, but older now. The Divine, the ever-present consciousness, is *"Ever again the wave sweeping through all things."* I am still "Yesterday's boy." Perhaps the soul is ever the young innocent: true, honest, clear-eyed, and genuine. Perhaps incorruptible. That is the True Self, the God within, the seed that remains in us.

Rilke, the older monk, reassures the younger one. He wants to reassure the younger brother that he is going through an awakening, a coming to consciousness at a deeper level. But he is not to lose himself in the wrong ways.

Rilke's line "now all flesh bares itself to you" is not referencing the negative "flesh" views of the Puritanical Christianity that sees the world and the flesh as evil and corrupt. "The Word was made flesh and dwelt among us" John wrote in his gospel;[6] Jesus was made flesh also to experience human life and human beingness. If the flesh is inherently evil and opposed to God, then Jesus could not be the "spotless lamb of God." This whole argument set off numerous theological debates centuries ago; it was settled by more lines drawn, more divisiveness, more dogma.

Rilke knows that "the great desire," the longing to connect with the Divine, also awakens the soul to the beauty and wonder of all life. We are not to forget who we are: we are in the image and likeness of God, a gift even the Angels envied in human beings. Rilke continues:

On pious images pale cheeks
blush with strange fire...
Your senses uncoil like snakes

awakened by the beat of the tambourine.[7]

Strange fire, senses uncoiling like snakes, the beat of tambourines and music are all human feeling, sensations, experiences our bodies feel in response to our soul. Walt Whitman championed the deep connection between body and soul:

> *That body of yours gives proportions to your Soul*
>> *somehow*
> *to live in other spheres;*
> *I do not know how, but I know it is so.*[8]

When one awakens to awe, to the awakening to transcendence, there is a flooding in of life and the visceral world. Rilke knows the confusion of being overwhelmed by the divine and the earthly. Awakening to the divine should also awaken all of our senses; the soul and the spirit pulse mightily through the body, the senses, and our feelings. As human beings we are body, soul, spirit and we desire unity and oneness within; not fragmentation, division, or self-destruction of parts or the whole.

Rilke sees in this younger monk a reflection and reminder of his own spiritual progress. Young initiates can easily get confused. I was confused myself many times. Do I question the elders? Do I submit? Stay silent? Speak up?

> *Now, like a whispering in dark streets*
> *Rumors of God run through your dark blood.*[9]

I remember as a young believer there at Patrick Air Force Base, there was a great sense that I was on to something in discovering Jesus. There seemed so much to learn, so much to process, so much to question and debate. It was confusing. Yet it was also an awakening, a coming to terms with the soul, the "whispering" and the rumors, the various theological sides and opinions.

The ocean is dark and the sky overcast. A few drops of rain get through the bough and branches above me. It is April and the foliage on this tree's branches has not bloomed yet. The rain is rather uncertain; so I stay a little longer under my covering.

The same "younger brother" is addressed in Rilke's next poem; it's actually a continuation of the first poem: *"I who came back from that same confusion..."*[10]

The older monk sees himself in the younger and knows the path. He went through and came back from the same confusion of the awakenings of body and soul. I know the confusion I had to come back from: of sorting out God through all this maze of contradictory theologies; of the inner awakenings, successive awakenings, of coming to terms with God and my Self, of finding peace with the Divine and the self. Rilke returned from his confusion; his own confusion of constructing, deconstructing, and reconstructing his faith. He returned and infused the old images with new life and new light.

> *I returned to paint upon the altars*
> *those old holy forms...*
> *But they shone differently*
> *fierce in their beauty.*[11]

The older monk went through the transformations, the awakenings, and he saw the beauty shining differently. The truth is, we should expect to "see the light" more than once in our lives. If you've only "seen the light" one time, you are probably missing something.

Just as he reminded the younger brother not to "forget who you are," he now says that he had to trust his own soul. They will want you to lose yourself, but you have to maintain the locus of control within yourself. You ultimately have to trust your soul, because down there in your soul is where the Divine Presence is, where the kingdom of God is within and with you. Now the older monk prays:

You, my own deep soul trust me.
I will not betray you. [12]

Trust your soul. At the core, at the very center of who you are in your soul, the Divine Presence abides there and always has. It's why we need to connect with our souls, be true to ourselves, that eternal soul that we can choose to quench, ignore, trade or feed, free and follow. The "spirit will guide you into all truth."

I am reminded of how the figure of San Pedro trusted me when he said: "You know what's right and good," and "Take care of this boy." Much like that line from the rock song that grabbed me when I was a sixteen-year-old: "Look to your soul."

It is about the longing and the Presence; the longing within for something that touches and engages the soul, something transcendent, divine; the Presence within and above that we sense and feel.

Rilke, as this older monk, does not disavow or debase his humanity, his human beingness. He embraces it as part of the wonder and beauty of spirituality. He writes:

My blood is alive with many voices
telling me I am made of longing. [13]

"Longing" is not simply feeling; it's passion, drive, desire. This is not asceticism, this is not rejecting the flesh as evil, this is not Buddhism's view that life is all suffering, that all earthly desire is bad, but rather this is an acknowledgement of life as it is: it's a gift to be a human being. This is Walt Whitman's celebrating life, reclaiming the body and soul together, celebrating life and acknowledging that "I contain multitudes."

Now, as the older monk, Rilke asks himself a question:

What mystery breaks over me now?
In its shadow I come to life.
For the first time I am alone with you—

You, my power to feel.[14]

The older monk is content with the mystery and the unknowable, the shadow of the Divine. The older brother is at peace with his soul, his body, and his power to feel, to experience and be fully human and fully soulful. This is about coming to terms with the power of feeling all our humanity, all of what it means to be "in the image and likeness" of the Divine Being.

I grew weary and felt stunted in "my first faith" with its closed system and circular reasoning. Its pillars were dogmatic, narrow propositional "truth" statements to provide its followers guardrails and parameters that explained how God works and doesn't work. I didn't think the system did God justice any longer. I don't think anyone system or religion does.

I did lose myself and I "came back from the confusion." "What chose *me* was the great desire." I am still "yesterday's boy," still kneeling in my figurative "monks robes." "My blood is alive with many voices." I "did not know I contained so much goodness."

EPILOGUE

I was visiting my son, Steve, and his family in California for Thanksgiving not long ago. I was also working through chapters in this book at the time. I had been going through a phase of trying to locate some guys from my time at Patrick Air Force Base. I was feeling bad about some of the "zealous" things I said to them and was hoping to apologize. I was having trouble finding them on any of the online search engines. Sadly, when I found my friend Ray, one of the few I figured would understand, I was reading his obituary.

Steve and I had some good spiritual conversations during those nights. It's nice when my children, now grown adults with their own children, can minister to me spiritually. I am glad my kids have not seemed burdened with the dark cloud of Evangelicalism that settled over me from my early zealous years.

During that week at Steve's home, I had a trilogy of dreams, three nights in a row; each dream, successively meaningful, related to my spiritual journey. Father Walsh would have loved it. I'll comment on the middle dream.

In the dream, I was puzzled by a small wooden cabinet I had that only had about twelve drawers. I was trying to organize my papers (writings, theology, spiritual insights, etc.) and I was frustrated that the cabinet was not sufficient.

Then, in came Stephanie and she set before me a new large wooden cabinet with a hundred drawers in it. It was just what I needed. She said that I could keep the smaller cabinet and use the new one for all the papers that didn't fit into the old one.

It all seemed so simple, but it was what I needed to do with my first faith and my newly reconstructed and enlarging faith. There have been a few people in my life who have helped me reorganize and reconstruct my faith. Stephanie was the travelling companion and mate I needed on the second half of my journey.

When our religion or beliefs seem to box us in or narrow our view of the Divine, we need to reexamine our faith. When our religion and our church become toxic and unhealthy, we need to step back and be honest with ourselves. I needed a much bigger filing cabinet and system.

RECENTLY, Stephanie and I were filming at a festival for a client's project. We were spending the night in a small town where we had done a lot of work and knew quite a few people.

It was late and we were sitting in a local wine bar with a few local friends. It was one of those musical chairs things, where over the course of two hours, a string of people came and sat down for a bit and we'd all switch chairs to chat with someone else before another few people came and joined in as others left.

At one point, I was sitting next to the senior pastor of the local church next to the festival grounds. It was a mainline church. The minister was kindly, dignified, gray-haired and about my age. I gave him my two-minute spiritual story of becoming a Christian, going to seminary, pastoring, and then leaving.

He was gracious and understanding. He appeared curious about my outward-bound journey and asked a few questions. He was surprised that I had taken an unorthodox path as I explained to him some of my "beyond the church" experiences. It seemed important to him that he be able to categorize me. Perhaps I didn't fit neatly into any of his labels. He concluded, "So, you're a contemplative." I was fine with that term; it was close and accurate enough.

I thanked him for staying in the church and for his years of service to the Church. I told him I felt that the Church never really follows the advice of Heb. 6:1-2 about moving beyond the elementary things. I asked him what he thought.

We wound up agreeing that the church often is like elementary school: it gets people oriented, gives them the basics, and is there for the ritual and the support.

I saw something of myself in him. I could have been him. If I had stayed all these years, I could have been close to retiring in a cushy, small-town church that was a relatively well-paying, easy gig. But I knew I wouldn't have been able to do it. Not now, not knowing what I now knew. I couldn't have gone the path I did and stayed a pastor.

I thanked him again for staying and for his service.

REIMAGINING THE CHURCH

There is the "God" we *think* we know. The "God" we know from our religious constructs, the beliefs we assent to, the "God" of our church and its statements of faith, the "God" of our popular cultures and times. The "God" we believe acts according to our beliefs.

Then there is the "God" we *don't yet know*; the "God" beyond our comprehension. There is the God that is beyond our constructs; the one who is inscrutable, beyond the limited containers of our belief systems; the God beyond our popular beliefs about this God or that God. There is the God who does not bend to our superstitions, church doctrine, national agendas, or personal will.

Perhaps it will take mankind a few more centuries or millennia to grow up, to mature collectively and evolve as a human race in order to stop warring, hating and killing in the names of our various "gods"—if our world makes it that long.

As more and more people leave their organized religions and churches, and the ranks of the "Nones" outpaces the old religious believers, there will rise up "new faiths" and "blended faiths."

I grew bored and constrained with my first faith. I awoke to the toxicity of my religious system constructed so to wall out the greater Divine Presence and keep me in. My Evangelicalism grew more and more inadequate for my spiritual longing. The image and voice of God within me needed a major overhaul.

As long as churches and religions continue insisting that their truth is the only truth, their Gods are the only Gods, as long as they continue fueling divisiveness and spiritual elitism, people will continue their disillusionment with religion.

In the distant future, there will be more global awareness and mankind will have outgrown the small-minded, regional and nationalistic religions that have divided us, driven us to senseless wars, and forced ancient, outdated beliefs upon us.

There will rise more "Spiritual Centers" that provide entry paths and orientation to various spiritual paths. Spiritual Centers that are not out to promote or profit from any one religion; but seek to give people the tools, guidance, and critical minds to make their own decisions about Gods, Goddesses, and beliefs. They won't think for you, but they'll give you enough food for thought.

TO STAY OR TO LEAVE

In one of Rainer Maria Rilke's *Book of Hours* poems, he imagines two men and their churches. In Rilke's short eight-line poem, he is not talking about two particular men, but two types of men. One man leaves and the other stays.

> *Sometimes a man rises from the supper table*
> *and he goes outside. And he keeps on going*
> *because somewhere to the east there's a church.*
> *His children bless his name as if he were dead.*[2]

The man who leaves "keeps going." He is searching for a distant or unknown "church" "somewhere." When the man leaves it is clear he is not sure where that somewhere is; it is only in a direction. This is the same type of man whom Rilke has been writing about: the one with an inner "longing," the one with "the great homesickness we could not shake off."[3] This is the man to whom the familiar "churches can look like prisons"[4] where "God is imprisoned and lamented like a trapped and wounded animal."[5]

The poem portrays another type of man in clear contrast to the man who leaves.

> *Another man stays at home until he dies,*
> *stays with the plates and glasses,*
> *So then it is his children who go out*
> *into the world, seeking the church he forgot.*[6]

Rilke knows there are more than two types of man, but he is addressing one thing. I believe Rilke's emphasis here is on the need to address the longing in contrast to the forgetting. There is nothing wrong with staying home; but beware of "playing" church. The problem is, the man who stays home "stays with the plates and glasses;" it is an image of maintaining a household; going through the motions; playing church.

Ultimately, this man's children see that he "forgot" what the church was all about. It became form without substance; ritual without meaning; going through the motions but not knowing why. In the end, his children needed to leave the church of their father. Dead orthodoxy and dogma can kill the soul, but it can also awaken the soul to seek, to search, to leave and keep going.

I AVOIDED WRITING this book as a "how to" or step-by-step plan. I wrote it as a memoir of how my spiritual journey unfolded for me. My journey is my journey; it's not a template or "how-to" plan.

However, there are steps and examples in every journey that can be descriptive and applicable. My journey may be my journey; but it is not unique. Many have written about the stages or passage of journey. The particulars may vary widely, but the journey is similar for many.

In the hero's journey, typically the hero returns from the journey with a boon or an elixir that he can share with others. Perhaps the boon or elixir is a secret that's been revealed, a new passage, a new land, a new answer. Perhaps the boon is more internal; the hero undergoes a transformation, a new maturity, a new understanding, a new wisdom.

The ways and rituals of our religions can be meaningful, the doors through which we enter. For some the church or temple is merely the foyer, or the threshold, and we find we need to move beyond for more of what we are seeking.

All our religions start as their own narrow road. When we get beyond our one narrow lane road, we see where the roads merge into one wider highway. The road naturally widens and embraces.

Is it too much to ask for the Divine Presence to meet us in profound and transformational ways? Is it too much to ask that at least once in your life you experience personally a touch from the other side, that you connect in a transpersonal way to the Divine, the Transcendent? To come away knowing what you only believed before in a way that no one can take away from you? To ask, to seek, to knock and actually have it opened unto to you?

I sought. I knocked. It was opened; and not merely theologically or figuratively. I opened and found that the narrow road widens out. The sum is greater than the whole of all the parts.

Rilke writes that:

> *We are cradled close in your hands...*
> *And lavishly flung forth.*[7]

Looking back, I see now that I was "lavishly flung forth." I didn't know the arc of my story until time revealed it. It was no small thing, but I needed a push.

I am content and grateful that after all the journey, I am able to return with a boon.

I'll close with my favorite traveler, Walt Whitman, from his most seminal poem.

> *I tramp a perpetual journey...*
> *Nor I, not anyone else can travel it for you.*
> *You must travel it for yourself.*
>
> *It is not far, it is within reach,*
> *Perhaps you have been on it since you were born*
> *and did not know it*
> *Perhaps it is everywhere on water and on land.*
>
> *You must habit yourself to the dazzle of the light*
> *and of every moment of your life.*

And I say to any man or woman
Let your soul stand cool and composed
before a million universes.[8]

NOTES

EPIGRAPH

1. *"Song of the Open Road"*
2. *Rilke's Book of Hours, II, 22 (Anita Barrows & Joanna Macy Trans.)*

PROLOGUE

1. *King Lear (5.3.325)*

INTRODUCTION

1. Ralph Waldo Emerson, "Emerson's 1838 address to the graduating class at Harvard Divinity School." (https://www.harvardsquarelibrary.org/biographies/emersons-divinity-school-address/)

1. HERE BE DRAGONS

1. Diane K. Osbon, ed., "Meister Eckhart," *A Joseph Campbell Companion* (Harper Perennial, NY, 1991), p. 115
2. Marlene Winnell, PhD, *Leaving the Fold* (Berkeley, CA, The Apocryphile Press, 2007), pp. 15.
3. *Ibid.*, p. 4
4. *Ibid.*, p. 5
5. *Ibid.*, p. 5
6. Thomas Wolfe, *You Can't Go Home Again.* (Internet: *https://quotes.pub/q/to-lose-the-earth-you-know-for-greater-knowing-to-lose-the-l-250678*)

2. THREE SCENES

1. Alice Miller, *The Truth Will Set You Free* (https://www.booksamillion.com/p/Truth-Will-Set-Free/Alice-Miller/9780465045853)

3. DOG TAGS

1. Joseph Stein, *Fiddler on the Roof* (Crown Publishers, Crown Edition, 1972.)

4. IN MY ROOM

1. Brian Wilson and Mike Love (songwriters), "Please Let Me Wonder," *The Beach Boys Today* album (Capital Records, 1965).
2. James Hendricks (songwriter), "Look to Your Soul," from Johnny Rivers' album *Realization* (1968, Imperial Records)

5. CIGARETTES OR A BIBLE?

1. Bob Dylan (songwriter), "Gotta Serve Somebody," *Slow Train Coming* (Columbia Records, 1979).
2. Matthew 11:28-29 (KJV)

6. MY WOODSTOCK

1. J. R. R. Tolkien, *The Hobbit.* (Tolkien Quotes: https://www.pinterest.com/pin/380624605978453360/)
2. Mrs. Cousin, "The Sands of Time," *The Baptist Church Hymnal*, 1900. Arranged by Mrs. Cousin from her poem of 19 stanzas for that collection. (From John Julian, *Dictionary of Hymnology, New Supplement* (1907), pp. 264.)

7. THE MONKISH BOYS

1. Luke 12:48
2. John 3:3 - KJV
3. II Corinthians 5:17 - NKJV

8. "SINNERS IN THE HANDS OF AN ANGRY GOD"

1. Joseph Campbell, *A Joseph Campbell Companion.* Selected and edited by Diane K. Osbon (Harper Perennial, NY, 1991), p. 30.
2. II Timothy 2:15.
3. Ezekiel 3:21 – KJV.
4. Jonathan Edwards, "Sinners in the Hands of an Angry God," Sermon from 1741 (https://www.blueletterbible.org/Comm/edwards_jonathan/Sermons/Sinners.cfm)

9. ROMANCING THE FAITH

1. Norman Greenbaum (songwriter), "Spirit in the Sky," (Reprise Records, 1969)

10. TWO DEATHS

1. II Tim. 2:15.

11. THE TEAMSTERS AND THE IVORY TOWER

1. Matthew 28:19-20.
2. Hebrews 13:2 – KJV.
3. Hebrews 13:2 – NLT.

12. CHURCH WORLD

1. Reza Aslan, *God: A Human History* (Random House, NY, 2017)

13. I HAD TO LEAVE MY FATHER'S HOUSE

1. Homer, *The Odyssey*. Translated by Samuel Butler (The Project Guttenberg eBook: https://www.gutenberg.org/files/1727/1727-h/1727-h.htm#chap04)
2. Genesis 32:22-31 – NIV.
3. Maria Popova, *Figuring* (Vintage Books, Penguin Random House LLC, NY, 2019), p.125.
4. Butler, Samuel, trans. Homer, *The Odyssey*, Chapter 4. (The Project Guttenberg eBook: https://www.gutenberg.org/files/1727/1727-h/1727-h.htm#chap04).
5. Ibid., Chapter IV
6. My verse: Nahum 1:7 - KJV
7. My verse: I John 4:6.
8. Nahum 1:7.

14. THE BALLAD OF FELIX MANZ AND PASTOR Z

1. John 13:35 - KJV.
2. Campbell, op. cit., p. 30.

15. DECONSTRUCTING MINDSETS

1. Andrew M. Greeley, *Confessions of Parish Priest* (Pocket Books, Simon and Schuster, NY, 1987), p. 13.
2. Revelations 3:10 – KJV.
3. II Corinthians 5:17 – KJV.
4. Winell, op. cit., p. 53.
5. Greeley, op. cit., pp. 474-475.
6. Ibid., p. 228.
7. Ibid., p. 475.
8. Winell, op. cit., p. 1
9. Greeley, op. cit., p. 484.
10. Ibid., p. 11.
11. Ibid., p. 13.
12. Ibid., p. 6.

16. FRANKENSTEIN AND ME

1. Mary Shelley, *Frankenstein,* Vol. II, Chap. 2 (Signature Classics, Barnes and Noble, NY; Sterling Publishing, Inc., Canada, 2020), p. 95. 123-124 .
2. Campbell, op. cit., p. 157.
3. Ibid., p. 179.
4. Shelley, op. cit., p. 95.
5. Ibid., p. 94.
6. Ibid., pp. 123-124.
7. Clint Ballard, Jr., Songwriter, "You're No Good," (Jubilee Records, 1963).
8. "My Evangelical Discipleship" verses in order: Rom. 7:18; John 3:30; Gal. 2:20-21; II Cor. 5:17; I Cor. 6:20; I Cor. 6:19; I Peter 1:16; Gal. 5:24; Luke 9:23; Matt. 6:25; Rom. 6:11; Prov. 3:5-6; John 15:5; II Tim. 2:15; Phil. 2:12; Luke 12:48; Phil. 3:14-15; Matt. 5:48
9. John Donne, "Batter My Heart, Three Person'd God (Holy Sonnet 14). (https://poets.org/poem/batter-my-heart-three-persond-god-holy-sonnet-14)
10. II Tim. 2:15.

17. ENCOUNTER ON THE BEACH

1. Walt Whitman, "Song of the Open Road," *Leaves of Grass, Second Edition* (https://www.poetryfoundation.org/poems/48859/song-of-the-open-road)
2. Walt Whitman, "Crossing Brooklyn Ferry," *Leaves of Grass* (https://www.poetryfoundation.org/poems/45470/crossing-brooklyn-ferry)
3. Ibid.
4. Walt Whitman, "To You," *Leaves of Grass* (https://poets.org/poem/you). (Note: There are two poems titled "To You" in Whitman's *Leaves of Grass*. This one is the longer one with the 1856 and 1881 dates listed. The dates indicate, respectively, the first edition and the last.)
5. Walt Whitman, "Song of the Open Road," op. cit.

18. YOU GOT NO SALSA

1. Campbell, op. cit., p. 30.
2. Karen Armstrong, *The Spiral Staircase* (Anchor Books, NY, 2005), p. 156.
3. George Fowler, *The Dance of a Fallen Monk* (Addison-Wesley Publishing Co., Boston, MA, 1995), p. 107.
4. Richard Schiffman, "When Religion Leads to Trauma," *New York Times,* Feb. 5, 2019 (https://www.nytimes.com/2019/02/05/well/mind/religion-trauma-lgbt-gay-depression-anxiety.html)

19. THE ALIENATED SELF

1. Winell, op. cit., p. 73.
2. Gal. 2:20 – KJV.
3. Joseph Campbell, *Pathways to Bliss* (New World Library, Novato, CA 2004), p.70.
4. Henry David Thoreau, *Walden.* (Marboro Books Corp., Publisher, Barnes & Noble Books, 1992), p. 9.
5. Jer. 19:9-10.

20. A FUNERAL AND A DIVORCE

1. Rainer Maria Rilke, Translated by Anita Barrows and Joanna Macy, *Book of Hours, Book I* (Riverhead Books, NY, 1996), p 83.
2. Winell, op. cit., pp. 70-71.
3. This is largely based upon Paul's verse in Romans 11:19 that "God's gifts and call are irrevocable"—which is conveniently lifted out of context.

21. NEW VOICES AND MENTORS

1. Walt Whitman, "A Song for Occupations," *Leaves of Grass (Book VX),* 1855.
2. Campbell, op. cit., p. 78.
3. J. R. R. Tolkien, *The Hobbit. Internet: Tolkien Quotable Quotes* (https://www.goodreads.com/quotes/134036-i-am-looking-for-someone-to-share-in-an-adventure).
4. J.R.R. Tolkien, The Hobbit (https://www.goodreads.com/quotes/113746-there-is-more-in-you-of-good-than-you-know).
5. Walt Whitman, "Passage to India," *Leaves of Grass.* (Marboro Books Corp., Barnes and Noble Books, NY, 1992).

22. NEVERTHELESS ME, MY SELF AND I... LIVE

1. Karen Armstrong, op. cit., p. 165.
2. Ibid., p. 165.
3. Joseph Campbell, *The Hero's Journey* (New World Library, Novato, CA, 2014), p. 35.
4. Bernie Brillstein, Frank Peppiatt, and John Aylesworth, "Gloom, Despair and Agony on me," *Hee-Haw*, recorded by Buck Owns and Roy Clark.
5. Karen Armstrong, *The Spiral Staircase* (Anchor Books, Random House, NY, 2005), p. 28.
6. Ibid., p. 28.
7. Ibid., pp. 28-29.
8. Winell, op. cit., p. 114.
9. Ibid., p. 15.
10. Ibid., p. 5.
11. Atria Books, 2018.
12. Winell, op. cit., p. 6.
13. II Timothy 1:7.
14. Carl Jung, *Memories, Dreams, Reflections*. Recorded and Edited by Aniela Jaffe (Vintage Books, Random House, NY, 1989), p. 211.
15. Ibid., p. 211.
16. Rainer Maria Rilke, "Autumn," *The Book of Images*. Translation by Edward Snow (North Point Press, Farrar Strauss and Giroux, NY, 1994), p. 85.
17. Walt Whitman, "Song of Myself," *Leaves of Grass* (Marboro Books Corp., Barnes and Noble Books, 1992)

23. ALCHEMY OF THE SELF

1. Walt Whitman, "Song of Myself," *Leaves of Grass* (https://www.poetryfoundation.org/poems/45477/song-of-myself-1892-version)
2. Fowler, op. cit., p. 301.
3. Jeremiah 17:9 - KJV.
4. Armstrong, op. cit., p. 105.
5. Fowler, op. cit., p. 107
6. Greeley, op. cit., p. 3.
7. Osbon, op. cit., p. 179.
8. Rainer Maria Rilke, "Moving Forward," *Selected Poems of Rainer Maria Rilke*. Trans. Robert Bly (Harper Perennial; Bilingual Edition, 1981), p. 101.
9. Joseph Campbell *Pathways to Bliss* op. cit., p. 68
10. Ibid., p. 70.
11. Geoffrey James, *45 Quotes From Mr. Rogers That We All Need Today"* (Internet: https://www.inc.com/geoffrey-james/45-quotes-from-mr-rogers-that-we-all-need-today.html)
12. James Hillman, *A Blue Fire*. Edited by Thomas Moore (Harper Perennial, Harper Collins Publishers, NY 1991), p. 119.
13. Ibid., p. 122.
14. Carl Orff, *Carmina Burana* (https://en.wikipedia.org/wiki/Carmina_Burana_(Orff))

24. ROOMMATES TOO LONG

1. Fowler, op. cit., p. 117.

25. A SECOND CALL TO ADVENTURE

1. Joseph Campbell, *The Hero with a Thousand Faces* (MJF Books, NY, 1949), p. 35
2. Campbell, *Pathways to Bliss*, op. cit. p. 131.
3. Ibid., p. 118.
4. Ibid., p. 133.
5. Rudyard Kipling, "The Explorer" (https://www.poetry.com/poem/33424/the-explorer)
6. Osbon, *A Joseph Campbell Companion*, p. 83.
7. Ibid., p. 84.
8. Ibid., p. 84.
9. Henry David Thoreau, *Walden and Other Writings* (Marboro Books Corp., Barnes & Noble Books, NY, 1992), p.75
10. Osbon, op. cit., p. 85.
11. Michael Pollan, *How to Change Your Mind* (Penguin Books, Penguin Random House, NY, 2019), p. 7
12. Thomas Moore, *Care of the Soul* (Harper Perennial, Harper Collins Publishers. NY, 1994), p. 213.
13. Thomas Moore, *The Soul's Religion* (Harper Perennial, Harper Collins Publishers, NY, 2003), p. 117.
14. Thoreau, op. cit., p. 75.
15. Ibid., p. 75.

26. ALL THE SEAS OF GOD

1. *The Rig Veda*, Book 1, Hymn164, verse 46.
2. Hebrews 6:1-2 – NIV.
3. Walt Whitman, "Passage to India," *Leaves of Grass* (Marboro Books Corp., Barnes and Noble Books, NY, 1992).
4. Exodus 3:14.
5. *The Bhagavad Gita* 10:20, op. cit., p. 54.
6. Ibid., 4:6.
7. Luke 17:21
8. *The Bhagavad Gita,* op. cit., 8:22
9. Ibid., 2:30.
10. Ibid., 4:9
11. Ibid., 7:10.
12. Ibid., 10:39.
13. Ibid., 9:18.
14. Ibid., 17:5-6.
15. Ibid., 11:5 & 10.

16. Ibid., 10:2.
17. Ibid., 9:23.
18. Ibid., 4:12.
19. Alan Jacobs, translator, "Poimandres," *The Gnostic Gospels* (Watkins Publishing, London, England, 2016) p. 130.
20. Ibid., p. 136.
21. Ibid., p. 137.
22. Ibid., p. 138.
23. John 16:12-13 – NIV.
24. Moore, *The Soul's Religion*, op. cit., p. 138.

27. MY WHITMAN LITURGY

1. Walt Whitman, "Song of the Open Road," op. cit., Stanza 5.
2. Thomas Moore, *The Soul's Religion*, op. cit., p. 117.
3. *"Crossing Brooklyn Ferry," st-8.*
4. *"To You"* (longer poem version).
5. *Song for Occupations.*
6. *"Song of Myself,"* st-1, st-3.
7. *"Song of the Open Road," st-5.*
8. *"Song of the Open Road," st-10.*
9. Walt Whitman, "To You," *Leaves of Grass*, op. cit.
10. Eknath Easwaran, *The Bhagavad Gita*, 10:42, op. cit., p. 57.

28. BEFRIENDING DREAMS

1. James Hillman, *A Blue Fire*, p. 241.
2. Robert A. Johnson, *Inner Work* (Harper San Francisco, Harper Collins Publishers, NY, 1986), p. 45.
3. James Hillman, op. cit., p. 241.
4. Robert Johnson, op. cit., p. 45.
5. Hebrews 1:1-2 – NIV.
6. Numbers 12:6 - NIV.
7. Acts 2:17 - NIV.
8. Romans 8:26 – NIV.
9. Robert Johnson, op. cit., p. 15.
10. Jung., op. cit., p. 394.

29. THE PARK BENCH DIALOGUES

1. Johnson, *Inner Work*, p. 21.
2. Campbell, *Pathways to Bliss,* op. cit., p. 131.
3. Johnson, op. cit., p. 14.
4. June Singer, *Boundaries of the Soul* (Anchor Books, Doubleday, NY, 1994), p. 279.

5. Johnson, op. cit., p. 14.

30. THE WOODEN SHARD

1. Russell Shorto, *Saints and Madmen* (Henry Holt and Company, NY, 1999), p. 197
2. Ibid., p. 208.
3. Ibid., p. 191.
4. Ibid., p. 212.
5. Ibid., p. 207.
6. Ibid., p. 207.
7. Pollan, op. cit., p. 152.
8. Ibid., p. 160.
9. Ibid., p. 161.
10. Ibid., p. 156.
11. Ibid., p. 157.
12. Ibid., p. 157.
13. Ibid., p. 52.
14. Ibid., p. 53.
15. Ibid., p. 55.
16. Ibid., p. 336.
17. Ibid., p. 349.
18. Ibid., p. 85.
19. James Fadiman, *The Psychedelic Explorer's Guide: Safe, Therapeutic, and Sacred Journeys* (Park Street Press, Rochester, Vermont, 2011).
20. William James, *The Varieties of Religious Experience* (Barnes & Noble Classics, NY, 2004).
21. Johnson, op. cit., p. 104.
22. Shorto, op. cit., p. 199.
23. John 6:53-55
24. Pollan, op. cit. p. 109.

31. "THE WIND BLOWS WHEREVER IT PLEASES"

1. Greeley, *Confessions of a Parish Priest*, p. 250.
2. John 3:8 - NIV
3. Popova, op. cit., p. 190.
4. Ibid., p. 373
5. Pollan, op. cit., p. 311.
6. Hermann Hesse, *Siddhartha*, Trans. By Joachim Neugroschel (Penguin Books, NY, 1999), p. 14.
7. Ibid., p. 15.
8. Ibid., p. 23.
9. Ibid., p. 36.

32. THE GODDESS I NEVER KNEW

1. Goethe, *Faust*, Quoted from *Goddesses*, Joseph Campbell, p. 225.
2. Thomas Wolfe, *You can't go Home Again* (*https://quotes.pub/q/to-lose-the-earth-you-know-for-greater-knowing-to-lose-the-l-250678*)
3. Campell, *The Hero's Journey*, op. cit., p. viii.
4. Whitman, "Song of the Open Road," op. cit., Stanza 5.
5. Quoted in Campbell, *Pathways to Bliss,* op. cit., p. 39.
6. Pollan, op. cit., p. 246.

33. INVITATION TO MY SILENCE

1. Rilke, *Rilke's Book of Hours*, op. cit., II, 5; p. 151.
2. Rilke, Rainer Maria. "Music." The Project Gutenberg eBook of Poems, by Rainer Maria Rilke. translated by Jessie Lamont, 1918. www.gutenberg.org/files/38594/38594-h/38594-h.htm
3. Rilke, "I live my life in circles." The Project Gutenberg eBook of Poems, by Rainer Maria Rilke.
4. Whitman, Walt. "Song of Myself," *Leaves of Grass*, Stanza 15, p. 35.
5. ibid. Stanza 16, p. 38-39.
6. ibid. Stanza 18, p. 39.
7. Bloom, Harold. *Introduction and Celebration*, ibid. p. x.

34. SETTING BOUNDARIES WITH "GOD"

1. Carl Jung, "Letter to Dr. Hans Schär; 16 Nov. 1951," *Letters of C. G. Jung: Volume 2, 1951-1961* (out of print), p. 28 (https://books.google.com/books?id=0UPLCQAAQBAJ&pg=PA28&lpg=PA28&dq=%22I+had–to+wrench+myself+free+of+God%22+Carl+Jung&source=bl&ots=KqZPFUlKry&sig=ACfU3U00hXSzMDKkGE98hqpd15hiArRO_Q&hl=en&sa=X&ved=2ahUKEwi9xYaBoc75AhVrkWoFHZrpDFMQ6AF6BAgCEAM#v=onepage&q=%22I%20had%20to%20wrench%20myself%20free%20of%20God%22%20Carl%20Jung&f=false)
2. Ezekiel 1:13-28.
3. Exodus 33:19–23.
4. R. H. Charles, translator, *The Book of Enoch the Prophet* (Weiser Books Publisher. San Francisco, CA, 2012), XVII.1.

35. SAN PEDRO CEREMONY

1. Campbell, *The Hero's Journey,* op. cit., p. 54.

36. TAKE CARE OF THIS BOY

1. "By Blue Ontario's Shore," *Leaves of Grass* (Marboro Books Corp., Barnes and Noble Books. New York, New York, 1992), Stanza 4.
2. Ross Heaven, "San Pedro, The Miracle Healer: An interview with an Andean Huachumera (San Pedro Healer)," Erowid.org, Nov. 25, 2008 (https://erowid.org/plants/cacti/cacti_writings1.shtml).
3. Michael Pollan, *This is Your Mind on Plants* (Penguin Press, NY, 2021).

37. THE GARDEN OF THE WORLD

1. Carl Jung, *Answer to Job* (Vol. 11 of *The Collected Works of C.G. Jung.* Bollinger Series, Princeton University Press, 1973 & 1991, p. 40.
2. Walt Whitman, "Children of Adam," *Leaves of Grass* (Marboro Books Corp., Barnes and Noble Books, NY,).
3. Whitman, "Facing West from California's Shores," *Leaves of Grass,* op. cit.
4. Whitman, *"As Adam Early in the Morning," Leaves of Grass,* op. cit.

38. A MOVEABLE SANCTUARY

1. Rilke, *Rilke's Book of Hours,* op. cit., I, 25; p. 89.
2. Rilke, *Rilke's Book of Hours,* op. cit., Book I, 4; p. 49.
3. I Corinthians 13:12 – KJV.
4. Ibid., I, 50; p.109.
5. Ibid, I, 12; p. 65.
6. Whitman, Walt. "Song of Myself," *Leaves of Grass,* The First (1855) Edition, Penguin Books, 2005. Stanza 21; p. 30
7. Mark 2:22 (NIV)
8. Whitman, "Song of Myself" Ibid., Stanza 50, p. 95.
9. Whitman, "Song of Myself" Ibid., Stanza 50, p. 95.
10. John 4:21ff. (NIV).

39. TO THE YOUNGER BROTHER

1. Moore, Thomas, *The Soul's Religion.* Harper Perennial, Harper Collins Publishers. N.Y, N.Y. 2003, p. 139.
2. Rilke, *Rilke's Book of Hours,* op. cit., I, 38; p. 97.
3. Ibid.
4. Ibid., I, 25; p. 89.
5. Ibid., II, 3; p. 141.
6. John 1:14.
7. Rilke, *Rilke's Book of Hours,* op. cit., I, 38; p. 97.
8. Whitman, *Leaves of Grass,* op. cit., "Think of the Soul," p. 469

9. Ibid., I, 38; p. 97.
10. Ibid., I, 39; p. 99.
11. Ibid.
12. Ibid.
13. Ibid.
14. Ibid.

EPILOGUE

1. Moore, *The Soul's Religion*, op. cit., p. 29.
2. Rilke, *Rilke's Book of Hours,* op. cit., II, 19; p. 175.
3. Ibid., I, 25; p. 89.
4. Ibid., II, 3; p. 141.
5. Ibid., II, 25; p. 181.
6. Ibid., II, 19; p. 175.
7. Ibid., II, 26; p. 183.
8. Walt Whitman, "Song of Myself," *Leaves of Grass,* op. cit., Stanzas 46, 48

BIBLIOGRAPHY

Armstrong, Karen. *The Spiral Staircase*
Anchor Books, N.Y., N.Y. 2004

Azlan, Reza. *God: A Human History*
Random House, N.Y., N.Y. 2017

Baer, Ulrich. *The Poet's Guide to Life: The Wisdom of Rilke*
The Modern Library; Random House Publishers. N.Y., N.Y. 2005

Bly, Robert. *Selected Poems of Rainer Maria Rilke*
Translation and commentary by Robert Bly
Perennial Library, Harper & Row Publishers. New York, New York, 1981

Buechner, Frederick. *Telling the Truth: The Gospel as Tragedy, Comedy and Fairy Tale*
Harper and Row, Publishers, San Francisco, CA. 1977.

Campbell, Joseph. *Goddesses – Mysteries of the Feminine Divine*
New World Library, Novato, CA. 2023

Campbell, Joseph. *The Hero with a Thousand Faces*
MJF Books, N.Y., N.Y. 1949

Campbell, Joseph. *The Hero's Journey*
New World Library; Novato, CA 2014

Campbell, Joseph. *The Masks of God: Creative Mythology*
Penguin Book, N.Y., N.Y. 1987

Campbell, Joseph. *The Masks of God: Occidental Mythology*
Penguin Book, N.Y., N.Y. 1988

Campbell, Joseph. *The Masks of God: Oriental Mythology*
Penguin Book, N.Y., N.Y. 1976

Campbell, Joseph. *The Masks of God: Primitive Mythology*

BIBLIOGRAPHY

Penguin Book, N.Y., N.Y. 1987

Campbell, Joseph. *Myths to Live By*
Penguin Books, N.Y., N.Y., 1993

Campbell, Joseph. *Pathways to Bliss*
New World Library; Novato, CA 2004

Cooper, Rabbi David A. *God is a Verb*
Riverhead Books. N.Y., N.Y. 1997

Dostoyevsky, Fyodor. *The Brothers Karamazov*
Trans. By Constance Garrett
The Modern Library, Random House, N.Y., N.Y. 1972

Edwards, Jonathan. "Sinners in the Hands of an Angry God"
Sermon from 1741 online:
www.blueletterbible.org/Comm/edwards_jonathan/Sermons/Sinners.cfm

Easwaran, Eknath. (Translator and Preface). *The Bhagavad Gita*
Vintage Spiritual Classics, Random House, N.Y., N.Y., 2000

Edinger, Edward F. *Ego and Archetype*
Shambhala Publications, Boston, MA, 1992

Fadiman, James. *The Psychedelic Explorer's Guide: Safe, Therapeutic, and Sacred Journeys.*
Park Street Press, Rochester, Vermont. 2011

Fowler, George. *Dance of a Fallen Monk*
Addison-Wesley Publishing, Menlo Park, CA. 1995

Greeley, Andrew M. *Confessions of a Parish Priest*
Pocket Books, Simon and Schuster. N.Y, N,Y. 1987

Hesse, Herman. *Siddhartha*
Trans. By Joachim Neugroschel.
Penguin Books. N.Y., N.Y. 1999

Hillman, James. *A Blue Fire. (Selected Writings by James Hillman)*
Edited by Thomas Moore

BIBLIOGRAPHY

Harper Perennial, Harper Collins Publishers. N.Y, N.Y. 1991.

Homer. The Odyssey. Translator: Samuel Butler.
The Project Guttenberg eBook: https://www.gutenberg.org/ebooks/1727

Jacobs, Alan. *The Gnostic Gospels*
Watkins Publishing. London, England. 2016

James, William. *Varieties of Religious Experience*
Barnes & Noble Classics. N.Y., N.Y. 2004

Johnson, Robert. *Inner Work*
Harper San Francisco, Harper Collins Publishers, N.Y., N.Y. 1986.

Johnson, Robert A. *Lying with the Heavenly Woman*
HarperCollins Publisher. N.Y., N.Y. 1994

Jung, C. G. *Memories, Dreams, Reflections*
Recorded and Edited by Aniela Jaffe
Vintage Books, Random House, N.Y., N.Y. 1989

Jung, Carl G. *The Undiscovered Self*
Signet, Penguin Group. NY, NY, 2006

Jung, Carl G. *Answer to Job*. Bollinger Series, Princeton University Press. 1973 & 1991.
    Princeton, N.J. 1973 & 1991.

Kierkegaard, Soren. *The Sickness Unto Death*
Penguin Books. N.Y., N.Y. 1989.

Moody, Harry R. and Carroll, David. *The Five Stages of the Soul*
Anchor Books, Doubleday, N.Y., N.Y. 1998.

Moore, Thomas. *Care of the Soul*
Harper Perennial, Harper Collins Publishers. N.Y, N.Y. 1994.

Moore, Thomas. *The Re-Enchantment of Everyday Life*
Harper-Collins Publishers, N.Y., N.Y. 1996

Moore, Thomas. *The Soul's Religion*

BIBLIOGRAPHY

Harper Perennial, Harper Collins Publishers. N.Y, N.Y. 2003

Osbon, Diane K. selected and edited by. *A Joseph Campbell Companion*
Harper Perennial, N.Y., N.Y. 1991

Pearson, Carol S. *Awakening the Heroes Within*
Harper San Francisco, Harper Collins Publishers, N.Y., N.Y. 1997.

Pollan, Michael. *How to Change Your Mind*
Penguin Books, Penguin Random House. N.Y., N.Y., 2019

Popova, Maria. *Figuring*
Vintage Books, Penguin Random House LLC, N.Y., N.Y. 2019

Reece, Erik. *An American Gospel*
Riverhead Books, Penguin Group. N.Y., N.Y. 2009

Rilke, Rainer Maria. *Letters on God and Letters to a Young Woman*
Translated by Annemarie S. Kidder
Northwestern University Press, Evanston, Ill. 2012

Rilke, Rainer Maria. *Rilke's Book of Hours*
Translated by Anita Barrows and Joanna Macy
Riverhead Books. The Berkley Publishing Group. N.Y., N.Y. 1996

Rilke, Rainer Maria. *The Book or Images*
Translated by Edward Snow
North Point Press. Farrar, Straus and Giroux. New York, New York, 1994

Rilke, Rainer Maria. The Project Gutenberg eBook of Poems, by Rainer Maria Rilke. translated by Jessie Lamont, 1918. www.gutenberg.org/files/38594/38594-h/38594-h.htm

Scott, Bernard Brandon. *Re-Imagine the World: An Introduction to the Parables of Jesus* Polebridge Press. Santa Rosa, CA. 2001

Sheehy, Gail. *Understanding Men's Passages*
Ballentine Books, N.Y.,N.Y. 1999

Shorto, Russell. *Saints and Madmen*

BIBLIOGRAPHY

Henry Holt and Company, N.Y.,N.Y. 1999

Singer, June. *Androgyny*
Nicolas-Hays, York Beach, ME. 2000

Singer, June. *Boundaries of the Soul*
Anchor Books, Doubleday. N.Y., N.Y. 1994.

Thoreau, Henry David. *Walden and Other Writings*
Barnes and Noble Classics. Marboro Books, N.Y.,N.Y. 1992.

Watts, Alan. *Just So*
Sounds True Publisher. Boulder, Co. 2020

Whitman, Walt. *Leaves of Grass*
Marboro Books Corp., Barnes and Noble Books. New York, New York, 1992

Whitman, Leaves of Grass: The First (1855) Edition.
150th Anniversary Edition; Introduction by Harold Bloom
Penguin Books, N.Y., N.Y. 2005

Winell, Marlene. PhD. *Leaving the Fold*
The Apocryphile Press, Berkley, CA. 2007

Yudelove, Eric Steven. *The Tao and the Tree of Life*
Llewellyn Publications, St. Paul, Minn. 1999.